DK 275 .B84 A3 1987
Bukovskii, Vladimir
 Konstantinovich, 1942-
To choose freedom

D1601010

TO CHOOSE FREEDOM

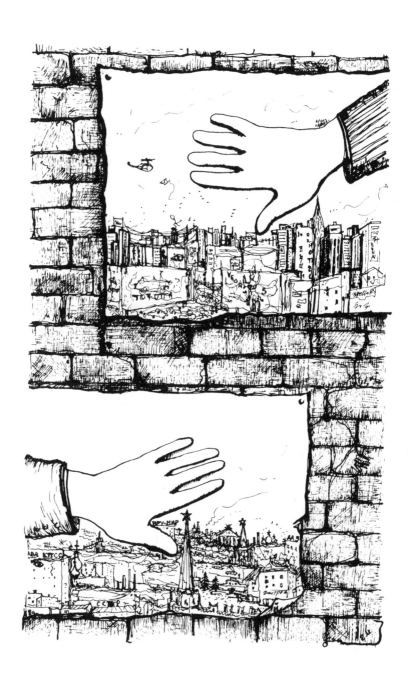

TO CHOOSE FREEDOM

Vladimir Bukovsky

Translated by Denise H. Wood
Edited by Alexis Klimoff

HOOVER INSTITUTION PRESS

STANFORD UNIVERSITY ♦ STANFORD, CALIFORNIA

The Hoover Institution on War, Revolution and Peace, founded at Stanford University in 1919 by the late President Herbert Hoover, is an interdisciplinary research center for advanced study on domestic and international affairs in the twentieth century. The views expressed in its publications are entirely those of the authors and do not necessarily reflect the views of the staff, officers, or Board of Overseers of the Hoover Institution.

Hoover Press Publication 344

Copyright 1987 by the Board of Trustees of the
    Leland Stanford Junior University
All rights reserved. No part of this publication may be reproduced, stored in a retrieval system, or transmitted in any form or by any means, electronic, mechanical, photocopying, recording, or otherwise, without written permission of the publisher.

First printing, 1987
Manufactured in the United States of America
91 90 89 88 87   9 8 7 6 5 4 3 2 1

DK
275
B84
A3
1987

Library of Congress Cataloging in Publication Data
Bukovskiĭ, Vladimir Konstantinovich, 1942–
    To choose freedom.

    Translation of: Cette lancinante douleur de la liberté.
    Includes bibliographical references.
    1. Bukovskiĭ, Vladimir Konstantinovich, 1942–
2. Dissenters—Soviet Union—Biography. 3. Political prisoners—Soviet Union—Biography. I. Title.
DK275.B84A3 1987   364.1'3 [B]   86-27507
ISBN 0-8179-8441-0
ISBN 0-8179-8442-9 (pbk.)

Designed by Lisa S. Mirski
Illustrations by Elena Mezincesky

3 3001 00752 7350

Contents

ONE has to have lived in this solitude without rest, in this prison without leisure that is called Russia in order to be conscious of all the freedoms one enjoys in other countries of Europe, whatever form of government they have adopted. When your son is discontented in France, use my formula and say to him: "Go to Russia." It is a voyage which every foreigner will find beneficial; anyone who has gotten a good look at this country will consider himself content to live anywhere else. It is always a good thing to realize that there is a society in which no happiness is possible, for, by a law of his nature, man cannot be happy unless he is free.

Marquis de Custine, *Russia in 1839* (Paris, 1843)

IF I express myself frankly, I risk being taken for a flatterer or else for a censor of too great severity; but it is only fair to recognize that it would be going against common experience and truth if one were to deny that many excellent things, worthy of imitation, are to be found here. However, this in no way prevents me from seeing quite a few things, and actually these are in greater number, which are definitely of another quality and from which may God preserve us. In a word, these comparisons make me conclude in all sincerity to Your Highness that if some of our young citizens, the ones who are capable of honest thought, who become indignant over the abuses and disorders to be found in Russia, all of which cause them great revulsion, nothing could better restore to them the love our country deserves than to dispatch them promptly to France. Here experience will teach them very quickly that all the tales about the perfection of this nation are pure lies, that men remain the same everywhere, and that people of intellectual ability and quality are just as hard to find wherever you go. Whatever the faults of our homeland, one can find there as great a happiness as in other climes, if one's conscience is at peace and if one's reason rules one's imagination, instead of being ruled by it.

Letter of Denis Fonvizin to Count Petr Panin (Paris, 1778)

Foreword

F EW individuals appreciate the value of freedom as keenly as Vladimir Bukovsky. He spent nearly one-third of his first 33 years in Soviet prisons, labor camps, and psychiatric hospitals. He dared to demand that the rights guaranteed to citizens in the Soviet constitution actually be respected and safeguarded. He still would be languishing in prison—or perhaps dead—but for the extraordinary efforts of strangers in the West who learned of his persecution and waged a worldwide campaign to win his release. Unable to resist the pressure of Western public opinion, Leonid Brezhnev released Bukovsky in December 1976, in exchange for Luís Corvalán, a Chilean Communist.

No one can deny that the West got the best of the bargain: Bukovsky has flourished in a climate of freedom. He consults with State Department officials in Washington, lectures extensively to college students, and appears frequently on television interview shows in Holland, France, England, and the United States. But by far his greatest impact on public opinion has been through his writings.

To Build a Castle, Bukovsky's first book, published in 1979, was a bestseller throughout Europe and critically well received in the United States; editions of this book have been published in eleven countries. Reviewers acclaimed the book for its shrewd insights into the Soviet regime and the human rights movement, but especially as a personal document that relates the story of how Bukovsky deliberately defied the KGB, was repeatedly imprisoned, and yet managed to maintain an unbroken spirit. Irving Howe wrote, "The sections of Bukovsky's book dealing with his experiences in Soviet prisons and camps are harrowing and brilliant, worthy of comparison with Dostoevsky's *The*

House of the Dead." Similarly, Philip Caputo observed that "Bukovsky's sense of humor, of detachment and irony, elevates his memoirs to a work of art."

In 1982 Bukovsky attracted a worldwide audience with an essay on "The Peace Movement and the Soviet Union." He boldly confronted the wave of antinuclear hysteria that was sweeping over Western Europe, the United States, and Japan. He argued that those who advocate unilateral disarmament by America and its allies are the pawns, knowingly or not, of Soviet foreign policy, and that if they succeed in their campaign they will leave the world at the mercy of Soviet military threats. An American reprint of the essay (following publication in the May 1982 issue of *Commentary*) sold more than fifty thousand copies.

A year earlier, in 1981, Bukovsky had written his second best-selling book. It was simultaneously published in two editions: the original Russian and a French translation, *Cette lancinante douleur de la liberté* (The piercing pain of freedom). Two years later a German edition (*Dieser stechender Schmerz der Freiheit*) was not only a bestseller, but also won Bukovsky the prestigious Konrad Adenauer Freedom and Literature Prize. When the French edition was published, it was hailed for its stunning portrait of naive Western attitudes toward the Soviet Union. Bukovsky's goals are to challenge Western readers to understand the totalitarian nature of Soviet society and to convince them that their own freedom cannot be preserved by evasion or wishful thinking. French reviewers also praised the book's verve and sardonic humor; these qualities are certain to appeal to American readers as well.

Although this translation appears five years after the original, the book is not at all dated. Nonetheless, this edition contains two epilogues that carry Bukovsky's insightful analysis from the Brezhnev era through the succession of Andropov, Chernenko, and Gorbachev. The first is a speech Bukovsky delivered in London in March 1985 at a conference entitled "Beyond 1984: Communism and Liberal Democracy," sponsored by the Committee for the Free World. The second is an address he gave at The Hague in April 1986 before an international symposium sponsored by the Dutch Institute for Public Interest.

To Choose Freedom enables Western readers to see the West from the vantage point of a man raised in a totalitarian society—a man who appreciates that liberty can be destroyed if taken for granted and left undefended, and who has dedicated his life to its defense. His message is one the West must heed while there is still time.

CHAPTER ONE

On Public Opinion
and Publicity

Here I am savoring Switzerland, my dear friends. The slightest breath of air seems to penetrate into my very heart, filling it with joy. How beautiful these places are! What magnificence! . . .

Fortunate Swiss! Should you not render thanks to Heaven every hour for dwelling in the embrace of sweet Nature, ruled by the benevolent laws of a brotherly Union, living in simplicity, and serving one God? Your entire existence is surely a delectable dream.

Nikolai Karamzin, *Letters of a Russian Traveler* (August 1789)

How pleasant it must have been, in the good old days, to travel about at leisure in a horse-drawn carriage! Should it strike the travelers' fancy, the coachman could be told to stop by some high alpine pasture where they could savor the rich aroma of the fields and, perched on a rock at the side of a road, jot down their travel impressions.

When a Russian travels abroad today, he usually does so precipitously, armed with a one-way ticket and a single piece of paper in lieu of all other documents: an "ordinary exit visa" permitting permanent residence in Israel. Thus is he reunited with the great family of Man. And of course he is in such a hurry that he cannot allow himself to think about sweet Nature. But by the time he gets to Vienna, even our present-day traveler would have plenty of material to fill the pages of his notebook: the endless visa formalities, the talks with the KGB concerning the situation in the Middle East, the customs inspection, the body search, the border guards, and finally Vienna itself. It all constitutes a series of events with at least some semblance of logical sequence and with at least a modicum of time to take them in.

I did not even have that. Only a few hours before, I had been arguing fiercely with my guards about my boots, and, convinced that I was being taken to solitary confinement or to be searched, had been concealing forbidden articles in my quilted prison jacket. At best, I thought, I would face a new trial. Only forty minutes ago, my handcuffs had been removed, but not without an altercation. And then all of a sudden here I am, in the West. Zurich. Zu-u-rich! I don't seem to remember hearing about such a transit prison . . .[1]

My first two weeks in Switzerland are almost a total blank—a few disjointed images, some vague impressions. That particular winter there had been much more snow than usual: a "white winter," the Zurichers called it. I seem to recall squinting continually. I was like someone coming outside after a long stay in the cellar. Another item that sticks in my memory is the constant problem I had with cars: I kept waiting for them to pass, while the drivers would wait for me to cross the street. It took me quite a while to catch on that pedestrians have the right-of-way here.

I took great care not to litter the streets, carrying my cigarette butt in my hand until I could find a proper receptacle. I was in the West, after all! And as for getting the coachman of legend to slow down a bit, so as to give me a chance to get my bearings . . . well, I had five or six television interviews daily, not counting meetings with the press.

"Don't let it get to you," my friends reassured me. "It's always like that at first. They'll eventually calm down and leave you in peace. Turning them down only makes matters worse, for they would simply hound you all the more. It's best to get it all over with at one time."

So I was patient. Rather like a boxer who after his tenth round in the bout is sponged off with a little water, given a few brisk rubs of the towel, and then pushed back into the ring.

But the last round seemed never to arrive, and the situation became more and more of a strain. There were trips. Nine days in Britain, twenty-four hours allocated to Paris, three days in Holland, a week in Germany, back to Zurich, back to London, back to France. Then off again to Germany. Airport to hotel, then hotel to airport. My memory of these times is of one continual plane journey. Each time the plane took off, I forgot the place we had just left and whatever it was we had done there. A marvelous state of being, serene and duty-free, when you can calmly sip your drink without a thought in your mind as you watch the clouds through the porthole. And what a wonderful panorama of clouds! Lucky clouds! Do you thank Heaven ceaselessly for your good fortune?

Maybe I have an unfortunate disposition, maybe it's a case of bad luck, but I seem to have spent my life doing what I least want to do, doing it against my wishes, forcing myself with clenched teeth. Was

---

[1] On December 18, 1976, Vladimir Bukovsky was exchanged at the Zurich airport for Chilean Communist Luís Corvalán. See Bukovsky's *To Build a Castle* (New York: Viking, 1979) for an account of his long struggle with the regime—ED.

this endless haste and the inability to finish anything what I really desired? Did I really want to argue with idiots, to persuade the fainthearted, to shout into the ears of the deaf? I had always sought rational, sensible occupations, ones that precluded haste: perhaps a manual trade, or something in science. I'd like to plane boards, making spirals of golden shavings, or chisel stones, or fashion delicately designed figures or jugs, or become a glassblower, or a fisherman standing in a stream up to my knees, casting my line.

Of course I wanted to be able to travel—but not the way we were doing it. Not to fly over three countries in the time it takes to consume one drink, and without seeing anything in the process. I wanted to be able to walk at a leisurely pace, to soak up the sights of the countryside, to breathe in the scent of the fields. I wanted to spend nights in a haystack or in the loft of a barn, to listen for the sound of the rooster at dawn and of the cuckoo at sunset.

One is almost led to believe that on the inopportune night of my birth, the Supreme Work Dispatcher, when he saw me approaching the gate of the heavenly camp, pulled out my file, and after the formalities of asking my name, first, last, and middle, rapped out with a scowl: "As for you, it'll be a lifetime of bouncing from pillar to post and minding other people's business."

As far as the Supreme Work Dispatcher is concerned, your wishes don't count for anything. He's only parceling out the chores that have to be done. Try protesting that one: there is no court of appeal higher than the celestial tribunal.

Here's an example of what I mean: I detest writing. It makes me ill. I lose sleep over it, it ruins my appetite, and every page costs me several months of my life. But there is no way out—here I am tackling my third book. I earned twelve years of prison for my first book; the second one cost me so much sweat that it could be the subject of another book; I hardly dare to think what will come of this third and, I hope, last book.

To be sure, what could possibly be more absurd than to find oneself suddenly in the role of a professional hero, who is, like a miracle-working icon, displayed in one city after another? The photographers trample each other as they retreat in a pack before you, blinding you with their endless flashbulbs. The TV cameramen become entangled in their cables as they thrust their menacing black-tipped microphones under your nose. What is it they are trying to read in my face, discern from my breathing? Why this ferocious pushing and shoving, as though their pictures would be better if they ruined their neighbor's? The entire throng continues retreating before you; there is nothing to be done but to smile inanely and keep breathing as normally as possible.

There is no hope of being just an ordinary guy. Everyone has such great expectations; you are supposed to come out with remarkable statements, profound reflections, handsome speeches, witty comments, reminiscences. At the very least you will be pinned to the wall and bombarded with questions. You no longer belong to yourself. Every minute of your life ends up being programmed a year in advance, just like a train carrying the mail. Whatever happens to you, the slightest misstep immediately becomes the center of attention. You will not be forgiven for a single mistake.

People have an astonishing need to create idols, only to abuse them later and knock them off their pedestals! Sometimes the most absurd fluke of luck, or perhaps a misfortune, can catapult you into the spotlight, and from that point on you become public property. The spotlight sweeps capriciously over our heads, suddenly illuminating one person here, another one there. Humans, just like insects, are irresistibly drawn to this light, which then becomes the criterion of everything: success, happiness, power, wealth.

This was my first significant impression of the West. Perhaps a better way to describe it would be to call it my first experience in perplexity. For us, back there in the USSR, *glasnost'*[2] was a weapon, a means for struggling against enslavement and arbitrary power. It was also a means for protecting oneself, rather like the lifeline that saves the mountain climber. It turns out that there is no single word in any European language that gives an adequate translation, for the word *publicity* has a very different meaning. The Russian word *glasnost'* has something cold and precise about it, rather like a scalpel; it is a word both solemn and dignified, conjuring up an official of the Duma, grave in his beard and long caftan, proclaiming an edict from the tsar in front of the Redeemer Gate of the Kremlin. *Glasnost'* is like an oath to tell the truth, the whole truth, and nothing but the truth. Publicity, on the other hand, has connotations to our ears of an unseemly free-for-all. It suggests something humiliating and even disreputable, as if you were led naked through the streets surrounded by a howling mob, and followed by urchins whistling piercingly. To have publicity puts you into the same category as a circus celebrity, a football hero, or a notorious cutthroat who has just been apprehended.

---

[2]*Glasnost'* describes the property of being open to public examination and discussion. It therefore suggests access to uncensored information and the ability to disseminate it—Ed.

I used to tell myself that is the way it has to be. It's something inherent to democracy, it goes with power being in the hands of the people. This must be why famous actors or pop singers can have a lot of political influence, and why it helps to be an actor if you want to be a politician.

I wouldn't say that such a conclusion grieved me particularly or tarnished my impression of democracy. It was all preferable to our Muscovite vampires. Yet my discovery made a strong impression on me, perhaps equivalent to what a Papuan would feel upon finding his war lance used as a decoration in a Parisian restaurant or a London pub.

It's far more than a matter of semantics. Back there, when I was at grips with the KGB or the prison guards, *glasnost'* was a life-and-death matter to me. Now that I am out of danger, *glasnost'* continues to be indispensable for those who remain in the USSR. To make use of *glasnost'* thoughtlessly would be equivalent to depriving someone of freedom or even of life. It was enough to recall the incredible stratagems, the huge risks, the tens of intermediaries it took to smuggle out of our prison the briefest of scrawls about those who depended on such *glasnost'*. And then when the information finally reached Moscow, one still had to convince a foreign journalist that what had reached him was worth reporting. Even that was not the end of it, for once the information got out to the West, some unknown editor or other kingpin had veto power over its ever seeing the light of day. But now it has turned out that our explosive *glasnost'* somewhere along the way became transformed into the dubious publicity.

Glasnost' is something objective, has nothing to do with any particular individual, is in the interest of everyone; publicity, on the other hand, is like a mark on your brow, it concerns you exclusively, and to pursue it is as ignominious as trying to soak a rich relative. None of us back there would have wanted any part of it. And besides, none of us pictured ourselves as doing anything heroic.

In a word, the Supreme Work Dispatcher had once again stuck me with the wrong job. No point in grumbling: each camp has its own way of doing things, and it's useless to grouse. Once I had accepted one invitation, there was no way to turn down all the others from competing organizations. If I granted an interview to one reporter, in the next second a whole pack would be on my heels. To turn them down would be taken as an insult. Worse, it could give rise to suspicions that your refusal is politically motivated. Meanwhile, friends egg you on: "As long as people are listening to you, make use of the opportunity to speak about such and such." Mentioning these individuals seemed to have little effect, but who wouldn't want to seize every chance to do something to help one's former cellmates, even if it was only to mention them by name?

In addition, this was a time when the Western public's interest in and sympathy for our cause was enormous. The desire to help and to understand was palpable. Our movement was advancing swiftly to center stage, becoming a factor in international politics and thus arousing formidable adversaries. It was not the time to take a holiday or to slow the pace.

But I did not feel that I fitted the role. Throughout this first period of freedom I felt profound unease, rather like a self-proclaimed doctor who is suddenly brought to the bedside of a gravely ill patient. I have neither the inclination nor the talent to appear on speaking platforms. A real speech is beyond me. What I manage to say seems stupid and awkwardly composed. The hardest thing of all is trying not to look at your audience, not to think of the consequences of forgetting what you want to say. You hope you will not go blank or stumble over your words. My nightmare was to imagine myself sitting speechless, confronting a hall full of silently expectant people. And as time went on, the problem only became worse. If only one could smoke in these places!

TV studios also unnerve me, but of course that is the very thing one must hide at all costs. On TV it's generally not what one says that counts, but how one says it. And I am a lousy actor.

On top of everything, I had been foolish enough to speak English at my first Zurich press conference. From then on, no one let me speak Russian again. At the time my English was pretty wooden, and I found it hard to express what I really wanted to say. It was real torture.

One other nuisance was that I had to wear a necktie. Never in all my life had I worn a necktie; it's an article of clothing I simply can't abide. The first time I ever got decked out in one was when it was put on me, by force, while I was handcuffed in the prison of Lefortovo, just before the flight to Zurich. But here I found myself, at every turn of the road, having to hang this rubbish around my neck.

One thing that came easily, however, was responding to questions. Perhaps I was accustomed to the interrogation process. And besides, the questions I was asked all over the world were pretty much the same. Before long, I could predict what was coming.

Nonetheless, there were two questions that could put me into a panic, for I had no idea at all how to respond. The first was "What do you do in life?"

What could I say? It was preposterous. I had once received a questionnaire from Who's Who International, and I got a headache trying to figure out what to say under which rubric. Were I to answer the questions exactly as they were formulated, I would end up merely giving my name and date of birth. Everything else would have had to remain blank. After all, none of the questions concerned the reasons for my prison sentences or the number of times I had been released and rearrested. I, for my part, had nothing else to say about my life.[3]

I couldn't very well enter these things under the "Hobbies" rubric, and in any case there was too little space there. Should I enter them under "Education" or "Membership in societies or clubs"? After agonizing over this for awhile, I ended up listing all my arrests under "What posts have you filled?" My releases from prison were recorded under "Prizes, decorations, etc." It was all pretty absurd. At least now I can put down that I am a student at Cambridge University.

The second question that I feared had to do with the reason why the prisoner exchange had taken place. Why had I been chosen? For the longest time, I could not find an answer to this question, and even now I am not wholly sure about the truth of the matter.

Indeed, why this exchange, and why me? We know too well the frame of mind of the "comrades in the Kremlin" to believe that this could have been a chance decision, and certainly it was not due to a burst of humanitarian sentiment. They are not the type to do harm to their own interests. For, however you look at the situation, the exchange was a substantial setback for them, politically speaking.

First, the very fact of an exchange constituted an implicit admission that there were political prisoners inside the USSR. Up until then, the leaders and all the propaganda mouthpieces had stoutly denied that anything of the sort existed. Second, this strange deal put the Soviets on an equal footing with the Pinochet regime, a regime that they had taken every opportunity to label as fascist. And though

---

[3]Bukovsky was first detained by the KGB in 1961 for his participation in unauthorized literary activities. In 1963 he was arrested for keeping copies of forbidden books and interned in a special psychiatric hospital for fifteen months. Released in 1965, he was rearrested later that same year for protesting in defense of the writers Sinyavsky and Daniel. He was sent, without trial, to a series of mental hospitals, including the notorious Serbsky Institute in Moscow. Set free in 1966 with the help of foreign pressure, Bukovsky was arrested once again in 1967, charged with organizing a protest demonstration, and sentenced to three years in a labor camp. During this period and especially after he emerged in 1970, Bukovsky did more than anyone else to publicize the suffering of perfectly healthy dissidents who had been committed to insane asylums for their political views. As a result he was arrested one more time (1971) and sentenced to seven years in prison and camp, to be followed by five years of exile. The unprecedented exchange of 1976 brought about Bukovsky's release from Lefortovo Prison in Moscow—ED.

we happen to know that the Soviet regime is a bit more fearsome—if only because of its capacity to survive, its aggressiveness, and the existence of well-organized supporters in countries all over the world— still, by lumping together the two countries, a real blow was dealt to the prestige and image of pro-Soviet forces everywhere.

Finally, it was obvious that the exchange represented a concession to the force of world opinion, a retreat in the face of the protest campaigns. The result could only be to strengthen the hand of those planning future protests.

The reaction of the Western communist press alone made it clear that the exchange had been a blunder.

> It is perfectly natural that Pinochet should have latched on to the project of exchanging Bukovsky for Corvalán. It's easy to understand that it was highly profitable for him. But it is hard to see how such a move could be profitable for the Soviets . . . Moscow not only gave away its trump cards to the Chileans, but it also admitted indirectly that Bukovsky was in fact a political prisoner . . . This line of action by the Soviet leadership has hurt the cause of socialism throughout the world.
>
> L'Unità (Italian communist paper)

> This exchange is grist for the mill of those who claim that democracy no more exists in the socialist countries than it does in the fascist ones. It is regrettable that the liberation of Bukovsky involved his expulsion from the country. Regrettable too that what took place was an exchange between a fascist and a socialist country, instead of being a simple act of justice.
>
> The Morning Star (British communist paper)

> Two men, two political prisoners were involved in a lamentable exchange. In our eyes, it is inadmissible to put men in a position of having to make the impossible choice between prison and exile. We feel such a transaction is outrageous.
>
> Georges Marchais,[4] L'Humanité (French communist paper)

> The actions of the Soviet authorities confirm that the regime is in no way superior to nor more humane than the regime of the fascist military dictator, General Pinochet. Pinochet has succeeded in presenting to the whole world an image of the Soviet Union as a country in which liberty is stifled as much as it is in Chile. And if the press of the socialist world celebrates the liberation of Corvalán as

[4]Georges Marchais is the head of the French Communist party—Ed.

a victory, all the while turning a deaf ear to the liberation of
Bukovsky, it means that the press has fallen into the trap set for it
by Pinochet.

From an editorial by Editor-in-chief of *L'Humanité*, R. Andrieu

Indeed, comrades, what is going on? You've fallen into the trap
set for you, you provide grist for the mill, you have given away all your
trump cards. Whatever for? Could it be in order to liberate Comrade
Corvalán? I will never believe that. Our tough old cookies in the Kremlin are anything but sentimental, and their comrades in Chile, Bolivia,
and Uruguay are especially useful to them when they are in prison,
for that provides a marvelous occasion to protest fiercely and to play
upon the sense of decency of trusting souls. But what to do with these
comrades once they are in Moscow? At the start, Corvalán had refused to be exchanged. It took an order from Moscow to make him
change his mind. Actually his prison was a fairly comfortable one,
and he gave frequent interviews to the press. Not quite the same
problem we had had, trying to smuggle out a few lines, passed from
hand to hand at enormous risk. Even if Corvalán had ended up being
killed, Brezhnev would not have lost too much sleep over it. Probably
just the opposite; it would have added one more communist martyr to
the list and could have served as fine edification for our youth.

And so what was the reason for this exchange? I kept racking my
brain for explanations, but none satisfied me. I was sure there was
some ploy involved in all this, some kind of snare laid.

It occurred to me that maybe they had been trapped by their own
propaganda. For the preceding three years, the Soviet press, as well as
the socialist and "progressive" papers all over the world, had demanded "Freedom for Luís Corvalán." How to respond now to a sudden offer to exchange him?

But Soviet propaganda could have found a way to turn down the
offer. They are masters at playing the moralists, the philanthropists.
Marchais came right out and said such an exchange was simply unacceptable. In fact, most commentators had given the transaction a
negative evaluation.

> The freeing of Bukovsky is a triumph for the protest movements. In
> no way can it be considered a victory for freedom.
>
> *The Daily Mirror* (London)

> It seems that international relations have been infected by the sys-
> tem of arbitrary arrest and abduction. International law no longer
> exists. The stage has been abandoned to warring bands who ex-

change hostages. It seems that a new era is upon us, the era of concentration camps on a world scale, mitigated occasionally by an exchange of prisoners.

Le Figaro (Paris)

Certainly it is better to exile political prisoners rather than letting them rot behind bars. But this trade in human beings between the Soviet Union and Chile is contemptible.

Berlingske Tidende (Denmark)

To sum up, it is evident that if the Soviets had chosen to turn down the offer, no one would have been critical. On the contrary, Pinochet would simply have been left with Corvalán on his hands and no more trump cards to play. And finally, if getting Corvalán were really a matter of great urgency, then this exchange could have been done discreetly without leaving any traces. West Germany regularly ransoms prisoners from East Germany, and there is no outcry.

Meanwhile, the Soviets continued to put their foot in it. At first the press in the Soviet Union and in the satellite countries kept mum about the exchange. Corvalán was welcomed in triumph. The only mention that was made of me, without in any way linking the two events, was to note that I had been "expelled" from Soviet territory. The first Soviet publication to make allusion to the exchange, four days after it had taken place, was our beloved *Literaturnaia gazeta*, which on December 22 published an article under the headline "News of the Week: Welcome, Dear Friend!"

Luís Corvalán is free! Luís Corvalán is in the Soviet Union! These words are rich in meaning. They proclaim the proud destiny of a man, of a Communist who is ready to sacrifice everything, even his life, for his convictions, for the sacred cause of the people. They speak of three years of prison, three years of continuous torture, and of the fascist Chilean regime that was ultimately powerless as all neofascism must be: they can throw a Communist in prison, or even kill him, but they cannot bring such a man to his knees! This event demonstrates, finally, the strength and power of world socialism and of the progressive public opinion of mankind, for both played a decisive role in securing the liberation of comrade Corvalán.

Moreover, did these fascist executioners really 'liberate' him? Not at all. He was snatched out of the bloodstained claws of the enemies of the Chilean people . . .

Today the open and covert admirers of Pinochet are trying to insinuate that the liberation of Corvalán is no more than a deal. He was, it is alleged, simply exchanged for the "dissident" (i.e., the Soviet-hater) Bukovsky.

We have learned that Pinochet had indeed expressed to a representative of a "third country" the passionate desire to receive this individual. The anti-Soviet essence of Bukovsky becomes even more obvious after this outburst of affection from the Chilean hangman.

One could say that they have mutually exposed one another.

The main thing, however, is that an illustrious son of the Chilean people and an indomitable Communist is free at last.

On the same day TASS announced that I had been "granted permission to leave the USSR" in accordance with my "own wishes." What kind of farce was this? They were like thieves caught red-handed. *Le Monde* had the following caustic comment:

> The Soviet press does all it can to hide the truth from its readers, but will it be able to suppress this truth for long? Announcements to the effect that the Chilean communist leader was released due to "broad international support" will evoke a snicker from those numerous individuals in the USSR who listen to foreign radio broadcasts.

As could be expected, Soviet propaganda let loose a broadside of slander in the wake of my departure. On December 22, TASS and *Literaturnaia gazeta* opened fire; then, on December 24, Radio Moscow featured a program entitled "Unworthy Uproar." On December 25, it was the turn of the daily, *Trud*: "A Criminal Decked Out As a Hero"; on December 26, *Izvestiia* presented "The Parable About a 'Martyr' and His Spiritual Fathers." It was the customary repertoire, and I was never described as anything else but a "common criminal" (naturally, since there are no political ones in the Soviet Union). And of course I was a student who had flunked out, who barely finished high school, who was kicked out of the university after only one year because of incompetence, a semiliterate who had an unhealthy vanity, who was trying to compensate for his intellectual weakness by proving himself in extremist acts, through provocation and hooliganism.

> Anyone with the least common sense will recognize the paranoid delusions evident in Bukovsky's dreams of conquest. We need to remind ourselves that Bukovsky had at one time undergone treatment, but this did not succeed in changing the aberrant character of his ideas.
>
> *Izvestiia*, December 26, 1976

None of this was at all surprising. And yet there were a few innovations. I learned that I had been sentenced for having created "an assault group of five terrorists trained to go into action." This group reportedly traveled to wooded areas for rifle practice. The Soviet papers kept contradicting each other as to the dates for all this. Some said it took place in 1965, others said it was 1970, and yet others placed it later. Subsequently, it seems, "fascist followers" and other centers of subversion supplied me with "foreign currency, electronic recording equipment, and cameras." And of course much was made of the special favor with which Pinochet was said to view me. Either he had just invited me or I had already left for Chile—or at least would be going momentarily. And each time the punch line was that I would soon stand revealed in my true colors, and that those who had been trapped into believing in me would be ashamed and would try to forget me as quickly as possible.

It was a pretty weak argument. Time would take care of it, for it would soon be apparent who I was and where I was going. And as for the line that I had failed to complete my studies, they would have done better to keep their mouths shut, for the story was not in their favor, and the Western press had written about it before. The gambit involving the "assault group" and my terrorist activities was only good for a laugh. Ironic comments were not long in coming:

The APN bulletin released in Brussels in French ascribes to Bukovsky the intention to struggle against the Soviet regime "by means of terror and the physical elimination of people." If this is true, it is incomprehensible why the authorities would permit such a dangerous individual to depart from the Soviet Union, and why they would provide him with a passport valid for five years.

Le Drapeau rouge (Belgian communist newspaper)

Bukovsky is accused of having created a group of five men as part of a plan to overthrow Soviet power. Fortunately there were not six of them or the poor state might have crumbled.

Die Welt

And was that all they could dredge up for their propaganda? If so, then why did they agree to a spectacular exchange witnessed by the whole world? Why should they provide such publicity for their enemy? No matter what *L'Unità* said, I knew perfectly well that the trump cards had been given to me, not Pinochet.

To be sure, there was my opposite number, Corvalán. The public's curiosity had shifted, with time, from a comparison of the Chilean and the Soviet regimes to a juxtaposition of Pinochet and Brezhnev, and finally to our two persons. We were asked what we thought of each other, what were the objectives for which we each were fighting, what was our vision of the future. The journalists were dying to sit us down at the same table and to get us to talk together. As far as I was concerned, I was quite ready to do so. But as for Corvalán, bound as he was by his membership in the party and by a natural gratitude toward those who had saved him, there was no way he could take part in this bourgeois fantasy. Representatives of the press suggested repeatedly that we meet together. Each time, I had accepted and he had refused. Agreeing to go to Moscow, he had in fact merely changed prisons, with his party comrades now serving as his new jailers. At his first appearance on Soviet television, he was forced to speak in a manner that made any subsequent conversation with the Western press pointless. He had to praise everything Soviet, approve the occupation of Czechoslovakia, and claim that there were no political prisoners in the Soviet Union. And when, at a Kremlin reception a few days later, he was kissed on both cheeks by Brezhnev, I really felt pity for the poor fellow. I even told the journalists that I feared we would soon have to start another campaign to liberate Corvalán by exchanging him for someone else.

Later, I learned that the apprehensions I had had about Corvalán's freedom and security were not without foundation. Someone I knew lived in the same building as Corvalán, who had been given an apartment on the fifth floor. As usual, the elevator was practically never in running order, which Corvalán found to be an inconvenience. Therefore, shortly after moving in, he asked a family living on the ground floor whether they would be willing to swap apartments. No sooner said than done. But almost immediately the KGB men arrived on the scene and made it plain to both parties that they were to move back to their former quarters. The one allocated to Corvalán had been carefully bugged before he moved in. It soon became obvious that Corvalán had little desire to live in the Soviet Union, and he left the country at the first opportunity. I believe his family still remains in Moscow.

After two weeks of feverish activity in Zurich, I was once again looking out a plane window at the white scene with snow-powdered pine trees and neat Swiss houses slipping away below me. I had not really had a moment to take in what was around me: neither the charms of sweet Nature nor the simplicity of the life-style. At the very most it had been a delectable dream. Or perhaps better said, an awakening, rather like that of a child who had slept with the happy assurance that in the morning he would find Christmas presents next to his bed. But the difference is that children don't ask Santa Claus whether they deserve these gifts.

◆ ◆ ◆

It is impossible to determine now who first had the idea of this exchange. I know at least ten people who claim to have fathered the plan and each can make a more or less valid case. It seems that it was in the air, perhaps circulating as a quip, then as a rumor, and finally as a serious possibility: why not, after all? Even in our prison the zeks[5] were furious when they read day after day the frenetic appeals for Corvalán's liberation: "What's all the bitching about? Acting as if their prisons were empty. If this guy Corvalán means so much to them, why don't they swap him for someone else?"

We do know for certain that back in 1973, just after Corvalán had been arrested, a Dutch woman came to the Chilean embassy in Holland, asking the ambassador to suggest this exchange to Pinochet. Later, in 1975, an Austrian journalist—acting on his own initiative and without knowing of this earlier action—made the same suggestion to top Soviet officials. As he tells the story, their reaction at first was as if it were totally out of the question, but at the next meeting they were more attentive and interested.

There is talk of a certain colonel or general in the Chilean general staff, a man of Russian origin, who is said to have tried "selling" the idea to Pinochet from the start and who finally succeeded in doing so. Since I have never met this man, I can neither confirm nor deny this version. And I learned to my great surprise, from a letter written by a Catholic priest (the letter was not addressed to me and came into my hands by chance), that this worthy member of the cloth, a procommunist—these things happen sometimes—had been party to the secret negotiations for the exchange of Corvalán. Corvalán is described as being held in Chile "under abominable conditions" and the letter suggests exchanging him for "some Soviet underling."

Whatever one makes of all this, the exchange was first publicly proposed in 1976, simultaneously by the Sakharov Committee in Denmark and by Sakharov himself at a press conference in Moscow. This was followed by negotiations, thanks to the good offices of a "third party," which is to say, the U.S. State Department. I learned subsequently that it had been Helmut Sonnenfeldt (Kissinger's deputy) who had been given this mission. Later still, through a mutual ac-

---

[5] *Zek* is camp slang for an inmate of the Soviet prison and labor camp system—Ed.

quaintance, Sonnenfeldt sent word that even though our ideas might differ on a lot of things, I should at least thank him for the exchange. It really is time to make up for this gaffe and to stop appearing to be ungrateful to the three individuals whom I have thoughtlessly not thanked before: Pinochet, Brezhnev, and Sonnenfeldt.

But ultimately it is not very important to reconstruct the minutiae of this whole affair, since the real reasons for the exchange are on quite another level.

◆　◆　◆

A campaign to affect public opinion is an extraordinary thing. Subjected as we are to a daily barrage of reports about human suffering, about horrors and catastrophes, it is surprising that human beings have not become completely indifferent to the misfortunes of others. Emaciated, dying children in Cambodia or Uganda, with protruding ribs and swollen bellies; Vietnamese refugees lost at sea; innocent people taken hostage; or perhaps simply a mother trying to save the life of her sick child, vanishing species of wildlife, or endangered cultural monuments: these facts and images cry out to us daily from TV screens and plead for our help from the pages of newsprint.

One would think that nothing could surprise us or goad us into action. In addition we each have our own troubles and misfortunes to deal with. And yet nearly every human misery still rouses waves of warm compassion. Families who are far from being rich tighten their belts to offer money, and even apologize for not giving more. Very busy people find time to compose moving letters; individuals collect signatures, hassle their governments, and use up shoe leather picketing embassies with homemade placards. People demonstrate in the hundreds, in the thousands, in defense of victims whom they do not know personally and who are at times in corners of the globe so remote that no one had ever heard of them before.

The limitless generosity and compassion of this impulse is perhaps the most gratifying phenomenon I have ever witnessed. It may be true, as some would object, that this describes only a minority, while the majority is apathetic and selfish. I know, however, that whatever does exist is already nothing short of miraculous.

The remarkable thing is the deeply rooted human urge to respond to a cry for help, to do something even if the outcome is uncertain. It is overwhelming, this sense of responsibility people have toward the suffering of others! Should this sentiment ever disappear, what we call humanity would also vanish—to be followed shortly thereafter by the human race.

In spite of this, strangely enough, people are not conscious of their own strength, they seem not to have realized that in the last analysis, it is they who make events happen. And in fact some of these campaigns have a carnival air about them: special buttons, lettered T-shirts, postcards, two or three placard-bearing processions. And then the miracle happens. The newspapers will comment gravely on "the victory for world opinion," but this seems much too abstract and too serious. So much so that people feel there must be a catch, that the trick was finally pulled off through secret diplomacy, through a deal or even an exchange.

It was only after visiting several countries that I was able to grasp the scope and the power of the campaign that had preceded my exchange. There was virtually no country where it had not existed. At each public appearance hundreds of people came forward to give me copies of petitions they had signed or clippings from the press. Members of parliament showed me transcripts of the resolutions they had passed, politicians let me look at letters of protest they had sent to the Soviet rulers. And at the same time almost every one of these people wondered why I had been freed.

Strange though it may seem, totalitarian regimes are extremely sensitive to public opinion, although they go to great pains to hide this fact. These regimes stay in power through fear and through the tacit compliance of the populace. Every individual is assumed to be totally defenseless vis-à-vis the state, utterly without rights, patently guilty. Under such conditions, the power of the word is immense, even if it is exercised outside the country. (It is not for nothing that they shot poets in the Soviet Union.) At the same time, both the men in power and the population at large are fully aware of the illegitimacy of the regime. The outside world has become the supreme adjudicator in this underground civil war. Rather like a gangster who, grown rich from the proceeds of his lucrative racket, strives to be received in high society by decking himself out in fancy clothes and imitating the habits of a respectable businessman, the Soviet regime wants to be treated as an equal by the world community. Long gone are the litany of superlatives about the USSR being the most just, the most happy, the most progressive, the most socialist society. Today, Soviet propaganda simply suggests that "things are no worse here" or asks rhetorically whether things are really better "there."

It's much the same in international relations. The aggressiveness shown by the USSR in foreign affairs is a direct result of internal instability and domestic awareness of the regime's illegitimacy. The regime avidly yearns to be accepted as a member in good standing of the world community, yet this is something that is intrinsically impossible. The regime has no use for allies or partners; it needs satraps and accomplices. Fear and silent (or strident) complicity are the principal factors in the projection of Soviet power abroad. (Come to think of it, there is not that much silent complicity; there is far more clamorous ideological support. To some extent this is engendered by the old myths about the happiest and most progressive society, but, since these myths have become tarnished, the main goal becomes channeling social energies in another direction, against South Africa, say, so that the USSR can continue to play the role of shining beacon.)

Another factor of considerable importance is the economic dependence of the Soviet Union on Western technology, credits, and tools. Add to this the current reliance on imports of grains, meat, and so forth. Throw in the persistent lack of stability in the East European satellites, and it will be clear how threatened the Soviets feel by simple things like badges and postcards—in other words, by that which goes by the solemn name of "world opinion."

But the Soviet rulers must conceal this dependence at all costs. What would be the point of depriving their people of free elections and a free press, if in the end they must yield to public opinion anyway, and, what is more, to public opinion *abroad?* For this reason the Soviet authorities do all they can to convince public opinion of the ineffectiveness or even the harm of any sort of open campaign. But, once it becomes apparent to them that a campaign is gaining ground and is not going to run out of steam, they quietly go about trying to find a solution to the problem. They do so very discreetly, so as not to appear to be bowing to public pressure, but rather doing it out of their own free will.

And so the Western myth of Soviet insusceptibility to external pressure has not arisen without Soviet encouragement. The Russians, it is said, are simply that way. The West, which measures everything by its own standards, is ready to write off any political action that does not produce the desired results in the course of two or three years. Efforts tend to be discontinued and discouragement sets in: exactly what the strategists in the Kremlin are counting on.

As for me, I was simply lucky. In nearly every Western country there were people who knew me personally or who had enthusiastically taken up the task of gaining me my freedom.

Cornelia Gerstenmaier, the founder of an association for the defense of human rights in Germany, acted with such vigor that TASS felt called upon to make several releases attacking her. For a long time the Soviets have considered Germany to be their private hunting ground, so they were particularly pained by Cornelia's actions.

In Great Britain, David Markham spent many weeks demonstrating in front of the Soviet embassy. Since my case was linked with the abuse of psychiatry for political ends, British psychiatrists and various associations offered me constant support (for example, CAPA, or the Campaign Against Psychiatric Abuse). Committees similar to CAPA were later formed in France, Switzerland, and Germany, and each offered a helping hand. Although the Congress of the World Psychiatric Association, at its meeting in Mexico City in 1972, shrank from discussing the documents I had gotten to it, numerous national associations and individual psychiatrists in various countries were deeply shocked by this shameful attitude—all the more so when the Soviets, encouraged by the timidity of the congress, gave me a twelve-year prison sentence for "calumny of Soviet psychiatry."

There was a powerful support movement in Holland, where Henk Wolzak had founded an association and where the University of Leyden had "adopted" me as its own "prisoner of conscience." This campaign was not without curious incidents. A family in northern Holland gave my name to their racehorse, which performed successfully in Dutch derbies. Gertrudis, the owner of the horse, regularly participated in demonstrations in front of the Soviet embassy astride her Bukovsky. One can imagine the fury of the ambassador!

And I must make special mention of Amnesty International, which acted with unstinting energy. The efforts of journalist Ludmilla Thorne were particularly helpful here. Together with Patricia Barnes (the wife of the well-known drama critic), she worked ceaselessly on my behalf, organizing meetings and supplying materials to the press. I am also grateful to the committee of American writers and journalists, which includes many famous people, to the scores of Russian friends who had emigrated by that time and dispersed to different parts of the world, to members of the Western press whom I had met in Moscow, and to members of the PEN Club, who enrolled me in their association in absentia. And I must not forget George Meany, who several times spoke personally on my behalf to Nixon, Kissinger, and Ford, or my faithful friends in Norway, painter Victor Sparre and journalist Leif Hovelsen. In short, it is impossible to enumerate all those to whom I am indebted for my sudden liberation.

This campaign, which was perhaps the most tenacious and vigorous of any to date, lasted six years, and became stronger and stronger. Matters came to such a pitch that six months before the new council meeting of the World Psychiatric Association, a meeting at which the Soviets ran the real danger of being condemned by the organization, the Soviet authorities needed to disencumber themselves of the most embarrassing cases. They had to defuse the mounting indignation of the world.

The turn of events was a total surprise to me. In 1970, when I set myself the task of gathering evidence about psychiatric repression, the situation seemed entirely hopeless. High-ranking Soviet psychiatrists declined to participate in our effort for fear of reprisal. Less well-known psychiatrists who joined us (the first one to do so was Gluzman)[6] were soon arrested. I did not put too much store in the Western specialists. How could they possibly understand the complexities of our life? How could they accept information about an unknown individual undergoing coercive therapy when this conflicted with the statements of the most eminent Soviet psychiatrists whom they kept meeting at international congresses?

By a strange twist of fate, however, it was in this area that we were destined to win one of the greatest victories in our twenty years of struggle. By its tragic character, the very act of locking up normal people in insane asylums for political reasons struck people's imaginations. It raised the issue of defining who was sane and who was healthy, and each person could easily picture himself in the place of the victim. Science and technology have become so omnipresent in our time, there is so much regulation of the individual by the state, such fear of losing one's humanity amid mechanisms and computer chips, that the psychiatric problem unexpectedly evoked a profound response. In a giant leap, we had broken from the neolithic age of the communist world to be catapulted into the computer civilization of the twenty-first century. (Isolated as we were in the labor camp at Perm, we had only the vaguest understanding of this process: at the time, Gluzman and I were collaborating on *A Manual on Psychiatry for Political Dissidents*.)[7] The subject became fashionable, provoking scholarly debate and much controversy in the press. The individuals whose cause I had defended had long been freed, and the scope of Soviet repression through psychiatry had lessened somewhat, but the protests reached a crescendo.

The Soviets now tried to save the ship by throwing some ballast overboard, but only succeeded in bringing more trouble on themselves. They exiled to the West nearly all those who had been in asylums for political reasons. These people were immediately examined

[6] Dr. Semyon Gluzman was the first Soviet psychiatrist to protest openly against the political abuse of his profession. The regime retaliated in 1972 by sentencing him to seven years hard labor, to be followed by three years of exile—Ed.

[7] An English translation of this handbook was published by Amnesty International in 1975—Ed.

by Western specialists and found to be perfectly healthy. They also let go several Soviet psychiatrists, who revealed the ways in which their profession was being manipulated. It all added fuel to the fire. The problem of psychiatric abuse acquired the status of an established concern in the Western world. It even became institutionalized: dissertations were written, bibliographies were compiled, commissions were charged with studying the problem. There were even some who were professionally interested in seeing more cases of psychiatric repression. In my opinion, it was the totality of these factors that finally overcame Soviet stubbornness. Realizing that the fever was not going to subside, they resigned themselves to freeing those whose fate caused the greatest clamor. They would then wait out the storm. And since, by chance, I had been at the very center of this storm, it was only a matter of time before I too would be freed.

It is worth recalling that the time was particularly favorable for such campaigns. The principle of human rights had suddenly gained great popularity, as usually happens after an infatuation with collectivist causes. Ten or fifteen years previously, when the first facts about psychiatric persecutions in the USSR had come to light—I have in mind the cases of Tarsis, Naritsa, and even earlier, that of Esenin-Volpin[8]—there had been virtually no response. But now a humanistic Renaissance was replacing the Marxist Middle Ages. The appearance of *The Gulag Archipelago* had riveted the world's attention on Eastern Europe. The concepts of "dissident" and of "dissident movement" became very important in people's thinking, providing a new faith for youth disenchanted by Marxist dogma. Even today, the topic can draw an audience of thousands in Italy and France. That which had been an unconscious impulse during the so-called revolution of 1968 now sud-

[8]Writer Valery Tarsis was committed to a mental hospital after publishing two stories abroad in 1962. Released after foreign protests, he wrote *Ward 7*, a novel based on his experiences in the asylum. The English translation of the book (1965) attracted attention to the issue of Soviet psychiatric abuse. Mikhail Naritsa, an artist and writer who had spent many years in camps and exile during the Stalin period, was arrested in 1961 for sending his novel, *Unsung Song*, abroad for publication. Interned for three years in a special psychiatric hospital, Naritsa later (1970) published a *samizdat* account of his arrest and imprisonment. Aleksandr Esenin-Volpin experienced both labor camp and mental-hospital imprisonment in Stalin's time. He was arrested again in 1959 after sending abroad a manuscript entitled *A Leaf of Spring*, containing poems and a philosophical treatise. He was placed in a psychiatric facility until 1961 and was recommitted after the publication of this text in the West. In the mid-1960s Volpin became one of the mentors of the human rights movement in the USSR, and another forcible hospitalization (1968) led to a public outcry that brought about his release. Volpin's many *samizdat* statements include vigorous protests against psychiatric persecution of political dissidents—ED.

denly acquired articulate expression, and our experience turned out to be both relevant and up-to-date.

In the twinkling of an eye, they all became dissidents: dissident Marxists, dissident Catholics, dissident artists, and dissident writers. No one was quite sure of the exact meaning of the word, but that did not matter. The essential thing was to be against the majority, to act on one's own, and to be persecuted. Psychiatry, the abhorred symbol of common sense, bourgeois conformity, and the establishment in general, was juxtaposed to everything new, revolutionary, and unclassified. That's what our problem became when viewed through the prism of the West.

It was an astonishing turn of events. For several decades, among them the darkest ones in Russian history, millions of human beings were exterminated as "enemies of the people," and those who were imprisoned in insane asylums considered themselves the lucky ones. Yet Soviet society then seemed a shining ideal to the youth of the West—young people just like those of today, who shudder in horror at descriptions of Soviet psychiatric prisons. In former times the progressive West saw our jailers as fighters in the battle against the establishment; while to us the Western establishment seemed the only defense against our hangmen. It's just like that old Soviet story about two ships passing each other at sea, one steaming toward the USSR and the other steaming West. The passengers on both vessels crowd the rails looking at each other and point significantly to their heads: "Those guys must be crazy!"

What in fact had changed? In fifty years, the Soviet regime may have become a shade less bloody, may have begun to look a bit more like a normal state, and had thus become more accessible to the foreign observer. During the same period the countries of the West had become more socialist, and had in some respects begun to resemble the Soviet Union. Communism and Marxism ceased being the ideology of rebels, having been absorbed by the establishment. Each side thought it recognized in the other its shadow or semblance. The paradox of the situation was that this politico-optical illusion was exposed thanks to psychiatry, thanks to our *samizdat*,[9] thanks to our desperate protests and to the harshness of the sentences we received.

Could we have expected such a reversal? Certainly not. We were of course dealing with a very specific problem, not with something symbolic. We were concerned about flesh-and-blood people who were

---

[9] *Samizdat* refers to the system whereby literary, political, or other texts that cannot be published in the USSR are reproduced privately (as a rule, on a typewriter with several carbon copies) and distributed chain-letter fashion—ED.

locked in specific psychiatric prisons, and we had to engage in a very real struggle to get them out. The West was far from being uppermost in our minds: we thought of it only as a possible means of support. But it is the way of all ideologies, religions, and beliefs to make symbols of actual events. For Jesus, too, the cross was probably an all too real wooden crosspiece, and the crown of thorns scraped his face in a very direct fashion.

In a democracy, every mass movement, whether it stands for the protection of the environment or the protection of a species of animal, inevitably becomes a political force that everyone tries to bend to his own goals. The Universal Declaration of Human Rights was promulgated in 1948 and does not seem to have caused any particular excitement in the succeeding years. But after we came upon the scene, suddenly socialists, Communists, Catholics, businessmen, and governments alike swore by this document.

The Soviets were unprepared for this new twist. Neither Marx nor Lenin had said anything about the rights of man. This time the initiative was not in the hands of the Communist Party of the Soviet Union—that alleged "vanguard of progressive humanity"—a most unfortunate development. Soviet authorities had missed the beginning of a new movement, unlike their management of the Movement for the Defense of Peace, which had served them as a docile tool during the 1940s and 1950s. Their lack of flexibility had left them isolated, faced with constantly growing public pressure. No matter how much abuse was heaped on South Africa or Latin America, it was not enough to deflect attacks on the USSR. I suppose that by accepting this singular exchange of Corvalán for myself the Soviets expected to turn around public opinion. That would explain why they hoped so ardently that I would take up residence in Pinochet's country.

Having recovered somewhat, the Soviet propagandists now launched a great hue and cry about "the hundreds of thousands of political prisoners in the U.S.A." ("Andrew Young has personally admitted it at the U.N."), the Wilmington Ten, the *Berufsverbot* in Germany, and torture in northern Ireland.[10] The leitmotif was familiar: "It's no better over there." And everywhere pro-Soviet "forces of world socialism" came back to life, proclaiming that everything was relative, that it was more a question of nuance, and that when all was said and done, life in the West was no cause for envy. Reassured, the statesmen went back to their deals, to their balancing, and to a healthy prag-

---

[10] At that time, Young was the U.S. representative at the UN. *Berufsverbot* refers to the West German prohibition against granting government-paid employment to adherents of extreme political views—Ed.

matism. Nonetheless, something very important, although barely perceptible, had changed in the world.

From then on, there would be ever more people walking back and forth in front of embassies with homemade placards, even though the total number of misfortunes in the world would not lessen from it. But as far as the Soviets were concerned, they simply had to find a way of getting rid of us.

◆　◆　◆

"No 'pravda' in *Izvestiia*, and no 'izvestiia' in *Pravda*" is the favorite pun among Soviet journalists: "There is no truth in *The News*, and no news in *The Truth*."

In point of fact, however, by reading Soviet newspapers knowledgeably, one can gain a fairly clear idea of political life in the West and of some specific events. But one needs to master the full range of Soviet symbols, all the journalistic tricks and clichés that allow one to read between the lines. One also needs to keep in mind that every publication in the Soviet Union is influenced by the interaction of two forces: on the one hand is Soviet ideological control, on the other is the desire of the journalist to elude this control, usually by pretending to be an overzealous idiot. *Homo sovieticus* is simply built that way: he has an irresistible urge to stick out his tongue behind the backs of the much-loved regime. The best technique is to play the well-meaning fool who wants all to work out for the best, but who manages to botch everything.

Certain simple souls are inclined simply to read the Soviet press backwards: they see it as a "mirror image" of reality. If the press vilifies someone, then that individual must be a fine person, and vice versa. If the press talks all the time about peace, it must mean that war is coming, and one should make haste to stock up on matches, soap, and salt before these items disappear from the stores. If the press boasts of a record harvest, one should expect famine. This formula has a certain truth to it, but such a simplistic approach deprives the reader of the bulk of the news, leaving him with a pretty thin idea of what is going on. The important information is encoded in the nuances and shadings.

News from abroad, for example, needs to be quoted from foreign sources, and the identity of this source is a crucial indicator. If the article states that "even the bourgeois daily, *Le Monde*, is forced to admit" or "even a newspaper as hostile to us as the *New York Times* states" or, to take an even stronger example, "*The Guardian*, which no one could accuse of being procommunist, writes," then the Soviets, or the "progressive forces," have chalked up a new victory. The reader is disconcerted: "They're supposed to be bourgeois and hostile, so why can't they at least refrain from applause?"

When the articles quote L'Humanité, L'Unità, or the like, that's a lot easier. Our reader will of course assail them, but with a certain relief and a tinge of scorn: "L'Unità is a shit-house, what could one expect!"

But if the article sinks to quoting Unsere Zeit or De Waarheid, and especially if it does so without mentioning that these are communist papers, the reader can be certain that a Soviet failure has occurred. "Aha," he celebrates, "you've been brought down a notch or two, my lovelies. And you have nothing better to quote."

The situation can be even grimmer for the regime when there is nothing at all to quote. On the contrary, their own people have to be brought into line for flirting with Eurocommunism. In these cases (which are rare enough) the report does not carry a dateline from abroad, appearing instead as a small paragraph, over the signature of A. Petrov or simply over initials.[11] In that case, the jubilation of the reader knows no bounds.

Finally, there is the category signaling a complete fiasco, when a press release is issued by TASS, as was done at the time of my exchange:

> It is to be regretted that certain voices have recently joined the anti-Soviet chorus in the West. Apparently bowing to fashion, a number of spokesmen have been repeating the charges about the alleged 'violation of human rights in the Soviet Union.' These individuals forget that this fashion in no way befits them or does them honor.

A wonderful statement! One would like to read such stuff every day! Soviet newspapers can be scanned much more rapidly than those published in the West. On average, a Soviet daily is rarely more than four to six pages long. The experienced reader simply has to read the headlines, identifying familiar clichés: "Ruses of the Enemies of Détente," "Anti-Soviet Sortie," "Provocative Ballyhoo," "Their Life-style," and so on. The rest of the paper, the reports on "Daily Labor," the editorial commentaries, and the feature articles, can be read by scanning diagonally, so as to grasp their aim. The information content is thin.

Vast numbers of people listen to the Russian-language radio broadcasts from the West. They constantly compare what they hear in these

[11] Such signatures are frequently used in Pravda for articles expressing the official point of view—Ed.

broadcasts with what they read in the Soviet press. Under these conditions, the official press ceases to be a source of information. Soviet newspapers resemble a clock that has stopped, but twice every 24 hours does give the correct time. In the same way, when from time to time the Soviet papers do publish something that is true, no one believes them any more. The press is the typographical image of the regime, and people read it in order to catch it at its lies, to gloat over a failure, or else to wonder: "How are they going to worm out of this one? What kind of stuff are they going to dish up about this situation?"

You would think that under such circumstances, the press would be wise to leave certain things unsaid and not try to pass failures off as victories. But that is quite impossible. Since the people already know the truth, silence on the part of the regime would be a sign of uncertainty, perplexity, and a loss of initiative. The regime feels constrained to "answer with dignity," to send out directives to millions of instructors, public speakers, propagandists, and other "front-line ideological workers," so that all of them will know what answers to give and what line to take with the population. No matter if this happens to be the stupidest explanation possible. The essential thing is not to remain passive, not to give the impression that the authorities are losing control of events.

It is considered important to maintain the same posture toward the West. Let the Westerners laugh at Soviet witlessness and let them try to disentangle the endless coils of Soviet lies. It does not matter. As long as a failure is not officially recognized, it has not taken place.

As he peruses his much-loved press, the Soviet reader can only shake his head in wonderment: "Who is ever going to believe all this nonsense? Perhaps we might be fooled at times at home, but in the West it'll be a different story."

That is where we make a mistake. The twaddle that is served up in the Soviet press is often more readily accepted by the West than by readers at home.

Because in the USSR we are consciously deprived of facts, we search for information wherever we find it. Over here, on the other hand, the public is surfeited with information, and as a consequence hears only what it wants to hear. One of the typical results of this difference is that we are far better informed about the West than the West is informed about us.

We know that we are constantly being deceived, so we are on the lookout for the lie everywhere. In the West, however, the public is not used to expecting deceptions, so it does not automatically search for it, and thus accepts information in a far less critical manner. Here is a curious example of what I mean. Some years ago, the experts announced that certain natural products, such as butter, meat, and the like, could be harmful to the human system. In the West, this caused the consumption of these products to plummet: various types of diets and the consumption of fat-free surrogate foods came into vogue. When the Soviet press reported the same findings, it only drew ironic smiles: the assumption was that the administration had to dream up something to justify the shortages of meat and butter!

The West has only a theoretical understanding of propaganda. No one, not even government agencies or persons engaged in counterespionage, can fully grasp the scope of the ideological war being carried on against the West. A classic spy à la James Bond will probably still be recognized as such (though to do so is not wholly in good taste, for the label "witch-hunt" can be applied), but people do not have the least idea what an ideological agent might be. For example, a highly respected Washington professor publishes solidly pro-Soviet articles in prominent journals. What is there to complain about? "It's his opinion," and in a democracy he has an absolute right to hold such views and to express them. What is wrong with that? Why not let the reader himself sift out the truth? We are touching on something of critical importance here: the criterion for truth. There can be three approaches to truth: truth is truth, one and the same everywhere; truth is somewhere halfway between two contradictory opinions; there are many truths, and each judgment is true in its own way.

Each one of these approaches can obviously be valid, when applied to different sorts of problems. Unfortunately, however, people brought up in different systems exhibit distinct preferences for the criterion with which they are familiar, and they tend to ignore the other two. I have often observed this difference when comparing the manner of disputation in the USSR and in the West. In our country, we would spend whole nights arguing until we are hoarse, trying to convince our opponent of our point of view, or at least thrashing out a single belief we could both accept. Nothing of the sort happens here. Both sides simply expound their points of view, define their terms, and detail their position, but there is no substantive debate. There might be an attempt to arrive at a compromise, but not to attain *the* truth.

It is not easy to explain this phenomenon. Perhaps after we rejected the communist ideology, we unconsciously adopted its attitude toward truth. Or perhaps it is that people in the West, brought up in a pluralistic society, are accustomed to the instrumentality of truth and are prone to compromise. (These observations of course relate to the so-called average person in both worlds: there are numerous exceptions.)

It is not difficult to picture the effect of Soviet propaganda on each camp. A Soviet citizen who is confronted by two opposing viewpoints will set about trying "to dig out the truth." The Westerner will either accept both opinions or try to arrive at a synthesis of both. There is no harm in an honest debate. But the Western pluralist, when faced by a choice between facts and deliberate misinformation, will end up accepting at least half of the Soviet lies. As the past master of propaganda, Joseph Goebbels, used to say, "For a lie to become credible, it has to be gigantic." In effect, then, if the lie is of monstrous proportions, the "middle ground" will turn out to be squarely within the lie.

If it were only a matter of credulousness, indifference, or Soviet agents, there would be hope in overcoming this communication block. But unfortunately the situation is more serious than that. The problems are rooted in the foundations of Western political life and in the idea that, as *Pravda* states, "the balance of power in the world has changed in favor of the forces of socialism." That is not merely a banal propaganda cliché. In any Soviet newspaper one can read about the "forces of peace, progress, and socialism," which must inevitably triumph, and about the "forces of reaction and of imperialism," which are destined to fail. It will not do to read these statements as mirror images of the truth, i.e., as statements that must simply be reversed.

One needs to spend some time in the West before one can appreciate the Soviet press. The Western papers are jam-packed with information, but it is all diverse and dissimilar. Try to figure out who represents the "peace forces" or the "forces of progress"! And identifying "the forces of reaction" is simply beyond possibility. This is the time to head for the nearest newsstand to pick up a copy of *Pravda*.

During the last two years or so that I spent in Vladimir prison, we had made it a rule to subscribe to virtually all the major Soviet newspapers and magazines. Each participant would go over four or five publications, and then the data garnered would be brought to a general discussion. Of course a lot of things remained contradictory or unclear, but when I arrived in the West, I found that many of my notions about it were astonishingly accurate. Needless to say, there were many quite elementary things about which I was uninformed, but what I did know was right on target.

Our prison community back in those times fell into two roughly equal camps: the optimists and the pessimists. Being a skeptic by nature, I naturally gravitated toward the second group. This was so especially in view of the way our debates would typically end, with the guard banging on the door and threatening us with solitary if we did not shut up, at which point the "optimists" would invariably throw out their crowning argument: "It is not possible that the people in the

West don't know what they are doing. They must have reasons about which we know nothing. They are not idiots!"

When I found myself in Europe, I discovered with a shock that I had been a starry-eyed optimist. When we were relative youngsters in the 1960s, we obviously did not read the Soviet press, and we certainly did not take it seriously. We believed that we were fighting the KGB and the party. All the others were supposed to be in our camp. As we got a bit older, we began to realize that our adversary was "Soviet man," and things became more complicated. And now it suddenly dawned on me that for twenty years, we had been fighting with practically the whole world. Had I known this earlier, I might have thought before I leapt in.

Twenty years ago, it is true, all this was not so evident. No one anticipated that our movement would gather such strength, so it seemed appropriate enough to give some sympathy to the weak underdogs. But now that our movement has engendered an international human rights movement in Western Europe with the subsequent public pressure on particular governments, and now that "the dissident factor" has begun to play a role in international politics, it has suddenly turned out that no political force is interested in lending us its support.

Our activities stick in the throat of one part of the Western establishment—the peace movement. These individuals desire above all to strike a friendly deal with the Soviets, yielding anything the Soviets might ask for. They argue that the Soviets will eventually get what they want anyway, so why not yield without a struggle? One should not arouse the "Russian bear."

Above all, one must trade, trade, and trade still more. The exports can be anything from Coca-Cola to human dignity. There is even the theory that liberation movements behind the iron curtain are dangerous: they might destabilize the balance of power and bring about war. Well-fed communism is preferable to hungry communism, and commerce is therefore a tool for building peace. Our movement simply hinders agreement between the sides. For proponents of these views, the difference between ideologies is irrelevant and may in fact be nonexistent.

For another section of the Western establishment (the "forces of progress and socialism"), we represent a knife held to the throat. For these individuals, the USSR is "objectively" an ally, and it is highly undesirable to criticize it in any form, for doing so is an indirect reproof to their own views. The witness we bear undermines their most fundamental assumptions. And in addition—in contrast to most Czech exiles, for example—the overwhelming majority of people emigrating from Russia do not support socialism, nor do they believe that socialism "with a human face" is possible. Our experience has been deeper, more cruel, and more prolonged. The Czechs can allow themselves to distinguish between a socialism brought in on the points of bayonets and an idyllic sort of socialism, whereas we do not have any such historical alibi. Strange to say, this has turned out to be an utter surprise for the "the forces of progress," who for a long time considered us to be a variant form of Eurocommunism. It seems that they had been led astray by our emphasis on human rights and nonviolent means, a position that was taken to be equivalent to a desire for a better, more humane, type of socialism. This probably explains why those very forces supported us at the beginning, contributing a great deal to the growing campaign in our defense. Once this misapprehension was cleared away, our attitude was perceived by many as almost a betrayal or even a deception. It was in any case a tremendous disappointment.

The above comments naturally pertain to those in the establishment, of whatever political stripe. The only ones who wholeheartedly supported us were the young people who were sincerely trying to find their own way, whatever their political allegiance, as well as individuals without any political orientation. But this represents a very substantial force, and together with the politically uncommitted sector of the press it makes up what is known as world public opinion. Our opponents do not even dare to challenge us openly or to engage in honest debate on substantive issues; they limit themselves to personal attacks. This is, of course, a method long used by Soviet propaganda, and it was therefore no surprise to us. The technique is known as "poisoning the source." The only difference is that when a Soviet reader finds a statement in *Pravda*, say, to the effect that Solzhenitsyn is a warmonger or Sakharov is an agent of world imperialism, all he does is roar with laughter. The Western public reads the press far less critically. Once something has appeared in print, the feeling is that there must be something to it.

♦ ♦ ♦

I usually try to avoid moralizing or the use of ethical labels such as "good" or "evil." And yet, in order to give a clear and succinct account of the present world situation, one ends up having to do just that. *Truth* is always naive and sure of itself; it takes for granted that it will triumph as soon as it is recognized. That explains why the forces of truth are usually so poorly organized. The *lie*, on the contrary, is cynical, shrewd, and splendidly organized. It does not labor under the slightest illusion about its own merits or chances of winning an honest victory; it is therefore ready to use any and every means.

In reality, efforts to block the introduction of the "dissident factor" into world politics, and attempts to liquidate it altogether, began long ago. I shall skip over the period when a communist-inspired terror of unprecedented scale and cruelty was simply ignored, and fugitives from this "paradise" were dubbed "capitalists and landowners," "fascists," or Western agents. It is staggering to recognize that Europe simply failed to take note of the extermination of some 66 million people in a neighboring country! As we have now learned, scores of books and hundreds of articles did address this issue at the time. They were written and published, but they passed unnoticed, because the invisible hand of the lie had managed to poison the credibility of the sources.

It became impossible to maintain silence after the Soviet government itself admitted the existence of these monstrous crimes. But there was soon a chorus of "specialists" who maintained that all illegalities had been removed by Khrushchev, and that the USSR was steeped in liberalism (this at the moment of the bloody suppression of the disturbances at Novocherkassk and at Aleksandrov).[12] There followed assurances that the dissidents were only a tiny group without any following and were therefore without the slightest significance. Since then the demise of the movement has been announced regularly. This has been going on for about fifteen years now.

During the 1960s, it took an immense effort to publicize any news about the arrests that were going on inside the Soviet Union. A Western journalist who was expelled from Moscow might well find himself fired by his employer when he returned home, or else transferred to an undesirable spot: he was considered inept for failing to get on with the Soviet authorities. Even at a later time (1970), my friend Holger Jensen, the Moscow correspondent of the Associated Press, was forbidden by his Washington office to write any more articles after his interview with me, and he was thereupon transferred to Vietnam.[13] It was the beginning of the era of détente, and the World Congress of Psychiatrists in Mexico City, under direct pressure from politicians, refused to schedule any discussion on the documents we had pro-

---

[12] There were serious riots in the industrial towns of Aleksandrov and Murom in 1961, and a major disturbance (crushed with great bloodshed) occurred in Novocherkassk in 1962. See the final chapter of Solzhenitsyn's *Gulag Archipelago*, vol. 3, for details—Ed.

[13] The interview focused on Bukovsky's experiences in mental hospitals and prison camps; it was published in the *Washington Post* (May 17, 1970) and other American papers—Ed.

cured for them. (Perhaps it would be more precise to say that the era of détente had begun in 1917.)

It took many years of exertion by honest men in both East and West before our voices were finally heard. Then came the forced emigration of hundreds of individuals active in the human rights movement, followed immediately by a spate of articles in the Western press about the poor adjustment these people were making to life in the free world. The implication was that sympathy for them was inappropriate, since a lack of freedom was their natural state.

There is yet another argument, an inspired debating stratagem. Since you have suffered at the hands of the regime, we are told, you cannot be objective or impartial. That's quite an invention, isn't it? To follow such logic, one must not give credence to the testimony of an inmate at Auschwitz, who has obviously suffered. Neither should one listen to what the Jews say about Nazi Germany: they have lost members of their families in the gas chambers, and how can they possibly be objective? Under these rules, who has earned the right to be heard? Defectors are not to be believed, victims cannot be objective, and the majority has been cowed into silence. There remain only the Soviet (or Nazi) authorities to reveal to us the full and impartial truth.

Solzhenitsyn is of course the number one target. One rumor had it that he has built his own little Gulag in Vermont, complete with barbed wire, if you please. In the next breath, he is reported on the way to see Pinochet. Or else it is suddenly discovered that he is the founder of a "New Right," or of a "National Bolshevik" party. The accusations are too numerous to list. In the course of three months in 1979 alone, I counted sixteen articles in the world press against Solzhenitsyn. Even inside the Soviet Union, he had not been considered worthy of a campaign of such scope. And of course I am talking about the noncommunist press.

The ultimate argument was always the same: we are all reactionaries. And so at last I learned the identity of those "reactionary forces" for which I had hunted high and low in the West. I had almost gotten to the point where I did not believe they existed.

When I arrived in Norway, it was not some communist tabloid but the leading newspaper in the country that featured a long article illustrated by two photographs. Beneath the picture of Solzhenitsyn was the caption "Bukovsky," and my photo was labeled "Solzhenitsyn." The article was larded throughout with phrases like "at the service of the forces of reaction," "servants of big capital," and so on. One might as well have been reading *Pravda*.

At about this time the British *Guardian* published an article by Dobkin, a correspondent of the Soviet news agency, Novosti. It was the usual display of civil discourse: I was both a terrorist and an agent of imperialism! At first I was delighted. Comrade Dobkin, I thought, now you are going to catch it; you forgot you are not in Moscow, my good sir. We are in the land of law here, and you will be brought to account for your slanders. Here was the chance to smoke out the source of the allegation about the "assault groups" to which I was supposed to belong. I was waiting for formal apologies from the *Guardian* before turning my attention to Dobkin. The case dragged on for two years. In the meantime Dobkin joined the staff of the Soviet embassy and was now protected by diplomatic immunity. Throughout this process I received press clippings from the United States, to the effect that I was an accursed reactionary who had stuck a "workingman's newspaper" with a lawsuit. The distance between this and *Izvestiia* was not exactly obvious.

One should add that the label of "reactionary" is dispensed with extraordinary ease. You earn it instantly, if you say (1) that you don't believe in socialism or (2) that you don't support détente. Three weeks after my arrival in Zurich, the local *Tages-Anzeiger* reported that I had "changed" with startling speed from a "political agnostic" into a "second Solzhenitsyn." This metamorphosis, the paper maintained, was brought about by the "reactionary milieu" by which I was surrounded and which had prevented any contact between me and "undesirable" members of the press. All of this was precipitated by my criticisms of détente. The author of the article had been sitting right beside me during my first press conference in Zurich, and he could not have helped but hear what I had to say about the marked deterioration of conditions inside the prisons once the Helsinki Accords were signed. The same article went on to claim that the reactionary forces had tried to enlist Plyushch, but that he had gone into hiding in Paris.[14] At that point in time Plyushch considered himself a Marxist, and thus was "approved" by the likes of *Tages-Anzeiger*.

Today it is amusing to recall the attempts to bring about quarrels between us, to enlist us in causes that were not ours, to group us according to whether we were "good" or "bad," and especially to classify us as "right" or "left."

Many years ago physiologist Ivan Pavlov designed the following experiment. He had conditioned a dog to expect food at the sight of a circle and to expect an electric shock at the sight of a rectangle. Thus trained, the dog was presented with a figure that was neither a circle

---

[14] Leonid Plyushch, a Ukrainian mathematician prominent in the human rights movement, spent three years in a special psychiatric hospital for his activities. He emigrated in 1976—Ed.

nor a rectangle, but something halfway between: an oval. The animal experienced a nervous collapse. When the West came into contact with the human rights movement in the Soviet Union, the reaction was in some ways similar. The prisoners of the spiritual gulag in the West, conditioned as they were to thinking exclusively in terms of "right" or "left," and divided by their astonishing ideological intolerance, could not seem to understand that they were faced by a radically new phenomenon. To our consternation, we learned that for them it was vastly more important to know with whom they might sit at the same table, speak at the same meeting, or sign the same petition than it was to grasp the essence of the speech or of the document they signed.

To us this seemed crazy. Just as a compass is of no earthly use at the North Pole, so traditional political labels are simply not applicable to the USSR. Who could claim to be more to the right or more to the left of Brezhnev? Even in the West such distinctions long ago ceased to make sense. What is there in common between the liberals of Japan and those of Germany, for example, or between the socialists of Great Britain and those of Italy? Where is right or left if Italian Communists are more conservative than British Labourites, or if American trade unions are seen as more "reactionary" than multimillionaires like the Kennedys or the Rockefellers? Such distinctions are preposterous nonsense; they serve only as a handy means for instituting intellectual terror. When the world is viewed in radically ideological terms, thoughts are replaced by labels, words lose their meanings, and the most loudmouthed demagogue ends up in the "progressive" ranks.

In the contemporary political arena, there is always the tactic of outpacing your adversary on the left by claiming he is a "reactionary": he will in effect be ostracized. And since every ideology needs its devil, the demonization of one's adversary begins. Little by little, a "climate of murder" is created around him, and before long a terrorist appears on the scene. In this way the derailed train inexorably tumbles into the abyss, each car dragging the next one to its ruin. Where should one locate the social democrats at present? They are now considered reactionaries! And what about the liberals? They have become "enemies of the people" and so are targets for terrorists.

And yet people here still press us with questions about how Stalin's Great Terror could get started; we are asked to explain how it was that Soviet communism lost its human face. The fact is that the West is in many ways ready for the same.

It was astonishing. We had emerged from a closed-off country where we had been deprived of all genuine political life. We arrived in the West feeling a bit like provincials who have stumbled into the nation's capital, and suddenly realized that politically we were several decades more mature. And although many of us have different political preferences, it will be impossible to divide us into "camps." We have been effectively cured of this kind of dangerous dichotomy, thanks to injections of sulphazine and the applications of "roll-ups."[15] We know of only one political camp, the concentration camp, where everyone gets fed the same slop. There is nothing to the left or right of that camp apart from the perimeter, with its "forbidden zone" where guards are trained to fire on sight. Our experience there has taught us that there is only one struggle in this world, that of the human against the inhuman, of life against the forces of death. Every last one of us is responsible for the final outcome of this struggle.

But it would be naive to imagine that the "forces of peace and progress" have gracefully accepted their lack of success in creating divisions among us. Having failed at that endeavor, they set about inventing their own dissident: a person whose views could be usefully contrasted with those of a genuine human rights activist. It was not a difficult task. In the last ten years, 250,000 people have emigrated from the Soviet Union, and the population of Moscow has long stood at 8 million people. So if one needs to restrain Carter in his campaign to defend human rights, one can easily find a spokesman who will announce to the press that Carter's attitude is positively harmful. And this would become prominent, front-page news, while a letter from political prisoners in support of Carter would appear somewhere near the back in the form of a brief summary, and not by any means in all the papers. Sakharov sends a message to the Belgrade Conference, and the *New York Times* inserts in the immediately following space on the same page a statement by "other dissidents" to the effect that Sakharov is a well-meaning but naive eccentric, a man isolated from the people, a general without an army.

No doubt the greatest discovery in this maneuvering were the brothers Medvedev (Roy and Zhores).[16] This in spite of the fact that they have never laid claim to the title of dissident, preferring to be considered advisers to the "doves in the Politburo." In the West, they were pronounced to be leaders of the "left wing of the dissidents." In

---

[15] Sulphazine consists of purified sulphur dissolved in peach oil. Intramuscular injections of this substance cause prolonged pain and acute hyperthemia (fever) and are used as "remedies for violent behavior" in Soviet hospitals. "Roll-ups" or "wet rolls" (*ukrutki*, in Russian) are another form of "treatment" whereby a prisoner is tightly wrapped in wet canvas or a wet bed sheet. The material shrinks as it dries, inflicting great pain and making breathing progressively more difficult—ED.

[16] Roy Medvedev, a neo-Leninist historian, resides in Moscow. Zhores Medvedev, a biologist, has lived in England since 1973—ED.

the course of my frequent international travels, I was astonished by the industriousness of those two brothers: they seemed to find time to get published in virtually every newspaper. Sakharov is nominated for the Nobel Prize, and presto, Zhores turns up in Norway to argue that it is inconceivable to give the Nobel Prize to the father of the H-bomb. A campaign is launched in defense of the imprisoned Helsinki group, and Zhores is ready with an explanation for a Paris daily newspaper to the effect that Western publicity endangers people in the USSR. Aleksandr Ginzburg is sentenced to eight years in special prison, and Roy hastens to announce that Ginzburg is a very unreliable person. When there is a hope that the abuses of Soviet psychiatry will be condemned in Honolulu, Zhores makes an appearance in the United States to announce that except for himself, and perhaps one other (Plyushch), no one has ever been hospitalized for political reasons. In a word, their productivity would do credit to a Stakhanovite. Just the two of them managed to kick up a ruckus the world over.

It was indeed an effective invention, letting the "dissidents" neutralize each other. Solzhenitsyn is a "dissident writer," and he is juxtaposed to X, some unknown or suspicious character who is also proclaimed a "dissident writer." It makes one think of Stalin's threat to Nadezhda Krupskaia: "We may have to find another widow of Lenin." The important thing was to present the dissidents as people who don't know what they want, and who spend their days squabbling with each other.

This was by no means a matter of a few isolated episodes: it was a superbly coordinated international orchestra possessed of great power. I am not at all asserting that the conductor's podium is situated in the Kremlin, but it certainly does seem that events follow a well-rehearsed pattern. Hard as things were in the USSR, we were confronted by a wall of reinforced concrete that nevertheless could be breached, given a sufficient level of persistence. Here, it is a wall of cotton wadding that envelops you on every side.

◆ ◆ ◆

I was not personally affected by this phenomenon at first. During the first three or four months, the democratic gods of publicity were in such a state of excitement that even the wall of cotton opened up for a time, and that triple-headed monster known as the "forces of peace, progress, and socialism" had to tap its foot and wait patiently for things to calm down. Only two third-rate communist papers spoke up, and those in countries where the Communist party is so tiny that it has to be financed directly from the Soviet Union: *Unsere Zeit* in West Germany, and *De Waarheid* in Holland. These papers are virtually unknown in their countries of publication, but they were the only ones the Soviets could find for their foreign quotations, no doubt to their great frustration.

After this first salvo, the Soviet press stayed silent for about a month, hoping that things would quiet down. But I had not gone to visit Pinochet, nor had the "soap bubble" burst as the Soviets had predicted. And so orders were issued to mount a counterattack.

One would have to be a well-trained Soviet reader to appreciate the consternation and fear of the authorities. During February, March, and April of 1977, the Soviets felt called upon to publish almost daily attacks on me. A brief list gives the idea: "Thick as Thieves" (*Trud*), "*Unsere Zeit* in Arms Against the Enemies of Peace" (*Pravda*), "Puppet Manipulated by Reactionaries" (*Izvestiia*), "Fawning over a Renegade" (*Sovetskaia Rossiia*), "Betting on Anticommunism" (*Pravda*), "In the Pay of NATO" (*Pravda*), "Truth About the Provocative Uproar" (*Izvestiia*), and "We Consider Him a Traitor" (*Komsomolskaia pravda*). The quantity alone points to panic. And as for the content of these articles, it defies the imagination. Only a month before, readers had been assured that I was a mental defective, a virtual fascist, one who had succeeded in repelling everyone I had met. But now they had to admit that the "Western press, radio, and television had continued to make a great fuss over this renegade." "Numerous leaders of the Christian-Democratic movement are taking part in this chorus of provocateurs." "Whom do we see among Bukovsky's friends in West Germany? Kohl, the president of the CDU." "Unfortunately, the anti-Soviet statements of Bukovsky get picked up by the radio and television of West Germany."

The reports with a British dateline (which also appeared in the Soviet press, with a month's delay) were more of an attack on the Conservatives than on me. The impression was created that I had either invented their policies or that their platform had been specially created for my sake.

One smart-alecky stringer (no doubt a closet anti-Soviet of the type who cannot resist the chance to thumb his nose behind the back of the master) wrote the following in *Izvestiia*:

> Mrs. Thatcher, who trumpets her anti-Sovietism at every opportunity, welcomed the new "fighter for freedom" with open arms. The reception was so ardent that it provoked a debate in Parliament. Mrs. Thatcher maintained in the House of Commons that the government ought to pay far greater attention to Bukovsky and to the information that he can provide about life in the Soviet Union.

Mr. Callaghan declared in response that the British government's views concerning the situation in the USSR are well known, and that the prime minister has not the slightest intention of *courting popularity* by an unnecessary meeting with the Russian dissident.[17]

The whole thing seemed unreal. "Ardent reception" by the opposition, lively debate in Parliament, a prime minister who could have increased his popularity had he chosen to receive me, but instead proudly abstained from such an easy way of ingratiating himself . . . What had become of the ignorant moron or the common criminal, of the terrorist and maniac? I can just imagine how much the Soviet reader of the press would have delighted in all of this.

This was followed by the culminating point of it all, a true gem of Soviet journalism, and the high point of panic. The statement by TASS was datelined Washington, D.C., March 2:

Jimmy Carter, the president of the United States, yesterday received Bukovsky, a man expelled from the Soviet Union, a common criminal who is also noted for his relentless opposition to the improvement of Soviet-American relations.

Before this meeting, Bukovsky engaged in conversation with Vice-President Walter Mondale.

That was the full extent of what *Pravda* had to say on the matter on that particular day. It was not the usual stuff: "Provocative Intrigues" or "Anti-Soviet Actions." The heading, "Reception in the White House," suggested something very different, perhaps a report on the Soviet ambassador's visit, or a meeting with a foreign minister. But then came the line about a common criminal who at the same time could influence Soviet-American relations. There was no explanation: the message was as terse and full of despair as an SOS. It was at this point that the "forces of peace and progress" sprang into action.

Up to that time, I had only met certain leaders of the opposition. The governments in power—whether the British Labourites, the German liberals and socialists, or the French Giscardians and Gaullists—were all careful not to receive me, in order not to distress their Soviet friends. Judged as I was by Western standards, it followed that I was perceived as being too conservative in Britain and Germany, too leftist in France. (I should add that in France the opposition also treated me gingerly, and I was welcomed primarily by reformed "leftists" like Armand Gatti, individuals who had become deeply involved in the struggle for human rights.) Brandt was too busy, Callaghan already

[17] At the time, Mr. Callaghan was the Labourite prime minister, and Mrs. Thatcher was the leader of the Conservative opposition—ED.

knew all about life in the Soviet Union (and also was too modest). Only the Dutch government was ready to give our movement its outspoken support.

Carter's gesture broke this blockade of silence and made things awkward for his opposite numbers in Europe, while his promise to make human rights a cornerstone of his administration must have sounded extremely ominous to their ears. At least in the beginning it appeared that in the long history of confrontation between democracy and totalitarianism, there had at last appeared a head of state who was willing openly to defend the values of our civilization. It threatened to deal a heavy blow to all three "forces" (peace, progress, and socialism) after a half-century-long policy of capitulation and secret agreements.

It goes without saying that the SOS from TASS was noticed immediately. The next day, a major American newspaper wrote:

> It is worth asking ourselves whether our country has the right to dictate to others how they should live. If we take on a mentor's role, it could lead other countries to exercise greater caution in their dealings with the United States.

After stressing the slanted nature of the new policy, the American journalist for some reason switched to events in Nicaragua. That is just the way the Soviets would have done it, and the article was deemed worthy of long quotes in *Pravda*.

Other newspapers, each just as "bourgeois" and "hostile," adopted a similar tone, trying to influence the president with dire warnings of "possible negative consequences." One would have thought Carter had ordered a general mobilization and nuclear alert. But as the well-meaning bourgeois anxieties and the hypocrisies of the "progressives" became more and more prominent, the tone of the Soviet press became ever more serene. And although the Soviet newspapers continued to chip away at Carter and myself for several months thereafter, claiming that it had been a case of interference in the internal affairs of another country, "action unfitting for a president," and so on, the Soviet reader could see clearly that the danger to the regime was past, and that they had gotten off with no more than a scare.

Why does Brezhnev not hesitate to embrace Corvalán before the TV cameras of the world, and no one, not even a spokesman for the Chilean regime, considers it an "interference in the internal affairs of another country," while our modest meeting with President Carter is taken as a "threat to peace and progress"? Why is the president of the United States not free to receive people who resist a totalitarian and repressive regime by strictly nonviolent means, men who are defending the very same principles that are written into the American Constitution and international accords? And why can the Soviets at the same time be permitted to send arms, money, and even troops to support their murderous puppets all over the world? And what does Nicaragua—a country where dictatorships from the right superseded dictatorships from the left about ten times a year—have to do with all this? Why did the American newspaper pretend to not understand the difference between a small dictatorship in a small country that menaces no one, and a totalitarian regime, master of half the world, that intends to impose its system on all of humanity and has been at war for the last fifty years, either openly or in secret, against all that is human?

One could line up such "whys" by the thousands without ever getting a satisfactory answer. "The forces of peace, progress, and socialism" do not deem us worthy of dialogue, just like the Soviet authorities. The only answer one can expect is lies, calumnies, and of course the charge of being "reactionary."

I am afraid that President Carter himself did not realize the significance of the event. The subsequent pressure brought upon him by France, Germany, and the above-mentioned forces within the United States soon put an end to his pronouncements on human rights. It seems that he did not grasp the potential consequences of this new policy. This certainly applies to the symbolic import of our meeting, which was essentially a fortuitous episode.

◆　◆　◆

Mike Wallace is more than a TV journalist: he's a real artist. Sprawled casually on his chair, he would ask questions that seemed entirely spontaneous: "Tell me, you've had two stints in psychiatric hospitals, and then served time in prisons and camps. And all that time you continued protesting. Maybe you really are crazy?" The television audience of millions was ready to tear him limb from limb for having put such a hypothesis into words. He played the role of devil's advocate brilliantly, asking the kind of questions that exist in the subconscious of many, but which we tend to suppress or drive away. By the end of the interview, after he had allowed himself to be completely "convinced," he shot one last question at me: "Would you like to meet with the president to tell him all that you have been saying to me?" (We had been talking about détente and its consequences.)

This exchange took place on "Sixty Minutes," a program that enjoys a great popularity in America, especially among young people.

They say it is watched by an audience of 40 million. I learned later that the White House had been literally swamped with letters, and at a press conference soon thereafter, Carter announced that he was ready to receive me.

I believe that two factors contributed to this decision. When the press analyzed the causes for Gerald Ford's defeat in the presidential campaign, one of the most prominent reasons cited was his refusal to receive Solzhenitsyn. Carter, on the other hand, had made the defense of human rights one of the principal planks of his campaign, a position that coincided with the views of most Americans after Vietnam and Watergate. The new president was also very conscious of public opinion. One had the impression that his concept of how to govern democratically was to respond blindly to public opinion polls. This image caused him a great deal of damage at a later point, since what is useful in a political campaign often seems to be inapplicable to the task of running a government. Even a perfect president cannot make decisions that will always be popular, and he certainly cannot please everyone. Of course he has to be true to the principles on which he took his stand, yet he cannot be governed by the passing whims of the electorate. It is also true that public opinion polls can be deceptive, since opinions often change the very moment a decision has been made. Those who are displeased will naturally make the most noise, and they seem to be everywhere. Thus it came about that Carter could change his mind several times the same day, and that is worse than any possible single decision. Right to the end of his time in office, Carter never seemed to get used to the fact that he was president, but seemed instead to perpetuate the patterns of his election campaign.

The second factor was that I had been invited to the United States by the AFL-CIO, a very powerful organization, which for many years had supported our movement. By tradition, the trade unions are viewed as almost a part of the Democratic party, and they vote mostly along Democratic lines. The AFL-CIO had contributed substantially to Carter's victory.

In spite of this, the situation remained unsettled right up to the last moment, and I was not at all sure the meeting would take place. One can only guess at the pressures exerted behind the scenes to prevent our getting together. Trudeau arrived suddenly in Washington on the date first chosen for the meeting, so it had to be put off by a few days. I have no idea whether this was a coincidence or a symptom of the vacillation in the White House. I was at that point leaving for Miami and a trade union meeting to which George Meany had invited me, and I remember thinking that my chances of meeting the president were getting slimmer and slimmer. But finally the uncertainty was over, and a State Department vehicle delivered me to the White House on March 1. Although I had waited for this moment for several weeks, the entire process now seemed strange, almost unreal, and in a certain sense even ridiculous.

While waiting for our hosts, the interpreter and I intently examined the walls, the ceilings, and the paintings in the Roosevelt Room. My interpreter was visibly annoyed. Sulkily, he kept repeating that his task was to translate only at the highest level, in meetings between presidents, heads of state, or royalty, but he was not ready to balk at this assignment. I sympathized as much as I could. Walter Mondale came into the room, shook my hand, and we sat at a table, the vice-president on a chair at my right while the interpreter and I sat together on a sofa. We barely had the time to exchange a couple of sentences, when I heard a muffled sound of rapidly approaching feet, rather like a troop of elephants that had gotten past the vigilant guards. The doors were flung open, the press burst in. Blinding flashes of light, numerous TV cameras, a veritable cyclone of activity. Mondale was clearly nervous. Out of the left side of his mouth he whispered to me: "In our country we have a free press . . . and it is a real power." I racked my brain to find some response of equal profundity so as not to look like a dunce under the gaze of all those cameras. But at this point the press began withdrawing as precipitously as it had arrived, getting off a few final shots as it retreated to the door. The room became astonishingly quiet. It took us a full minute to regain our normal sight after the dazzling flashbulbs and to lose the silly smiles we had worn for the photographers.

The conversation was quite lengthy. I did most of the talking, and the vice-president took notes of some kind, occasionally interrupting to ask questions. I wanted to explain the major peculiarities of Soviet psychology, a misunderstanding of which usually leads to errors and defeats. I was especially eager to point out the fallacy inherent in the concept of détente as it was then interpreted by both sides. Having spent a lifetime in a country where hostility to the surrounding world has been elevated to the rank of official philosophy, and where every schoolchild knows that the war (whether hot or cold) against the "capitalist" countries must continue without respite, we are astounded by the untroubled serenity of the West, an attitude that borders on irresponsibility. Even though we were fairly well informed about the West, this went beyond anything we had anticipated. To encounter this way of thinking in the man on the street is surprising enough. To discover the same frame of mind among statesmen is truly frightening.

"Try to figure out what makes these men tick," my friends advised me. "Use your prison experience to reckon, for example, what sort of an interrogation it would take to break down their defenses."

I am afraid that my specific experience proved less than useful in the case at hand. These people did not have to fear any future interrogation, and in any case, personality does not carry much weight in modern politics, since a gigantic apparatus is at work, whether in the East or the West. At a later time I had the opportunity to meet with deputies, advisers, senators, members of Congress, as well as with their staffs—i.e., with the apparatus. The conclusions I drew from all this were in no way reassuring. These people were probably better educated than their opposite numbers in the USSR and without a doubt they were far more humane. But from all I could see, they did not have anything like the Soviet experience of a fierce struggle for existence, the kind of struggle that scorns all moral values.

For a person to have reached a certain level in the Soviet system, he has to have crushed a score of competitors, to have climbed over heads or even corpses, and to have mastered all the tricks of skullduggery and deceit. So often we wonder how it is that our poorly educated Soviet leaders, who have often not even mastered correct Russian, nevertheless manage to govern a huge empire and to keep the rest of the world cowed with fear. Actually there is no mystery to all this, and there is no need to think there are gray eminences lurking in the shadows. To be a Soviet leader one does not need to be highly educated or cultured. In fact, such qualities could only be a handicap. Psychologically, they belong to the criminal type and, for this mentality, success is based on cunning and experience. A gangster boss does not need to have read Tolstoy or Shakespeare in order to terrorize an entire camp. The fifty-year relationship between the USSR and the democratic West is astonishingly similar to the relationship between professional crooks and the rest of the inmates inside a prison: the former systematically rob and terrorize the latter. The resemblance is striking, in fact. There is the same naive faith that the problems can be resolved by the payment of a suitable ransom; the same desire to demonstrate friendliness and to emphasize that one has only non-aggressive intentions (carried to the point of unilateral disarmament); and, above all, the same wonderful theory that if only one remains quiet, avoids "provoking" the bandits, and studiously looks the other way when the other guy gets beaten up, everything will be fine. We have seen this behavior repeated hundreds of times, and we are well equipped to state that it is invariably doomed to failure.

To deal with the Soviets, the Western world would be far better off to appoint a tough old sheriff from Chicago rather than a professional diplomat with Harvard diplomas: it would be someone who understood a criminal mentality. But how does one explain all that to the president of the United States in fifteen minutes?

Toward the end of my conversation with Walter Mondale, President Carter came out to join us. In my remarks I made no specific appeals, and limited myself to saying that the campaign for human rights needed undeviating persistence to have any hope of achieving results. One had to take into account the specifics of Soviet psychology. One must not count on early success, nor should one change this policy if success is not immediately forthcoming. It was already clear that the Soviets would go to great lengths to show that they were impervious to outside pressure. They were even capable of increasing their repressions in order to discredit any effort to influence them. They could always count on somebody in the West picking up this motif. One must not yield an inch to such maneuvers. If the present line could be held for several years, the Soviets would begin to retreat.

I do not know if I succeeded in expressing all this clearly enough to the president, but he assured me that he was firmly determined to carry on in the same spirit, not to yield in any way. Human rights was to him not a passing political slogan, but one of the pillars of his foreign policy, not only in his relationships with the USSR but with other countries also. He impressed me as a warm, sincere human being, and we parted on a positive note. I naturally thanked him for having invited me: by this gesture he had accorded both honor and support to our entire movement.

The two men left the room. I searched my heart to see if I could have made better use of the fifteen minutes that fate had put into my hands. I'm not sure that I could have. Even twenty-four hours would not have been long enough to say all there was to say. What is more, it would have been useless. At this level, people do not try to convince each other or present long lectures. They only *exchange views*, articulating their positions and making comments that had been prepared in advance for the press release. It is hardly reasonable to expect significant results from these political ping-pong games.

"Do you wish to take part in a press conference?" asked the press attaché. But my interpreter protested so vehemently (there were no royalty or presidents in attendance) and my English was still so shaky that I declined. And anyway, what would be the point? One can't explain much at a press conference either.

The lawn of the White House was crowded with reporters when the Secret Service men helped us to our car. The press was holding cameras above their heads, thrusting their black clublike microphones in our direction, and shouting something. As for me, for the first time in my life, I felt the full extent of my muteness. I was like a fragile Christmas tree ornament carefully wrapped in cotton wool.

◆   ◆   ◆

Later on, it was often said that President Carter had tried to diminish the effect of our meeting by downplaying the drama, not posing for photographs with me, and not scheduling a joint press conference. I don't think that was a calculated move at all. More likely it was the result of a lack of organization and planning. And in the eyes of the Soviets it would not have made much difference whether we had been photographed or not. The crucial thing was that the meeting had taken place. That in itself signified "a hostile act" to them, a challenge, an open gesture of support for one of their internal enemies. Once the president had decided on this step, there would have been no particular reason to stop halfway and thus evoke the discontent of the press. Moreover, the official White House photographer took pictures throughout our meeting.

It is much more important to know whether the president had fully grasped the ramifications of his policy on human rights, whose centrality to his new course was being proclaimed by this gesture.

Our age, perhaps the bloodiest in human history, has brought with it a problem that has so far proved insoluble, but must be resolved if we are to preserve our civilization. Totalitarian regimes and ideologies are a deadly threat to the democratic countries, a threat that grows in intensity as modern technologies of transportation, communication, and warfare have made the world a much smaller place. We have all become neighbors. The problem is how the democracies can defend themselves without renouncing their traditional principles, that is, without slowly becoming a likeness of their adversaries.

The logic of such a metamorphosis is very straightforward: if there exists a "world bandit," then there is need for a "world policeman" to stand up to him, someone capable of fighting with the bandit on his own level and therefore not squeamish about methods. Anything less will be ineffective. But after a certain time, the impartial observer can no longer distinguish the policeman from the bandit. By this logic, then, democracies cannot hope to defeat totalitarianism in equal battle without turning into the image and likeness of their enemy. On the other hand, all attempts to "negotiate" with the bandit simply increase his strength and one's dependence on him.

And so our world finds itself caught between two extremes, both of which are sure roads to defeat. It is not surprising that the tendency has been to vacillate, at times following one of these roads, then changing course to follow the other. In the process, the world has been slipping deeper and deeper into the quagmire of despair.

Each change of policy is naturally presented by the politicians in power as a radically new course that has no real alternative. We are warned that we shall revert to the Cold War if we reject détente; in the 1940s and 1950s, we were warned of the opposite menace. The fact is that the Soviets benefit in each instance. Although it is true that they don't make great gains during "cold" periods, the ground is prepared for their future successes. For the West, such a period involves the imposition of certain limitations, an increased level of militarization, a constant threat of war, and inevitable support for certain "stable" dictatorships—each of these policies calling forth popular discontent. There follows a period of growing opposition and pro-Soviet illusions, a propitious climate for Soviet subversion. In the context of mounting public pressure, it becomes a question of renouncing either democratic principles or the Cold War. In the periods of "thaw," the Soviets restore their crumbling economy with the help of credits and goods from the West, consolidate their influence in various unstable regions of the world by playing on the disaffection of the people, and proceed to seize new territories, which in turn brings about a new "chill." For over half a century this merry-go-round has been in operation. And it should be noted that all the variations in temperature have occurred only in the West. Within the Soviet Union, "cold" is the rule.

There seem to be only two variables in this dismaying formula. First of all, the Soviet conquests have so far been irreversible and the Soviet sphere of influence has therefore continued to expand. This is facilitated by fear and rampant defeatism in those Western countries that are not yet occupied (in some cases one hesitates to call them free). Second, the Soviet system is slowly but surely deteriorating: despite all Western efforts, it is becoming increasingly difficult to stave off the collapse of the Soviet economy. Just as slowly, various resistance movements are gaining strength inside the Soviet bloc, and they will destroy the system sooner or later if they are supported and encouraged. These movements have exposed a crucial fact about the system: the regime is becoming internally decrepit, inflexible, and increasingly incapable of defending itself in the ideological struggle.

Given these considerations, the "human rights policy" turns out to be a marvelous discovery, perhaps the only possible solution to our fatal dilemma. It enabled us to take "moral" stands that did not lead to the negative consequences of the Cold War (human rights must be respected everywhere, not only in the USSR), it offered support to the

resistance movements, presented an ideological challenge to the se-
nile Soviet regime as well as to pro-Soviet elements in the West, and
permitted the West to recast its entire strategic policy with a new emphasis on democratic regimes rather than dictatorships. As a final
plus, this policy in no way precluded a strong defense, for it is a human right to defend oneself.

The greatest benefit of all lay in the fact that the West was finally
acquiring some semblance of an ideology capable of standing toe to
toe with communism. In the United States, it could serve to unify the
country after its deep crisis and could even help to restore the nation
to its leading role in the world.

Obviously, all this would have to be carefully detailed; each case
and each country is different and concrete application of the policy
would have to be individually adjusted. And it would clearly be
impossible to embark on a completely new policy instantly. To do
so would merely destabilize policies already in place without imple-
menting the new one. Last but not least, such a radical change of
course could be put into effect only with great skill.

In no way am I calling President Carter's sincerity into question.
But my impression was that there was little apart from this quality. He
did not even have a well-informed entourage. He failed to grasp the
dimension of his task and seems to have decided to make the White
House into an annex of Amnesty International. Lacking any thought-
out program, he abandoned under pressure everything that was of
real worth in the human rights concept. Three years later, when the
invasion of Afghanistan signaled the end of détente, neither America
nor Europe was ready. The former policies were no longer valid, but
no alternative had been prepared.

It would be unfair to blame President Carter alone. To be the
president of the United States is by no means an enviable position: I
would not wish it on an enemy. People in the West make tremendous
demands on their governments, often expecting that which they could
very easily do for themselves. This is especially true in the United
States, where elected officials seem to exist primarily to be badgered,
pressured, besieged, and accused of every sin under the sun. Years of
their time in office have to be set aside preparing for the next election,
and what sort of serious work can be accomplished in the time remaining, especially if a policy line has been set during the preparatory
phase? Inertia in a large country is directly proportional to its size,
and the monstrous bureaucracy does pretty well what it likes—it is
the Frankenstein of our age. It has been a long time since presidents
and prime ministers have actually governed. The world is run by the
"establishment" and the myths it creates. Today, these are the myths

of "the forces of peace, progress, and socialism." In human terms, I feel only sympathy for President Carter. I imagine that he is all too familiar with the sense of muteness with which I left the White House.

Whatever the reasons, the cooperation that began with such fanfare did not get very far. I wasted two hours trying to persuade Andrew Young to bring up at the United Nations the problem of genocide with respect to a number of small ethnic groups in the USSR. I offered him documentation on the Crimean Tatars and on some other colonies of the Soviet empire. Young yawned with boredom. All of our other appeals, counsels, and recommendations were equally in vain. It was only toward the end of 1980 that a new rapprochement occurred in the wake of an all-too-predictable crisis. At this point Carter implemented almost all the suggestions we had made three years earlier: a reduction in trade, an embargo on a number of products, a partial scientific boycott, and the boycott of the Moscow Olympics. But it was already too late.

◆　◆　◆

The meeting with President Carter did have one totally unexpected result. Because of it I learned the main reason for my mysterious exchange and the explanation for the enigmatic behavior of the Soviet authorities. The story was told to an acquaintance of mine by one of Brezhnev's closest aides, and it is unimpeachable both in terms of the source as well as in terms of the typical Soviet lunacy that it involves. The moment I heard it, I knew immediately that I had gotten to the bottom of the mystery and that no other explanation was possible.

Two weeks or so after the reception in the White House, Brezhnev expressed disquiet about the new American policy and demanded a full report on my activities based on what was appearing in the Western press. After studying this account, he looked severely at his aides.

"Comrades, what in the world have you done? You assured me he was touched"—he pointed significantly to his temple—"but this makes clear that he is not cracked at all; he keeps making public appearances and speaks well . . . How can you let activists like that out of the country?"

Talk about embarrassment! It seems that the Kremlin had actually been convinced that I was a paranoiac. That explains why they had let me leave with all that fanfare. It's easy to imagine the effect it would have had on supporters of our movement had it been true.

It is a wonderful story! Even the all-powerful Soviet leaders can fall victims to their own lies; even they need an independent press and freedom of speech, so as not to make silly blunders. Within the party bureaucracy feedback turns into a vicious circle. At the beginning, in the 1960s, they had given orders to treat us as clinically insane individuals, and when a subsequent report referred to us in these terms, they believed it!

So this was how my fate was decided.

It really is useful for the Russian traveler to get news from his distant fatherland. It clarifies the mind.

CHAPTER TWO

On Liberty

*If none was to have Liberty but those who understood what it is, there
would not be many free men in the world.*

Lord Halifax

F EW things can be more hopeless than trying to compare the life of
two antithetical systems such as totalitarianism and democracy.
Every attempt complicates the problem further, and every statement
seems to be both true and false. I have not even been able to find a
more or less appropriate metaphor.

I have just written the phrase "antithetical systems," but is that an
accurate description? How can they be totally opposite? There must
be some ways in which they resemble each other. So perhaps it is
more useful to simply speak of systems that are different. But if that is
true, the differences ought to be measurable, or at least describable. It
should be possible to indicate scales and gradations. It is enough to
start on this path to discover yourself in the company of those clever
Western commentators who claim that there really *are* no differences,
but only a few nuances.

It all reminds one of the efforts scientists have made to compare
human beings with monkeys. Everything seems alike: from the body
structure to the functioning of the respective systems. Even the brain
does not seem to differ substantially. As long as one restricts oneself
to measuring organs and analyzing details, the difference does not become apparent. But if one steps back to gain some perspective, the
unbridgeable gap between the two species becomes clear. In this case,
just as in the comparison of systems, there were common ancestors.

The clearest demonstration of this biological difference between
two worlds can be obtained in a natural setting. The behavior, the reactions, and the impressions of a Soviet citizen who turns up abroad

will be far more eloquent and informative than a whole library of scholarly books on comparative politics.

What does a Soviet citizen know about the West? What are his expectations? After being subjected for several decades to raucous propaganda about the perpetual crisis of capitalism—exploitation, terrible contrasts, slums and unemployment, death from hunger, discrimination, and the cruel power of capital—he more likely than not sincerely believes that he is heading for paradise. For such a person, the West resembles a gigantic *Berezka* shop,[1] where he can find *everything*, and to which he now has access because he is now also a "foreigner." It is a place where he no longer needs to try to obtain hard currency by hook or by crook, for all money is now hard currency. And what does he mean by the word *everything*? First of all meat, sausage, blue jeans, and all sorts of clothing. Not to forget caviar, lox, records, books, quality furniture, automobiles . . .

But no matter how he strains his imagination, however hard he tries to recall all he might have seen at international exhibitions in the USSR, he soon realizes that the reality exceeds all his expectations. The typical image of paradise is of a place where you can get all the things you have lacked, the things you have not even dared to dream about. But when he is faced with piles of footwear, bales of clothing, dozens of varieties of sausage, meat in unlimited quantity, to say nothing of a multitude of goods, products, and objects about which he knows nothing, the Soviet citizen stands overwhelmed. Not infrequently, especially among the women, this can lead to a form of psychosis. They suspect that all this plenty is the result of a mistake, an error in distribution, and that the supplies will soon disappear, to be replaced by the usual empty shelves and immense queues. And so they embark on a frenzy of buying, build up huge stockpiles, and are unable to stop. Others succumb to a psychotic distrustfulness. To have all these goods within reach, displayed on the streets and dangling over the heads of passersby, exhibited in every store window, can only mean that it is not for real. It is all for show, as in the Soviet store windows, but no one will buy it. That explains the huge accumulations of stock that draw no queues and virtually no interest. One has to be clever to search out the "real" goods, the kind that are kept hidden under the counter or in places known only to the initiated.

In a word, a crisis of one's value system occurs. That is what happened to me at the Zurich airport as I stood over the bag containing

[1]In the Berezki stores, purchases may be made only with "hard" (foreign) currency. Access to these stores is prohibited to ordinary Soviet citizens—ED.

my prison gear. I was overwhelmed by the thought that my most precious treasures—the penknives, razor blades, and books, which represented a fund accumulated over many years—had turned to nothing before my eyes. I had spent much effort hiding these objects, sewing them into the lining of my clothes, trembling lest they be discovered each time there was a search. Fool that I was, I had even taken along a rag for washing the floor.

The Soviet citizen spends a large proportion of his life worrying about how he is going to find, acquire, or unearth the most elementary things. Tremendous skill, cleverness, and ingenuity is required to achieve what in the West might take five minutes. And all this experience and acquired knowledge suddenly becomes worthless.

Therefore, the first reactions upon reaching paradise are confusion, consternation, and demoralization. As a Russian proverb says: Too good is not so good either. Just try choosing something specific from among the endless array of goods, all of which are unfamiliar to you! I once spent an exhausting hour at a counter stocked with twenty-four different varieties of olives, without being able to reach a decision. Olives are admittedly not crucial to one's survival, but the same type of choice needs to be made day in and day out. Accustomed as we are to the uniformity and standardization of the Soviet world, we are simply bewildered by the variety, by the unexpected bustle in the streets on any day or week, by the crowds of people (especially young people) who don't seem to be in a hurry. The impression is of a holiday or a fair, and the adjective that comes closest to describing the reigning atmosphere, as we perceive it, is "carefree." There is none of the crush and tumult of perpetually irritated crowds of people who must make use of every free minute to accomplish the hundreds of minutiae that make up our life.

In the streets of Soviet cities I had never seen so many young people who seemed to be at leisure. In my country one meets mostly grandmothers with children, and retirees in the morning. Then, at the midday break, the streets are flooded with a crowd of sullen people. This ebb and flow continues until nightfall, with jostling crowds taking the place of city life. There is not much for young people to do in the streets. The few cafés that do exist are jammed full, and to get in you have to wait in line for an hour or so. And in any case, not much fun is to be had there: after you've eaten your shish kebob and finished your bottle of wine, you've got to move on so as to make room for the next person. All that is left is to go to the movies. To be sure, there is always the organized leisure that one receives at "houses of culture" and various clubs with their inevitable sections on singing, photography, dancing, and sports. But it is all so artificial, so controlled, so banally conventional, that it in no way provides a social life or real entertainment. Only the sporting groups achieve any sort of popularity. For the average Soviet citizen, life is filled with incurable boredom and a feeling of emptiness, alongside an extraordinary preoccupation with various details of everyday living, each of which can grow into an insurmountable problem. This is the root of the inordinately high incidence of crime and the ubiquitous alcoholism.

Another thing that strikes us immediately when we arrive in the West is the absence of drunks. I am not talking about people who are somewhat tipsy and are having fun with friends. This is a common enough sight, and most people will indulge in a daily glass or two of wine or a couple of drafts of beer in the company of others or by themselves. It is the attitude toward drinking that is so radically different. The goal is not to get soused, drunk to the point of passing out and losing all human traits—as it is in our country—but rather to be agreeably high for a certain period of time so as to unwind and to make one's talk more jovial. One does not typically run into people who stay dead drunk week in and week out; it is rare to find unconscious bodies lying on the sidewalk, something that is a routine part of the landscape in a Soviet city.

It's really not accurate to use the word *alcoholism* to describe the recent trends in our country. It might be more appropriate to speak of a sort of popular psychotherapy. People drink to reach the stage of stupefaction as quickly as they can, so that all the stored-up anger and frustration can be vented on the first passerby. Socializing has been reduced to drinking. When you meet an acquaintance, it is impossible not to have a drink and, once you start, it is impossible not to get drunk. Anyone who chooses to stay sober arouses suspicion: what is he trying to hide?

But once we have crossed the frontier of our much-loved homeland, many of us lose our old habits. Vodka is sold everywhere and the price is reasonable—no need to split the cost of a bottle or to drink it in some doorway. You can drink to your heart's content, nobody cares. But strange to say, it's hard to enjoy drinking any more. The alcoholic atmosphere is missing. The parties astonish us by their tedium and lack of spontaneity. In England, especially, they resemble exercises in collective masochism. Each one takes a turn at adding something to the conversation, evidently to avoid total silence. But despite these efforts, there are painfully awkward pauses, when the faces express panic or the yearning to say goodbye and get out.

I should add that this is typical of parties for people who know each other only slightly or not at all, and who may in fact have come precisely to make acquaintances. In all other instances, the Soviet citizen is struck by the relaxed style of people in the West. This ease shows in everything, in their manners, the way they dress, even in the way they walk and gesture. These characteristics, though hard to define, enable us to pick out a foreigner in the streets of Moscow. What produces all this? The answer suddenly dawns: it's got to be *freedom*! These bloody foreigners have never felt an invisible presence at their backs or sensed the eye of the state observing their every gesture. It never crosses their minds that someone might come up to them and ask "What are you doing here?"

In fact, this is not something that happens to us every day either, but each day we are on guard expecting it, and when it does happen we are not surprised. Unconsciously, even when occupied with the most innocent of tasks, the Soviet citizen is formulating phrases in his mind to explain, to justify, or to prove something in his unceasing inner argument with the mythical and ever present THEM. You will never catch a Soviet citizen off guard, not even if a surly-faced and self-assured character grabs him by the collar, twists his arm, and drags him off to you-know-where. At this point our Soviet man will let every inch of his body express complete docility, together with a nice degree of surprise that is always ready for use along with the following phrases: "But what is going on? I was only walking by . . . I was simply going to the store . . . here is my shopping bag . . . check it for yourself . . . hey, take it easy on my arm! ow! Let go! you don't need to twist it off; I am not trying to run away." Meanwhile, in his mind he is turning over all the possible reasons for this arrest, trying to figure out how they could have come to the fore and what is the best way to react. No one, under our system, is without some reason for being pulled in, unless one speaks of newborn infants.

It is the THEY concept in action. We don't talk about the "government." We say "they" or "the regime." There is no word in the West that expresses in the same way the all-encompassing power wielded by the state. In the West there is the parliament, the government, the municipal authorities, the university administration; the power of the media, of the trade unions, of the police, of customs; a whole network of authorities and powers that spend a good proportion of their time fighting among each other. For the most part the public ignores their existence, and their presence is of little interest, since THEY are not a factor in day-to-day activities. Above all, there is no need to ask THEM permission to do something each time you want to do it. In the West, authority usually operates on the principle of limiting certain actions rather than on the idea of granting prior permission for action of any kind.

As a result, the normal process of doing something does not involve thinking about authorization first. If you run into a snag, people don't say to themselves, as they do with us: "That stinking regime! It stops us from doing anything!" Only the communist propaganda spends its time cursing Western authorities.

Everyone knows that the West is considered free. Everyone has heard about political parties, parliaments, and the independent press. In fact, most Soviet people rather overestimate the degree of political freedom that exists in the West. It is other things that really surprise us, unexpected details that ought to seem perfectly natural, but psychologically are hard to reconcile with what we customarily imagine.

One night, as I was walking along a London street, immersed in my own thoughts, my eye chanced on a sign by the side of a massive churchlike building that I was passing. The perfectly conventional signboard read "Jehovah's Witnesses," and something else that I could not see, so overcome was I with surprise, almost panic. The "jehovists" here? Those "fanatical sectarians" that our regime uses to frighten children? That most clandestine, most secret of all the sects in the USSR? One can meet real flesh-and-blood Witnesses only in the camps and prisons, but even there they cover their tracks. Their reputation is legendary: there are prison tales about their fabulous power of organization, their miracles of ingenuity, their skill for staying underground. Fellow prisoners relate that even in the tightest prison, and under the strictest security, they manage to receive copies of their *Watchtower* (printed in Brooklyn), and a recent issue at that! The regime regards them with a dread bordering on superstitious horror, and for this reason any Witness who is arrested can count on a long sentence. And here I was standing in front of a building and a signboard. So anyone can drop in and have a cup of tea with them?

Perhaps my analogy is a bit exaggerated, but imagine your feelings if you saw written on the side of a building "Cosa Nostra Ltd., Headquarters of the Mafia." The Witnesses are treated in our country pretty much as the Mafia is in the West, and the same mystery surrounds both.

It is paradoxical, but true, that one becomes conscious of freedom not by seeing protest marches, strikes, parliamentary debates, or a great variety of newspapers, but rather by becoming aware of details to which people in the West pay no attention. In Zurich, I was struck by the courtesy of the drivers, the picturesque gaiety of the streets, the many street-corner musicians who seem to play for their own pleasure more than for money. Each person is struck by something different, something special: for example, the copying machines in every station and in each post office. All you need is a coin, and no one checks to see what you are copying, no one watches to report you to the authorities. For us it is incredible, and one can imagine how our *samizdat* would have flourished under such conditions.

It is hard to express the feeling that pierces you suddenly and is a mixture of pain and fright. "My God, that is what liberty is, and I am free." Like someone bewitched, our man stands in front of a Xerox machine or the sign in an airport that announces flights to Rome, Vienna, Frankfurt, New York, Copenhagen. It is all incredible.

I like to observe people, the way they walk, their gestures, their method of communicating, the expressions on their faces. I learn more that way than through their words. Words are impersonal, sometimes empty of meaning, and worn through use. All too often they serve to confuse and to conceal the speaker in a cloud of fog. They are a means of self-defense. That is why people are so afraid of being silent around each other and talk ceaselessly, erecting barricades of words. Whenever I observe a crowd in some large international airport, I am always pierced by the same stabbing pain of freedom. My God, how young they are, don't they ever grow up? They are rather like tropical plants who know nothing of the murderous power a fierce winter can have. So much naive energy, such a happy thirst for sunshine! Even the elderly have a rosy complexion and are full of energy. When death comes, they must be tremendously surprised.

What to say about the children? They are probably better brought up, they seem much calmer and don't keep hassling the grown-ups, who in their turn are not forever scolding them. The children don't seem to have that perpetual itch, that impatience to be the constant center of attention. The parents don't seem to feel the continued need to teach the children, they are not always correcting them or threatening them with punishments. The children are left far more to themselves, for they have plenty to occupy their time. Never in all my life have I seen such a profusion of toys, games, and entertainments. What was it like when we were young? We could go to the skating rink, we could get into fights, or we could play war. Here one could spend half of one's life at Disneyland. When I look at this plethora of electronic games, from which the youngsters can't seem to detach themselves, I feel sincerely deprived. Compared with these kids, we had no childhood to speak of. But then adulthood comes later too, and the blue-eyed, rosy-cheeked naiveté practically never disappears. This is most true of Americans. Perhaps it's a law of nature: does one need to confront difficulties to mature fully? Or perhaps, on the contrary, innocence is a natural state for humankind? Maybe the bitterness that comes from experience only corrupts the soul and makes us into cynical old men at an early age?

Once, in the fall of 1970, two youngsters of about nine or ten came to my front door. "We're collecting money to send books to children in Vietnam," rattled off one of them smartly, looking at me with clear eyes. Noticing my hesitation, he repeated with a slightly reproachful voice: "Books . . . for children."

How was I to respond? I could not after all explain to these kids the complexities of the Soviet involvement in Southeast Asia or tell them bluntly that the money they were collecting would go neither for books nor for children. On the other hand I could not stomach the thought of simply giving them some money and saying nothing at all, knowing as I did what the money would be used for. Perhaps it would be only ten kopeks, but it was not a question of the amount. A bullet does not cost much.

A friend who was visiting at the time saved the day, turning down the kids on some pretext or other. I would not have been able to decide what to do, probably I would have ended up refusing to give anything, without an explanation. This incident stuck in my mind for some time, especially the reproachful tone of the speaker. I hated myself for my indecision, for the unease about the whole question, and in my soul I cursed the Soviet authorities who had made everything so complicated.

To my great astonishment I learned a couple of weeks later that these clear-eyed kids had actually been raising money to buy themselves ice cream. By chance they rang the doorbell of their schoolteacher, who called their bluff. I was not so terribly surprised at being taken in by these boys, despite all the sharpening of my wits by prison experience—I was much more stunned by the profound cynicism of these kids, by their very grown-up understanding of how to use adults' hypocrisy. The rascals knew perfectly well that no one would dare to turn them down and that their victims would not press them for an explanation. If, at ten, one is skillful enough to make use of the official ideology, it shows an astonishing level of cynicism already. What can be expected from the grown-ups?

And now imagine a meeting of the Democratic party in the United States, where grown men and women sob openly as they listen to a speech delivered in tones of pure demagoguery à la Goebbels. The speaker is a well-bred and elegant millionaire describing the plight of the unemployed. The reserves of naiveté among his listeners seem to be unlimited.

It is for such reasons that we find it hard to take many of the problems of Westerners seriously. Reading about these things back in the Soviet Union, we would merely shake our heads in perplexity, for envy and irritation were the only feelings these articles provoked in the average Soviet citizen. It all reminded us of the story of poor

Moishe, who, hungry and dead-tired from the many chores in his destitute village, drags himself to school and is barely able to stay awake in class. "Tell us, Moishe," asks the teacher as he strides around the classroom, "how many legs do cockroaches have?"

"I wish I had your worries, sir," answers Moishe with a sigh.

What else can one say when you hear people complaining about traffic jams during rush hour, or about the difficulties that millions have losing weight, or about the vices of the "consumer society"? As for us, we'd be delighted to have something to consume. If you don't like it, don't consume! What's the problem? Who is there to blame except oneself?

"Consumerism" is seriously considered one of the evils of capitalism, as if, under socialism, people subsist on nectar, like bees. Advertising comes in for particular attack, since a magical power is ascribed to it, a power so great that it is said to control modern society. Perhaps life in the USSR has immunized us against believing any kind of advertising (only worthless goods get this treatment, whereas quality products disappear from the shelves the minute that people learn they are on sale). Personally, I rather like the TV ads. They are often clever and imaginatively done. But I don't recall a single instance of buying anything I didn't need, just because of advertising. Some people in the West seem far more susceptible: they go into a store to buy some toothpaste; before they come out they have spent everything they had in their pocket. And then they complain about the "consumer society."

There is a Russian proverb: "The person who has eaten his fill doesn't understand the person who is famished." The opposite is also true. When a person arrives in the West from Soviet Russia, it takes him a while to realize that the "others," the Westerners, are not a race apart: he is now one of them. The new life takes getting used to.

Or take the matter of scale. If it is months since the Soviet city you happen to live in has had any meat for sale, it will not occur to anyone to speak of a "problem," to say nothing of a "crisis." At best, the Soviet papers will refer to a "temporary difficulty." In the West, however, crisis follows crisis. Unpracticed as we are, we find them impossible to detect. Newspapers proclaim an energy crisis, for example. Not a difficulty, mind you, a *crisis*. "Damn!" you say to yourself, "things must be really bad." But the very first thing that strikes you when you approach New York by plane is the glow of light in the sky. You'd think someone had set off a nuclear bomb for fun, everything is so bright. Lights have been added in every possible place, everything that can be turned on has been turned on, just so people wouldn't have to write about the crisis in the dark.

Perhaps our imagination is too lively. When we hear of the "urban crisis," some scene from the last days of Pompeii comes to mind, with panic-maddened crowds, fires breaking out everywhere, buildings collapsing on all sides. And we can't imagine a "government crisis" at all, except perhaps as a shoot-out between cabinet ministers.

In the West there seems to be an extraordinary tendency toward exaggeration. The slightest event receives a dramatic twist. I have no intention of following the fashion of blaming everything on the press: the newspapers merely satisfy their readers' thirst for sensation. As the Russian saying puts it, no point blaming the mirror if your mug is awry. But Westerners seem to be built in such a way that they never consider themselves to blame for anything. The very idea seems blasphemous, almost like an attack on democracy. No one wants to admit that a good half of the "crises" are due to this simple reason.

An endless protest march moves through the city, red banners aloft. "What do we want?" barks one of the leaders through a megaphone. "Money!" roars the crowd in response. "When do we want it?" "Now!"

Drivers and pedestrians wait with casual indifference for traffic to be restored; their faces don't even seem to show impatience. But I can't keep from smiling. Do those demonstrators really think they are the only ones who need money and need it right away? No doubt Rothschild has the same thought every morning. Yet they seem to be seriously convinced that their need is the greatest. There is not the slightest trace of humor. They believe the world owes them something, they've been trained to think that way. The essential thing is to make demands. Result: galloping inflation, recession, unemployment, "crisis." And of course everyone, except them, is responsible for the state of affairs.

It is an amazing faculty human beings have of projecting their inner problems onto the surrounding world and demanding that the world be remade! It's like a puppy chasing its tail. The fundamental assumptions of the two societies are diametrically different: in the USSR, the individual is automatically in the wrong, the state is always right. In the West, an individual is persuaded that he has the right always to be happy. If he falls ill, those who are healthy are responsible; if he is poor, it is naturally the rich who are to blame. It is a purely childish egocentricism along with an equally infantile refusal to accept any restraints. One day, the students in my college at Cambridge mutinied, occupying the administrative offices and organizing a sit-in. The reason: one of them had insulted a member of the service personnel and had been barred from the college pub for a month. People back home would have split their sides with laughter had they heard of this. These students would have been kicked out of the university in five minutes flat, drafted into the army, and made to spend the rest of their lives "being taught by hard labor," without ever again getting the chance to go on with their studies.

This is simply the first example that comes to mind. There are thousands of others to draw on, and in the last analysis it is none of our business. We are enjoying the hospitality of the West and it is not up to us to judge our hosts. But we do get indignant at the hypocrisy, the double standards, the lack of the slightest desire to understand the other point of view. Let's say some eccentric decides to cross the Atlantic in a washtub, for no particular reason except that he is bored. The whole world buzzes with anxiety, naval vessels change course to help him, helicopters rush to his aid from all sides. Our man strikes picturesque poses for the TV cameras, causing the ladies to swoon. But at the same time thousands of Vietnamese men and women are fleeing from persecution and terror in leaky boats, perishing at sea after weeks of fighting hunger, thirst, and the elements, and nobody seems to care. Captains of passing ships are even forbidden to take them aboard so as not to deal with potential immigrants.

Or consider the example of nurses demonstrating in Rome. The usual red banners, the usual chanting, but the main slogan of the demonstrators is as follows: "We demand the same working conditions as Soviet nurses." Some demand! What do they know about working conditions in the USSR? I wouldn't even have wished the life of a Soviet nurse upon my KGB interrogator. A life to be envied? Ridiculous. To resemble a Soviet nurse, the Italians would have to earn five times less, abandon their trade union, and juggle two to three jobs to make ends meet.

You can just hear the Soviet citizen grumble: "Send them to the USSR for a year or two, that will put some sense into their heads. No good trying to explain it all: it goes in one ear and out the other. They have too much freedom in the West, freedom that has not cost them anything." It is particularly galling for old camp inmates to see young people with dyed hair, a ring in their nostrils, and decked out like parrots. "A spell in camp would do them a world of good. The fun they'd have . . ."

◆   ◆   ◆

But it is a lot easier to get accustomed to affluence than to empty shelves, to freedom than to prison. The fact is that liberty is a natural state, not something the Martians have brought us. After a couple of years in the West, the Soviet man begins to feel perfectly at home, almost as if he'd been born there. The keenness of the early impressions begins to fade, the sensation of being on a permanent holiday dissipates, and the acute awareness of freedom comes less and less frequently, until it disappears altogether. It isn't that one is disillusioned, but one's enthusiasm abates to a certain degree, as a result of which one makes several surprising discoveries.

It suddenly becomes clear that one never has enough money, that one must keep counting, calculating, economizing. How this has come about is a mystery. We have the same money as before, perhaps a bit more, the prices have not changed all that much, but still we don't have enough cash. "What's going on?" we marvel. "We don't seem to be laying out money for anything special, we simply live like everyone else. Where the devil does the money go?"

The fact of the matter is that the art of economizing is unknown to us. In theory, there are only two situations when one can dispense with counting money: if you have unlimited amounts of the stuff, or if you have none! Accustomed to the second possibility, we had unwittingly slipped into an aristocratic life-style.

In economic terms, the Soviet population can be divided into three rough categories. First come those who live entirely on what they earn. Official salaries are so low that they are barely sufficient to cover the food budget alone, even if the husband and wife both work and their aged live-in parent contributes his or her pension. How these people manage to survive is a mystery that I have never been able to solve. On payday they settle their debts, then turn around and borrow some more from their friends and colleagues. It is a merry-go-round that lasts a lifetime. It is true that one can get along on very little: potatoes, bread, canned fish. The crunch comes when shoes have to be resoled, and sometimes this has been done so often that the shoe repairman refuses to try again. Even worse when the husband drinks up his paycheck, a not uncommon occurrence. When the children have grown up enough to hold paying jobs of their own, things become a little easier. But whatever the circumstances, it is not essential to know how to save money, for in any case there is nothing to buy. Besides, frugality is not part of the Russian character.

"Damn it all," says the average guy to himself. "Rich we've never been, and this is not the time to start trying. The old lady will make out somehow." And he drinks up the wages with his pals. When he gets home there's an enormous row, perhaps even a fight, but lo and behold, they manage to muddle through. Women are the prop and anchor of Soviet families, and their economizing consists basically of buying the cheapest possible products. It is a situation of no money, nothing to buy, and no temptations. You wear the same clothes for years as they get mended, patched, turned inside out.

The majority of the people, however, add to their salaries by various unofficial or illegal means. For example, they steal from their place of employment anything that can be used at home or disposed of on the black market. It's not by chance that one of the worst curses you can hurl at someone in our country is: "May you have to live on your salary for the rest of your life!"

To get some sense of the scale of illegal gains, one needs to be reminded that the average monthly salary is 140–50 rubles, while a pair of women's shoes costs 70–90 rubles—which suggests that only high-ranking party members can afford to buy them. Since the price of an automobile is some 5,500 rubles, you need three years without eating to be able to buy one. Yet in the street you see a lot of cars and women wearing nice shoes. Articles not offered in the stores can be gotten on the black market, albeit at a huge price. Measly blue jeans that cost just a few dollars in the West are worth 150 rubles in the USSR, that is, a whole month's salary. And yet people snap them up.

But money earned on the black market is volatile: quickly earned, quickly spent. It's even dangerous to put it aside, for if the authorities find out, it will only get confiscated. Anything left over is better spent on drink. In a word, the average Soviet person lives from day to day and makes no plans for the future. But then our whole life-style bears the stamp of impermanence, unreality, emptiness; we are like people living in a waiting room. A woman I knew never got around to buying herself teacups, she always drank out of glass jam jars. "What difference does it make?" was her explanation.

It is only the high party functionaries, the established scholars and scientists, and the recognized representatives of the arts who make up the privileged category, with a future not limited to today. But even they don't need to save money: there are stores that exist entirely for them, they have access to imported goods, they can travel abroad. These privileges and many others make their lives even less real.

The retired colonels of the Ministry of the Interior and of the KGB make up a separate group. It is probably the one social stratum that leads a well-ordered existence, with a sense of preparing for the future. They cultivate strawberries on their dachas, and their high fences evoke the respectful envy of their neighbors.

In sum, the average Soviet citizen does not know how to live on a budget, as an Englishman might, who will walk two miles to a pub because the beer costs two pennies less than the one next door to his home. "It doesn't matter," the Soviet man would say in this case, "I don't have any money anyway." But life in the West is such that if you don't count your pennies, no amount of dollars will prove to be enough. The street is full of temptations: something to attract your eye wherever you look. In other words, it's a sure road to financial ruin to keep one's Soviet habits and to try living like everyone else. "How strange it is," says the Soviet man to himself. "My whole life in the USSR I never counted kopeks, and here I am having to economize."

Another discovery for us is the huge bureaucracy in the West and the amazing docility with which people accept it. Of course it can in no way be compared to the one in the Soviet Union. Back there, it is omnipresent and interwoven with the fabric of the party. There are probably at least ten files on each Soviet citizen, and if you happen to run afoul of the system somewhere, you draw the monolithic ire of the state in all its forms, starting with the janitor and the policeman on the corner, right up through the courts and high government officials. A person who does not have the proper papers simply doesn't exist. If you weren't issued a certificate, you are a nonperson. But at least you can always resort to a bribe, or have some higher-up put in a word for you, a method far more powerful, as everyone knows, than any commissioner. (Maybe the same thing is possible in the West, but we don't know the ropes.) On the other hand, bureaucrats in the West are far less dependent on their superiors, and one cannot easily frighten them with a threat of complaining to their boss. Moreover, there does not seem to be any place to lodge a complaint, and no one seems to be required to respond to you. This is perhaps the greatest failing of Western bureaucracy, for the mentality of functionaries is the same all over the world. The lower the rank he occupies, the more he wants to show his power; the less a "client" can teach him a lesson, the more impudent he becomes. In the Soviet Union, the power of the functionary is limited by his fear of his superiors, of various inspection committees, and of the men who dream of replacing him. This restraining factor seems to be lacking in the West. What can a bureau chief do if his subordinates are united in a trade union? There is very little leverage on the bureaucrat here. If you want to complain to the president, go ahead; the official couldn't care less.

There are only two ways in the West of exerting influence on the bureaucracy: the courts or the press. But you can't go to court for every problem. It is as time-consuming as it is expensive. Neither can you expect the newspapers to write up every little incident. As a result, the Westerner is practically helpless vis-à-vis the bureaucracy and has little resource against its arbitrary actions. Just as in the USSR, the functionaries stick up for each other when a case comes up, for a common front is the natural defensive reaction of all bureaucrats. In the West this reaction is probably even stronger, for it is reinforced and virtually legitimized by the concept of loyalty to the department or corporation.

The great difference between Soviet bureaucrats and Western ones is that the latter cannot arbitrarily kill you, or put you in prison, or cause you grave harm. The courts will protect you in these cases. But they can certainly torment you in lesser ways without fear of reprisal.

A young man, the son of two Parisian friends of mine, wanted to spend two weeks in the United States. You would think that is an easy matter in the free world: buy your ticket and off you go. But no. At the American embassy, where he stood in line for several hours, the official didn't even want to discuss it: "We have no guarantee that you plan to return." It was like a slap in the face. The style in the Soviet Union is not much different: it's not their task to establish the criminality of your intentions; you have to prove your innocence. As the saying goes, try to prove you are not a camel. And what would constitute a guarantee? Money? The statement of a sponsor? It was quite unclear.

I was very busy at the time, so I suggested the first thing that came to my mind—send a letter to Muskie, who was then secretary of state. The result surprised me by its similarity to the tactics of the Soviet bureaucracy. The letter was forwarded from Washington to Paris, where it landed on the desk of the very people he had been arguing with. Once again he was refused a permit, although in more polite form. No response ever came from the State Department.

Perhaps it is because of what I have been through in life, but this sort of thing can really drive me through the roof, even though I might not be personally involved. Bureaucratic arbitrariness simply puts me into a cold fury, and hypocrisy even more so. None of these people had ever required that I present guarantees. When you stop and think about it, the situations of myself and of this young man were the same. We were both émigrés, only I was a bit older and had influential friends in Washington. I could get them raked over in the press and he couldn't.

In short, I took personal affront and phoned Washington. Several of my friends readily sent wires to the American embassy in Paris. But nothing doing: officialdom was not budging an inch. After complicated maneuvers and several exchanges of telegrams between Paris, Washington, and London, I had a rather strange conversation with a Miss Jackson of the American embassy in Paris. Her basic argument was that any young émigré of eighteen years of age and without a permanent job would obviously try to stay illegally in the United States. I assured her that my friend had no such intention, since his family was living in Paris, and he had been employed during the last several months.

"I know both him and his family well enough to be certain that there will be no complications. I guarantee it. Is my word a sufficient guarantee?"

No, it was not sufficient for her.

"If he were twenty-five years old, and had worked at the job for several years . . ."

"Does that mean you don't allow entry to tourists who are younger than twenty-five? There must be a lot of people in his shoes. You'll have to admit that it is hard to find an eighteen-year-old who has held a job for several years."

"Quite true," she countered. "Our task is precisely not to allow such people to enter the United States. We refuse entry to thousands like him."

A fine task, breeding anti-American sentiment in young Europeans!

"But what are the guarantees that you require of me? If you don't trust me or my friends, what should I do? Appeal to the president of the United States?"

"The president can do nothing about this. He has assigned us to do this work. Nobody can change anything. Your friend simply belongs to a category of people to whom we are obliged to refuse a visa."

What to do? Just like her opposite numbers in Moscow, this woman was not handling people; she was dealing in categories.

And this is merely an example picked at random.

◆ ◆ ◆

But our biggest discovery of all is that the West, as such, does not exist. We are in the habit of endlessly repeating the phrase about the way things are "in the West." Living in the USSR, our idea of this mythical land is rather like a comfortable hotel or a living room where well-groomed people say clever things to each other. Even when we handed *samizdat* materials to foreign journalists, we never bothered to inquire to which Western country the materials should be sent. No matter, we reasoned. The people in the West would figure it out.

Some day, experts will write learned papers about the origins and the many meanings in the Russian language of the word *West*. In any case, the subject is too complex to be handled here. But I shall note in passing that the term has nothing to do with geography. Japan and

Australia are part of the West, while Cuba is not. In the eyes of most of my countrymen, Finland is "the West for all that," but East Germany is definitely not. The twentieth century plays tricks with our language, with the meaning of words.

Not only is there no political unity between the countries of the West, but no common trait that could be easily articulated. This mythical unity is perceived only from the USSR, and it disintegrates the minute the Soviet frontier is crossed. I'm afraid that even the concept of "Western culture" is a figment of our imagination. In England, only specialists are aware of recent developments in French culture (and vice versa). The same is true of Italy with respect to Germany or of Spain vis-à-vis Holland. In the United States, Europe is far away from most people's consciousness. Far fewer people are skilled in foreign languages than we had thought, with the exception of the residents of the smaller countries like Holland, Switzerland, and Norway. Despite the way that fashions, pop songs, and opinions migrate from one country to the next, and despite the many millions of tourists who visit the major European countries yearly, national vanities are of striking intensity. It seems to be a tendency of the times that national traits are increasing at the expense of cosmopolitan ones.

In any case it is quite absurd to speak of "Western culture" today at any level above mass-produced consumer goods. Indeed, national traditions and temperaments vary a great deal. Here is a typical example. My book *To Build a Castle* was to appear in nine countries almost simultaneously. Each of the editors asked me to abridge some part for their particular edition. Their requests were so different that I was afraid the end result would be nine different books. It was clearly more than a publisher's whim in each case, but rather reflected a distinct national trait. The Danes wanted to delete one chapter entirely, while the Italians featured this very chapter in a major magazine. The French wanted to see more political commentary, while the British and the Americans suggested that it be cut. The Spaniards recommended deletion of all the more lively episodes so as to leave nothing but abstract analysis. In the end I refused to agree to any changes, feeling that a book should be the same for everyone, and that those who did not like its contents had the option of not reading it. A book is not a suit, after all, and it cannot be altered to fit different sizes. And yet I suppose my various editors were not entirely wrong, for they know a great deal more about their reading public than I do.

It is hard to discover the source of our mistaken image of the monolithic West. Is it simply because all the countries that make up this category are democracies? But then freedom is identified with variety, to the extent that it allows people unrestricted development of their own characteristics. Perhaps we have fallen into the habit of seeing the world as divided into "them" and "us." Or perhaps it is simply that we are so used to a lack of variety, to a dull uniformity? Probably all of these reasons play a part. Nowhere outside the USSR, with the possible exception of Jerusalem, do people still have such a habit of thinking in geopolitical terms. In opposition to our dreary uniformity we have imagined a uniformity of luxury. Such are the limits of human imagination.

But there is another and more serious reason, and it can be related to the above-mentioned story of the poor Jewish boy Moishe and his teacher. Compared with our misfortunes, all else seems pretty minor. We mentally "try on" the Western countries for size the way we would try a new suit. It doesn't much matter whether it's a morning coat or a kilt from Scotland: it's all clothes to a naked man.

When one is in Penza, or Riazan, or some other faraway corner of Russia, the differences among the Westerners seem so insignificant that the concept of the West is almost palpable, so great is the contrast between life here and life over there. But once you have crossed the frontier, the perception typical of Riazan quickly fades away. It's the West, all right, but it happens to matter a great deal what part of it one chooses to settle in.

When a Soviet citizen emigrates, he doesn't pause to think about his exact destination. Where to? To the West, of course, where else? If we don't like one spot, we can always go to another. That can't be much of a problem, the point is to get out of the USSR. But the real choices turn out to be very limited. There are so many limiting factors: knowledge of languages, employment opportunities, the proximity of friends, immigration policies, and so much to get used to. For an émigré, the problems of the West seem to grow tenfold. Every move is a step into the unknown.

Small children fare best with all this; they learn the language in no time, the life-style too, and two years after their arrival it's hard to tell them apart from the natives. Adolescents have a harder time of it—at this age they are painfully self-conscious and have difficulty communicating. Here they are faced with the additional language barrier and trying to cope with the nostalgia for friends left behind. My nephew had a further problem: during his first two years abroad he was gravely ill. That made it impossible to send him to an ordinary school or to take him elsewhere to meet people his own age. He became quite downhearted. I decided to make him a present of a puppy for New Year's, so as to provide him with at least this companion. I was living in England at the time, while my nephew was in Switzerland, where I was planning to visit for a few days for the holidays. It was difficult in a phone conversation to settle on the exact type of dog he wanted. But it was clear that he preferred a big dog, the biggest in the world. Fine. The reference book informed me that the largest canines are mountain dogs from the Pyrenees, huge shaggy monsters with white fur that resemble polar bears.

It was easy to arrange. I found a kennel in England that bred this kind of animal. By November, the puppy was sent by plane to Zurich and took up lodging in the apartment. He was a small fluffy creature, about the size of a rabbit.

Taken up with my studies, I did not return to Zurich until a year later, during the Christmas holidays, where I beheld the following astonishing scene: slumped in the most comfortable chair in the living room was a monster morosely gnawing on a bone. Whenever the bone would happen to fall out of his mouth he would look around the room with a questioning gaze, and then would give a short, imperious bark. At this point the family would race to his side to retrieve the bone and put it back in his menacing jaws. The explanation I was given was that in Switzerland it is categorically against the law for a dog to bark (in any case the owner of the apartment had made this a condition), and the clever animal had seized on this situation to virtually enslave the entire family.

There was no end to problems. All the furniture had been gnawed, shoes and gloves chewed and spit out. What was to be done? To give the dog away to strangers seemed akin to betrayal. I decided I would take him with me to Cambridge, where I had a small house and a decent-sized garden. There he could bark to his heart's content. But it wasn't as easy as it seemed.

The English are convinced that every dog who gets rabies must have contracted the disease abroad. Unthinkable that there should be an English variety. As a result, it is easier to smuggle drugs into Britain than it is to bring in an animal. Every quadruped is required to spend *six months* in quarantine. (Of course their masters are allowed to visit them regularly, in the manner of calling on relatives in prison.) This pleasure is offered to you at 40 pounds a week, a sum equal to the wages of an unskilled worker.

Faced with the alternative of either placing man's best friend in a prison or giving him away to strangers, I settled on the second course. My principles as a former convict did not leave me any other choice, and it proved impossible to find an apartment in Zurich where dogs had freedom of speech. The British were firm in their refusal to recognize the English bloodline of this dog and would not repatriate him. Poor beast! Without realizing it, he had been caught up in a typical émigré quandary: one place is easy to enter, but you can't bark; in the other place you can bark your head off, but they won't let you enter. Fortunately, we found some kind people who took in the unfortunate animal.

◆ ◆ ◆

So here we are, dispersed all over the world. Each one has found himself a spot as best he could. The time of the early excitement has passed, and so has the period of discoveries, disappointments, and critical comparisons when one exclaims to anyone who will listen: "Why, that is just like it was at home!" or even: "Back home, this was better." It's astonishing how quickly human beings forget the unpleasant aspects of the past or manage to see them in a heroic light. Everyone agrees that war is horrible, for example, yet old veterans abound who remember it as the best period of their lives. Looking back thirty-five or forty years later, that experience seems imbued with the fullness of life, the events seem to have a higher purpose, and human bonds have a special quality. In the same way a former convict at times acknowledges with a sigh that prison was not without positive aspects.

I am convinced that homesickness is really a longing for a past that always seems preferable to the present. To the man sentenced to die, each moment gone by seems better than the one just beginning; the oldster rambles on about how the winters were fiercer and people were braver in his day. The émigré has much in common with these two examples, for he too cannot retrace his steps. He is faced with a maddening limitation not unlike the locked door of a prison cell. But if it is suddenly opened, one look at the dirty streets, rough-hewn fences, and morose passersby is enough to dissipate the dreams of freedom that had been cherished for years. (In the camps, I met some men who had fled the USSR, but had later returned in search of their past. They told me that when they actually crossed the frontier, they had a sense of having made a terrible mistake. The further they moved into the country, the less they found what they had dreamed about, and in the camps they were now yearning nostalgically for Paris, Rome, or London.)

How strange. Only a year ago, we were highly exercised about the inability of Westerners to understand the abyss that separated our two ways of living. We railed at those clever types who claimed there were no differences, only nuances. But now we are no better ourselves. Only yesterday we denounced the indifference, the apathy, the selfishness, the narrowness of interests, the desire for peace and comfort at any price, and the inability to appreciate the freedoms that had come by inheritance—yet we are becoming exactly like the people we had criticized.

The metamorphosis sets in with extraordinary speed. In all of my previous life, I had never had my own roof over my head or a key to my own door that I could at last lock from the inside. But no sooner had I acquired these things, no sooner had the latch clicked shut on my front door, than I felt a complete indifference for the rest of the world. I sank into my armchair, turned on the TV, and lost all desire to move. Just let me sit and sit, while *they* entertain me with their programs. It was an almost physical need to forget, to shut myself off from the world. If the phone rings, I won't answer it. Nor will I come to the door if someone knocks. Let them all go to the devil with *their* problems! It goes without saying that any intrusion into my fortress from the outside world became a great issue. "The rats!" I'd say upon finding the electric bill in my mail box. "They've raised the prices again!" And when I would run into friends out of my distant past, by about the third glass we would start to reminisce about events that now appeared in a distinctly romantic light. From the viewpoint of our present life, the past does indeed seem fantastic.

And then, after the fourth glass, we would begin to argue, each one defending his present country of residence. For one thing, we did this because we are Russians, and a Russian cannot live without arguing. Second, at this final stage of his metamorphosis, an émigré becomes a fervent booster of his new homeland, a more zealous patriot by far than the native inhabitants. And third, we argued because the traditional ideas about national traits turned out to be false. Only after a few years of living in these countries does one recognize the absurdity of the usual ethnic generalizations.

What nonsense the various nationalities have said about each other, and about themselves too! Russians are hardly in a position to sort this out. I have the hardest time in these arguments that follow the fourth glass, since with the exception of Portugal, Luxembourg, Malta, Monaco, and Andorra, I think I have visited all the other countries. But there are two countries that I feel bound to defend with particular ardor: Switzerland, which gave me my first view of the West, and where my family still lives; and Britain, where I have been living for four years.

What gets dished up the most often about Switzerland is the incredible orderliness, cleanliness, and boredom that is said to be typical of the country. One could add prosperity to the list. I suppose that if you have absolutely nothing to do, and are quite incapable of finding distraction for yourself, believing that it is the duty of others to provide you with entertainment, if chaotic train schedules and filthy streets are your idea of variety, well, then you probably *will* be bored in Switzerland. But for the person who is genuinely busy, for whom each minute counts, there is no better place to live. And I would add that there are just as many, if not more, ways to find entertainment in Switzerland as in other countries. One must not forget that four different nationalities are united here under one roof. That is already fascinating in itself for anyone who cares to look around. It doesn't suit your taste that the Swiss are not always going out on strikes, that you rarely see "explosions of popular anger," and that it is hard to find the same "problems" that exist elsewhere? The Swiss are simply rational people who don't want to cripple their country financially for no reason at all. In addition, their prosperity derives from the fact that they work better and more conscientiously than is the case in some other countries; they do this instead of demanding ever more money from their government, for they lack the naive idea that money grows on trees. Instead of pursuing the idle dream of a social structure where no one works but everyone eats and has a good time, they are willing to work hard. This seems to be an unusual discovery for the twentieth century, as simple as it is inspired.

At the same time the Swiss are by no means insensitive to the misfortunes of others. They are warm people, affable and ready to lend a helping hand, as my family has had the chance to experience. They have an admirably efficient system of charitable institutions and their medical insurance program makes socialized medicine unnecessary. Their ideas of charity are rather old-fashioned for our enlightened age: for them it is a moral duty and not a legal obligation.

And, finally, Switzerland is perhaps the only country in the free world that has a responsible attitude toward its own security. Rather than taking shelter under the "umbrella" provided by others, or hiding their heads in the sand like an ostrich with the silly notion that "if we are not armed there will be no war," they have fashioned one of the best-equipped armies in Europe. History has taught them that neutrality must be securely defended if it is to be taken seriously by others. Up to a certain age, each Swiss male is required to do military service every summer, and every household is required by law to have certain food stocks on hand. And all this gets done without either pacifist or militarist hysteria; there are no childish disputes about where missiles can be placed—near your village or near mine. As far as I have been able to observe, Switzerland is the only European country truly ready to defend itself, and I can assure you that for this reason the Soviet army will never try to invade it. What would be the point of fighting for each rock in the Alps, losing precious time and resources, when it is possible to overrun an Italy or Germany with almost no effort?

No, it is not boredom that Switzerland evokes, it is envy. Let's see the other countries organize their societies as well, and only after that let's talk about fun.

In a certain sense, Britain is the exact opposite of Switzerland, and I cannot think of much that the British could be envied for. At the same time, there are even more fictions about the British than about the Swiss, many of them made up by the British themselves. There is the hoary legend about the English being cold, full of reserve, stiff, and almost devoid of emotion. What rubbish! Nowhere else have I met people as vulnerable, as emotional, and as eager to communicate. The trouble is that the English are terribly shy and full of complexes; they dread making moves that could be interpreted as an imposition. In psychological terms, they are introverts. One has to be a very poor observer of humanity to ascribe these traits to stiff haughtiness.

It is possible that my relationship with the British was made easier by the fact that I am Russian; how they get along with each other may well be a more complex matter. But Russians as a people are reputed not to stand on ceremony, and for this reason there seemed to be no barrier of conventions standing between me and my English friends, a barrier that can be formidable in England. In this respect, they almost seem to have set obstacles in their own path. But in reality they are incredibly fond of talk, at times excessively so, and their use of language is masterful. It is no accident that English is lexically one of the richest languages. When I was studying English during my prison days, I never ceased to be astonished at all the variety: why so many synonyms? Where Russians would use adjectives and a few suffixes, the English would have a separate word for every shade of meaning, thanks to which they can be extremely precise in what they say. They greatly prize language that is succinct, witty, and out of the ordinary.

Another legend about the English that is just as persistent and just as false ascribes to them a great deal of common sense, skillful pragmatism, business acumen, and a touch of pedantry. In Russia this nonsense has even entered folklore, and a celebrated folk song, "Dubinushka," has the following lines:

> To help the onus of his labors,
> The clever Englishman devised machine upon machine.
> But our Russian *muzhik*, when the work gets him down,
> Sets to singing his cherished "Dubina."

In point of fact, the English are incredibly impractical. Life in Britain seems to have been designed for maximum discomfort. The great period of British inventions began with the steam engine and ended with the early automobile. This probably explains the strong attachment the British have for these machines, and why there are endless exhibitions, museums, and collections of them. It's a peculiar national nostalgia. One might say that the secret dream of the English is to transform their entire country into a museum, while they collect tickets at the door. They want neither to break with tradition nor to innovate, and modernization or change of any kind arouses fierce resistance. A formerly advanced and industrialized country is turning into a backward and underdeveloped one before our eyes. For the most part none of this bothers the British too much (or if it does, they are good at hiding it).

In any case, the first impression striking a foreigner in Great Britain is the extraordinary slowness with which everything is done. A taxi that was promised in five minutes arrives on the scene forty-five minutes later; the driver will be genuinely surprised to find you angry. A train can stop in the middle of the countryside and remain there for several hours, and the passengers don't exhibit annoyance or impatience, or make any attempt to find another means of transportation. It is as though no one is in a hurry or has anything to do. If you expect to have furniture or some of your other purchases delivered to your home, you should be ready to wait for several months. A check deposited in Cambridge is credited in London only three or four days later. It would be quicker to go there on foot. Even the phones are extraordinarily slow; one must dial the number at half the speed normally used on the Continent. In a word, it is a completely unbusinesslike country, one certainly not suited for people who have things to do.

You could say that it is unsuited also for ordinary working people. All the shops close at five o'clock, that is, exactly at the hour that the offices shut, so there is no time to get one's groceries. The only way an employee can buy bread is during the lunch hour. Naturally enough, there will be lines and a great crush. And one must still have time to grab a bite. After this, one is laden down with packages for the rest of the day.

About two hundred years ago, some smart aleck had the bright idea of introducing *bank holidays* in England, days when the banks would close and everyone else would also cease working, evidently out of protest. Such a response is easy to understand. Banks are the last institution that would seem to need any holiday. On the days they are open, they function only from 10:00 AM until 3:30 PM, a sort of permanent bank holiday. It goes without saying that they are shut on Saturday and Sunday. These wretched accountants' holidays arrive quite unannounced, like all natural disasters. It is as complicated to figure out when a bank holiday will occur as it is to calculate the Jewish Passover, the difference being that it happens six times a year and always at a time of greatest inconvenience. So if you earn money while in Britain, keep it under your own roof or bury it in your garden, for getting it out of a bank can be impossible.

This probably explains why the English are not so profit-minded. I must confess, against all the impulses of my British patriotism, that I have avoided buying goods manufactured in Great Britain since I first noticed the "Buy British" posters. Rather absentminded by nature, I never used to pay attention to the country where the things I purchased had been made. After becoming aware of the publicity, though, I began to pick out exclusively British-made articles in my desire to help. I was cruelly punished for my pains! The products were of poor quality, overpriced, and usually designed to be as impractical as possible. For example, you can't replace the light bulb in a lamp without breaking the lampshade. And for heaven's sake don't try to get anything repaired! The end product will be fit to throw away anyway, and you will have spent money and nervous energy for nothing.

A rather typical scene: the largest bookstore in Cambridge, a university town, ignores the syllabi and lists of recommended books distributed by the professors, even though the courses in question may have been in existence for years. To get the book you need it is easier to go to London. The only shop that stays open in the evenings in Cambridge is run by an Italian. The place is always full and it offers stiff competition to the dozens of large and small English stores, many of which are on the verge of bankruptcy.

Of course, the country sustained tremendous damage from the socialism that was relentlessly introduced for many years, but of this more later. But that alone cannot explain everything. Each year British universities graduate thousands of historians, philologists, and other specialists who have virtually no chance of finding employment in their field. Yet thousands of new students are recruited for the same fields of study the following year. This does not happen for engineers, technicians, or specialists in modern production techniques, but it does for lawyers, historians, and Latin scholars. Most of them swell the ranks of the unemployed (something easily foreseeable), and few of them find jobs as managers in different companies or as civil servants. Why do they persist in wasting time this way, and why cannot efforts be made to teach them something useful from the start? And this is happening in a country of more than two million unemployed, where a dozen firms declare bankruptcy every day (in part because the management is unqualified). In a word, Great Britain gives the impression of a slowly sinking ship, the crew and passengers of which all pretend that nothing is wrong, desiring to go under with dignity.

To a degree this paradoxical situation can be explained by a typically British attitude toward misfortune and adversity. The English seem inclined to fatalism; one is not sure whether this is an inborn feeling or an acquired one. They believe that one must wait out hard times just as one waits for bad weather to change. They have a point about the latter: the British Isles make up perhaps the only country in the world where conversation about the weather is not due to a lack of some more fascinating subject, for the weather has for centuries continued surprising everyone by its caprice. What can one do about it? The typical British reaction is not to take it seriously, to ignore it. Thus every winter, with a terrible regularity, fifteen to twenty people freeze to death in their beds. Yet that in no way convinces the British that serious steps ought to be taken to install even rudimentary heating systems. They simply do not believe, or rather do not want to believe, that serious cold snaps can occur.

Another aspect of this popular philosophy is to regard inconveniences and difficulties as a sort of moral hygiene. I think that deep down the British view comfort as something shameful, something akin to corruption. A striking example is British cooking, which has become legendary. One would think there is not much you can do to a piece of meat to make it unpalatable. My knowledge of the culinary arts is virtually nil, but I don't believe I could spoil meat sufficiently to make it resemble British cooking. It is not at all a question of different tastes. The British are quite realistic about what their grub is worth, and when they want to eat half decently, they go to an Italian, Greek, or French restaurant. By British lights, eating should simply not be a pleasure, lest it lead to moral decline. By way of contrast, consider the French, gourmets to the point that they can spend all they earn on food, just as the Russians spend their salaries on drink.

As a biologist, I am inclined to think British fatalism is inborn rather than acquired. It may be tempting to explain everything by the weather, by the ingrained habit of coping with a difficult climate, by a kind of "acquired helplessness," but I would still maintain that natural, inborn reactions are more important. In very rough terms, the animal world exhibits two types of reactions in the face of danger or difficulty. One is the active response of either flight or aggression, which is in each case an attempt to modify or eliminate a dangerous situation. The second type is the passive response known as "freezing." A hedgehog attacked by a fox rolls up into a ball covered with sharp quills; a turtle hides its head and limbs and offers only its armor to its enemy. In the same way, an Italian or a Russian, when faced with a financial crisis, will attempt to make money on the side or will steal, if worst comes to worst. When faced by the same problem, the Englishman will scrounge and economize, but will not try to change the situation. And certainly he won't work.

This is especially obvious now, when the government is making huge efforts to overcome the inertia and passivity of the population. For England to pull itself out of the ever-worsening economic crisis, it will have to change its character. There needs to be more activity, a more active search for profit, a greater attempt to find opportunities for work, and a looking toward the future rather than to the past. As the Russians put it, "a wolf who doesn't run, doesn't eat." But how can the hedgehog grow wolves' legs? The English have "frozen," have withdrawn into their shells, and the reforms of the Conservative government evoke greater and greater immobility. "You can roll me over all you want," the hedgehog thinks to itself while the fox tries vainly to get past the prickly quills, "but you'll never get to my belly. You'll tire out before I do. You'll give up." The hedgehog is certain that all troubles come to an end. All one has to do is to roll up in a ball and wait.

Much also could be said about the traditionalism of the British, about the island psychology of a people who even at the end of the twentieth century cling to the naive idea that no calamity can reach across the Channel. But none of this explains the mysterious attachment we feel for this country. For all my grumbling about the blundering inefficiency of the British, only here do I feel a keen interest in people and in the world around me. For the most part the British are noticeably more civilized than their neighbors. They are wonderful actors and witty conversationalists. They have originality and know how to appreciate that quality in others. It is a race that thinks. One can tell the Americans the same thing twenty times over and they never seem to lose interest or enthusiasm, but the next day they will ask you the very same questions. But if you happen to run into an Englishman whom you have not seen for two years, he will remind you of your last conversation with him and proceed to tell you his further reflections on what was said.

The English are not wealthy (far from it), but they are amazingly responsive to the misfortunes of others. They are ready to pass the hat for the most extraordinary variety of causes, whether it concerns their own country or some faraway corner of the globe. For them charity is not a habit, not an automatic response to traditional or religious demands, but rather something like a need. At the same time it is not a question of easing the conscience by giving away money to right and left. The Englishman must first assure himself that the cause is a good one; he needs to feel himself a concerned participant. I know a man, for example, who, upon learning of the misfortunes of the Vietnamese boat people, sold his house and dedicated himself completely to organizing help for these refugees. What is most striking in these instances is that the British then seem to be transformed: they become practical, efficient, and full of common sense, almost as though they had awakened from lethargic sleep. Perhaps in everyday life they lack a cause that seems worth serving?

Once they choose a principle to follow, the British will stick to it at whatever price, a quality that endears them to me most of all. When his principles are at stake, an Englishman shrinks neither from difficulties, nor privations, nor even from that most important threat—of being taken as a silly oddball. A seventy-year-old man goes to prison for the fifth time because he refuses to wear a motorcycle helmet. Interviewed on TV, he is asked about his persistence. "Don't you think it's a bit much, five times in prison, all because of a helmet, and especially at your age?" "But it's a limitation on my freedom. What right does Parliament have to decide the acceptable manner of death for me?"

Perhaps this could happen in other countries too. The point is that in England this way of reasoning will provoke neither laughter nor ridicule, but rather understanding and sympathy. "Here's a man of conviction," the British will say. And for them that justifies everything.

When an event deeply shocks the British or really arouses their indignation, they are simply superb. It is at such times that one senses the strength of this people, a quality that evokes unqualified respect. A friend of mine, a psychiatrist by training, left the USSR so as not to be forced to contribute her professional knowledge to the goal of political repression. But the Soviet authorities did not let her ten-year-old youngster leave the country, in the hope of using the boy to put pressure on the mother. Over a period of more than four years, all of Britain fought for the boy. The newspapers reported the latest developments, the radio and TV felt duty-bound to tell his story again and again. Elderly people wore out shoe leather walking in front of the Soviet Embassy, carrying placards and presenting petitions. The boy's birthday was celebrated publicly in the streets, with cakes baked in his honor and pieces distributed to passersby. The indignation was so widespread, and the will to obtain justice was so boundless, that finally the Soviets capitulated, to the great joy of all. Name me another country that would fight for an émigré with such tenacity. Where else in our cynical century are there people who allow themselves the luxury of having principles and of sticking to them?

And so, when I return to Cambridge after being away on a trip, I have the impression of coming home. I can always curse the inconveniences and the slow pace of life in this country, but I will not allow others to do the same in my presence. I permit myself to poke fun at the British or to be caustic at their expense but I will not allow "foreigners" to do so. Strange, isn't it? I must have been born here in one of my earlier incarnations.

◆ ◆ ◆

If there are plenty of foolish ideas about the British, the Swiss, the Italians, and the Germans, what one hears said about the Russians tops them all. That is why after the fifth glass has been drunk, the arguments among Russian émigrés inevitably return to the question of how we are different. In what sense are we to blame? What is the elusive something that makes the people here free, while we in Russia are all slaves, from Brezhnev on down to the last prisoner?

I don't have in mind those well-known differences that lie on the surface. Few people today can be unaware of the fact that we are in the grip of a ruthless dictatorship of a single party whose tentacles spread out into every corner of the society, and that, together with the all-powerful, all-knowing KGB, this coincides almost literally with the society depicted by Orwell's *1984*. By definition, totalitarianism is the extreme concentration of all aspects of power: political, administrative, economic, military, and spiritual. But to be aware of this is not enough. Inevitably the next question is: how can such a monster continue to survive at the end of the twentieth century? What is the source of its strength? Is it true that every country deserves its government? Maybe there are qualities in us that make the existence of this monster possible or even justified, qualities that are not found in more civilized peoples?

There are many platitudes and clichés that at first seem to explain everything perfectly well. But none of them hold up to close analysis. It's rather like the story of the hundred-year-old man who is interviewed by researchers from the gerontology institute in the hope of learning the secret of his longevity.

"It's all a question of abstinence," declares the old man in a moralizing tone. "All my life I never drank, never smoked, never womanized."

Suddenly there is a terrible commotion next door, with things falling over, curses, and a woman's cries.

"What is going on?" ask the startled gerontologists.

"Pay no attention," explains the old man with an embarrassed air. "It's just my older brother who's come in. He's a worthless character who spends his life smoking, drinking, and wenching."

One typical bromide has it that people in the West are kinder and more tolerant. It is certainly true that one meets a lot of very kind people here. Soviet twaddle about the cold and selfish capitalistic world is as far from reality as the stories about the droves of unemployed dying of hunger. Empathy for the sufferings of others and a readiness to help are purely human traits and do not depend on the form of government. But how is one to make comparisons? In my country, we might have five people living in one room, yet it would never cross anyone's mind to place the paralyzed grandmother in an old folks' home. We couldn't face each other after that. In the West, it is almost the rule. In the best of cases, the old people are allowed to live out their days in the house they have always occupied, while the younger generation moves elsewhere. There is a card for Christmas, another for Easter, and a short visit every three or four years. Of course this is also possible in our country, but it would be frowned upon. One would earn the reputation of being a person who cannot be counted on when hard times strike.

Perhaps the difference lies in the fact that there is so much hardship in our country that most people have tasted it. And for that reason, they are more likely to share their last possessions.

In day-to-day living in the West, one indeed finds more tolerance, or in any case less irritability, than in the USSR. There, if you dial a wrong number or step on someone's toe by mistake, you can expect a storm of insults. The lack of common courtesy in everything having to do with service is notorious. Here, on the contrary, you will hear (and say) more "thank yous" and "beg pardons" in one day than you would in a whole lifetime in Moscow. Interminable hours standing in line, constant difficulties, and a life without a future result in a human being so filled with anger that a mere touch by another is sufficient to make him explode. That is the source of the ingrained coarseness, the pushiness. If you want the salesman to pay any attention to you, you've got to give him an earful. A person who is gentle and polite simply will not survive in our country. Aggressiveness probably derives from the same source.

Almost every college at Cambridge has its own disco, and there are a few more in town. Alcohol is sold till closing time, which is two or three o'clock in the morning, right at the bar. Yet in the course of three years, I have never heard of a serious brawl. In any case, no one has been killed or maimed. When the town boys roughed up one of the students one night, it was considered an extraordinary event. Inconceivable that such a situation could exist in Soviet Russia, where any fellow who comes to even the most unpretentious dance will always carry a knife. Alcohol is never sold at nighttime, except in restaurants, and carrying a knife is punishable by one year in prison. Yet in spite of this, hardly a month goes by without a murder or a stabbing. And that is not counting the ordinary sort of fights. The hostility between the "locals" and the "outsiders" sometimes grows to warlike proportions.

It goes a lot deeper than irritability or intolerance. Nor can it be explained by an innate aggressiveness. What can adolescents find to do, when there is no social life to speak of, or any meaningful future? Hooliganism can thus become the one accessible means of self-expression, or communication, if you prefer. It becomes their subculture. The intellectuals have their outlets: *samizdat*, the struggle for human rights, and hostility toward the KGB as the symbol of authority. The young workers have only crime, and for them the police personify the government. A similar phenomenon can be observed in certain slums in the West. But the difference is that the entire Soviet Union is one vast slum, the only exception being a few model islands, disinfected and ready to be shown to foreigners.

Psychologists consider frustration, especially sexual frustration, as the most frequent cause of aggressiveness. Soviet society, with its official prudishness and hypocrisy, has not only banned pornography, but views sex in general, especially among adolescents, as outside the law. When you consider the atrocious conditions in which most Soviet families have to live, often crowded into a single room, the practical opportunities for sex are few indeed. Thus the great frequency of gang rapes by bands of youths in the public gardens, in the hallways of buildings, and even in courtyards. In the West, this is a rare occurrence.

Despite our very high incidence of crime (in all the years of Soviet power, we have never had fewer than 2.5 to 3 million prisoners, that is, roughly 1 percent of the population), it would be inaccurate to conclude that we are innately aggressive. The major reasons for crime are social. In the United States, for example, where living conditions are immeasurably better and where the incidence of crime is considerably less (there are approximately 400,000 persons in jail), the number of murders committed per year is higher than the Soviet average. At the same time, the level of crime among Americans of East European stock is considerably lower than the national average.

One day in New York I was waiting in line for a taxi, when it suddenly started to rain heavily. The line instantly disintegrated into a tangle of brawling people. Approaching cabs were literally taken by assault, the women being the most violent. They charged into the middle of the crowd, shouting hysterically, and pushing everyone else aside. One might have thought we were aboard a sinking ship, and it took police intervention to restore some semblance of order. I've seen similar scenes repeated elsewhere in America. It is always risky to generalize from such incidents, but you would not have been able to see anything like this in our country in recent decades, despite the tremendous overloading of the public transportation system. There can certainly be a lot of pushing and shoving due to the crowds, some people will perch on running boards, others will swear mightily, but the basic order in which people have lined up will nevertheless be maintained. And we are totally without the feminine aggressiveness that seems to be the special attribute of America.

In the question of crime and tolerance, it is interesting to compare the attitude of the state and of society toward criminals. One day upon turning on my TV set, I heard an extraordinary announcement. It was the secretary of the Home Office, who in Britain has the reputation of being a "reactionary." He declared that since the prisons were overcrowded, it would henceforth be necessary to reduce the number of prison sentences and to increase the rate of early releases. (At this point, there were some 45,000 people behind bars, or about 0.08 percent of the population.) Besides, the cost of maintaining a prisoner is 200 pounds per day, he said, too much of a burden on the treasury.

"My God," I thought, "I must be dreaming! This cannot be reality! Any moment now the guard will wake me up by banging on the cell door with his keys. When I tell my cellmates about this, they are going to double up with laughter! The very idea! Too little room . . . too expensive . . . These dreams are really something!"

Soviet prisons are made of rubber. There are at least five inmates occupying the space that was designed for two under the tsars. Overcrowded prisons are never a problem. You herd a group of prisoners together under guard and order them to build a camp for themselves within two weeks. Our country produces enough barbed wire to surround them with, no problem there.

Two hundred pounds per day boggles the mind. Why, the entire Politburo would hang itself from the walls of the Kremlin if anything like that were to happen in the USSR. Prisoners are supposed to bring in a profit for the state, to enrich the people's economy. For 200 pounds, the camp supervisor would lock himself in too, and would never leave his cell.

There is a real reactionary minister for you!

On the other hand, the attitudes of society toward criminals is noticeably harsher here than it is in our country. The death penalty exists only in very few countries, and in some of the American states, where it is carried out reluctantly. It has been abolished in Great Britain, but there continues to be quite a powerful movement that is attempting to have it restored. In general, people in Britain believe in punishment. Even corporal punishment in schools has not been officially abolished, though it is rarely used. Curiously enough, parents seem to prefer institutions where it is still practiced; there is a waiting list for these institutions, and they usually prosper financially.

In the Soviet Union, the death penalty is the punishment for at least a dozen crimes, including some that are not crimes of violence, such as bribe-taking, large-scale fraud, "betrayal of the motherland," "disruption of the functioning of corrective-labor camps," and so on. The cruelty of the state's repressive machinery has at times attained levels of outright terror directed at the population, but we know that even this did not lessen the incidence of crime. On the contrary, morals only regressed, and punishment lost its value as a deterrent. In the course of half a century, so many people—those innocent of any crime as well as genuine criminals—have spent time in prisons that being arrested is no longer perceived as shameful. In order to restore its value as punishment, the regime has attempted to make prison conditions intolerable, and to keep the prisons at the bare edge of survival. The result has been a great deal of sympathy for prisoners among the society at large, and a general loss of faith in the efficacy of an ever-mounting spiral of cruelty.

Bitter experience has taught us that from the point of view of psychology, punishment makes no sense at all. If the criminal does not feel guilt, punishment is simply a form of torture; if he does he is already punished more than the state could ever succeed in doing. Men are not like Pavlov's dogs; their consciousness is not formed by reflex. A man is not going to submit to being trained. He finds a way out, he pretends, he develops clever ways to defend himself, but all this does not affect the inner man. In a word, punishment only succeeds in corrupting, embittering, or breaking a man.

The desire of society to protect itself against individuals who disregard the rights of others is quite justifiable; such individuals must be isolated and prevented from committing further crimes. But when society exacts retribution from a criminal, it is as hideous as the crime itself.

A case in point is the instance of Jimmy Boyle, who is serving a life sentence in Scotland. He was born and raised in one of the slums of Glasgow, where crime is an everyday occurrence. I am not a proponent of the view that poverty necessarily leads to crime. The tales of sentimental writers like Victor Hugo about a man who stole a loaf of bread out of hunger and then went on to become a hardened criminal are pure bunk, and can be believed only by people who don't have the slightest understanding of the criminal mind. Criminals are extraordinarily ambitious people, who will not wait for hunger to set in before they act. Those who possess that sort of patience will never steal anything but bread. The criminal world is a subculture with its own heroes and scoundrels. To get to the top of the heap in this world, one needs to possess unusual qualities, which by the way are not necessarily antithetical to common human ones. But it is certainly true that a person growing up in the slums has a much greater chance of becoming a criminal. The prevailing atmosphere of such places is undoubtedly closer to the psychology of the criminal world. For strong-minded and ambitious personalities, a career in crime is very likely.

But to get back to Jimmy Boyle. During the 1960s, he became one of Scotland's most famous gangsters. Condemned to life in prison for murder, he could not be subdued even there. There began an endless series of conflicts with the prison authorities, mutual cruelties, and more punishment. He spent many months in solitary confinement, sinking to the level of a wild animal, and his life sentence was extended by twenty-five years. It is hard to say where all this would have led, had the authorities not opened a special experimental unit in the Glasgow prison to deal with incorrigible criminals like Boyle. The plan was very simple. The men would in essence be left alone and granted a certain amount of independence, together with fairly lenient living conditions and access to books, radio, TV, and to means of expressing themselves.

It goes without saying that the first reaction of the convicts was defiance and suspicion; they saw it all as a new trap. But the months went by without any unpleasant surprises. Little by little, each one found himself some sort of an occupation: drawing, making things. Jimmy started to sculpt and to read. The guards left him pretty much to himself.

The outcome does not surprise me. I have had many occasions to observe that even the most hardened criminals, when left to themselves in a prison that has a good library, begin to rethink their past. They have a long sentence ahead of them, plenty of time on their hands; they realize that they are no longer so young and that life has somehow passed them by. The natural question is, why? Maybe boredom is the original motivation for starting to read, but eventually it begins to sink in that the small realm in which he had been king is but a tiny segment of an immense world—a world that is vastly more interesting than the one he had known before, and a world in which he too could use his gifts. In this world he could meet far more striking individuals than his fellow thugs or his prison guards, and the values and ethical norms of his criminal microcosm don't apply to it. In a word, he experiences a crisis of his subculture.

Jimmy became a sculptor, wrote his life story, and became famous for things other than his criminal feats. He even got married. And it was at that point that society began to take vengeance on him. After thirteen years in prison, of which seven had been spent in the "special section," where he had an excellent behavior record and had never crossed swords with the administration, he was eligible for parole. But society furiously protested such an idea. A campaign was launched to prevent his release; it was based on the argument that he was dissembling, playing the role of a reformed convict. The "special section" came in for severe criticism at the same time. How could criminals be allowed to have books and television, while many ordinary honest people could not afford these things? Call this a prison? It sounds like a resort! And where is punishment? There was no end to the talk, and the "special section" came within an inch of being eliminated. At one point I had publicly to come to its defense. Finally, in order to let emotions subside, Jimmy was moved to another prison, allegedly in preparation for his later release. The "special section" was allowed to stay open, but one wonders for how long.

So much for tolerance in a democratic society. Political tolerance is even less in evidence. It suffices to recall the various "Red brigades" and "Red armies," the endless clashes between the left and the right, the mutual smear campaigns among political parties, the furious harassment of individuals by the press, and the "demonization" of one's opponents. At least in the Soviet Union, intolerance is artificial and imposed from above. It arouses not the slightest enthusiasm.

One day, in the Vladimir Prison, my cellmates and I raised the question of what should be done to the leaders of the party and what might be suitable punishment for them. Out of the eleven prisoners in our cell, only one suggested the death penalty, another proposed a public flogging, and one thought they should be put behind bars and subjected to recordings of their own propaganda on a round-the-clock basis. The rest were in favor of a formal public condemnation of their criminal policies but without any sanctions against individuals. And not one of these eleven expressed an interest in being either the prison warden or the executioner of these hypothetical prisoners.

It is of course hard to predict how the entire population would answer such a poll. We do know, however, that terrorist acts are remarkably rare in the USSR.

◆ ◆ ◆

Another illusion, this one generated and promulgated by our own human rights movement, concerns the belief that people in the West have a profound sense of law. Our basic idea was that democracy depends on every member of society being aware of himself as a citizen or, in the elegant phrase of Aleksandr Volpin, as a "subject of law." This led directly to our concept of the "sovereignty of the human conscience," and thus to personal responsibility. It followed that passivity or silence in the face of a crime that one had witnessed were forms of collaboration with the criminals. We sincerely believed that every person in the West carried these democratic principles within himself, together with a lofty sense of the limits of his own rights. Such consciousness, we thought, existed in our country only in the most rudimentary form, and for that reason we first of all had to overcome the "Soviet man," or in any case his primitive level of legal consciousness.

I remain convinced that this is the only possible road to democracy from the world of totalitarian tyranny. But our image of the West was in this respect very far from the truth. Perhaps people were different here when democracy was instituted, with traits that later disappeared due to natural selection, but today the levels of legal consciousness for the average man in the Soviet Union and in the West are not significantly different.

I must say that I had begun to suspect this fact while I was still in Moscow. It was disturbing to note that foreigners arrested by the KGB in connection with our activities caved in and "sang" much more readily than did Soviet citizens in a similar situation. It is normal enough to experience fear in a foreign country with a sinister reputation, especially in the hands of a secret police with an even worse name. But one would have thought that the sense of right and wrong does not depend on geographical location and that the Universal Declaration of Human Rights applied equally to the whole world. I am not speaking here of some information that might have been blurted out by accident or in a moment of fear. I have in mind the full confession of guilt, legally phrased, confirmed in writing, repeated in front of witnesses, sometimes even on Moscow TV. The foreigner caught in the act of importing or exporting "forbidden texts" not only reveals the names of those who gave him the materials and of those for whom they are destined, but goes on to confess that he committed a crime against the Soviet Union, namely "agitation with the aim of subverting or weakening Soviet power."

With some rare exceptions, these people don't seem to remember either the Universal Declaration of Human Rights or the Helsinki Accords. Moreover, the trick used by the KGB to disarm virtually all of them is even more ludicrous.

"Come now," says some semiliterate major, "you claim not to understand the criminal nature of your acts, and yet you concealed them and acted conspiratorially. So you clearly tried to escape detection, isn't that so?"

And after consulting with their inner sense of right and wrong, about 95 percent of them agree that they are guilty. It does not take a great legal scholar to figure out the fallacy of this argument: after all, any housewife tries to keep her money safe from thieves and locks her front door at night without committing any crime. For a man convinced of the rightness of what he is doing, who has been brought up since childhood in the awareness of the laws, there should not be the slightest hesitation. How is it that these people conform so easily to our rules the minute they set foot on Soviet territory?

When one lives in the Soviet Union, one is always trying to find a rational explanation for certain disparate facts about the West that filter in to us. In a pinch we explain inconsistencies by the inadequacy of our information. The readiness with which elected governments give in to terrorists who have taken hostages always disturbed us profoundly. Perhaps we had missed something? In principle a government does not even have the right to enter into negotiations in these cases, for this would mean recognizing the bandits as a valid negotiating partner. Why hold general elections if the nation can in effect be controlled by an armed maniac? After all, authority is not an object that can be temporarily handed over to one's neighbor: "Here, hold this for a minute. I'll be right back."

But after spending some time in the West and seeing the voters' attitude toward elections, nothing surprises me any more. Almost half of the voters don't go to the polls at all: they don't care. A certain proportion votes out of a sense of obligation to their party, just like in the Soviet Union. The rest generally vote not for what they desire but against that which they fear. For the right, so that the left does not come to power, or vice versa. And why vote for the splinter parties, if they have no chance of winning? Only the English probably read the pre-election statements. Can this be a responsible way for a citizen of a democratic country to choose his elected representatives?

It is amusing to hear in this context that everyone is dissatisfied with the mediocrity of the people in politics, with their lack of any kind of guiding principles or conceptual framework, with the absence of any real choice between candidates. Indeed, except for Sadat, the Pope, and Mrs. Thatcher, the professional level of Western political leader is alarmingly low. In France, most of my friends don't vote, claiming that it is pointless. Despite an abundance of parties that seem to exist mostly for their own pleasure, there are only two significant forces, and both are in effect pro-Soviet. For one of them, the biggest enemy is for some reason the United States, reminding one of Krylov's fable about the mice who declared that there is no more terrible a beast than the cat. In the opinion of this camp, the "grandeur of France" depends on constantly acting to the detriment of the free world, inasmuch as the latter makes no attempt to occupy France or to exile her into Siberia. For the other camp, the greatest friend on earth is the Soviet Union. In spite of this, as best I can judge from the press and from my fairly numerous public appearances in France, the population is not at all pro-Soviet, far from it. The gap between the desires of the voters and the policies carried out by the government is immense: the two entities seem to exist independently of each other.

The voters are discouraged and can see no reason for going to the polls: nothing will change anyway. But is it not true that these same voters have brought about the situation by acting on the principle of the lesser evil? Do they not have the right (and the duty, I would add) as citizens of their country to pave the way for a government that corresponds to their convictions? The answer I got to these questions frightens me by its similarity to the reasoning of a Soviet man: "What can one individual do all by himself? What can even a small group do? The majority will go right on as before, no matter what I do."

An even more striking example of the sense of law in the West is the attempt to legislate the question of abortion. It certainly is an extremely complex question, and I don't have the slightest intention of going into it in depth. Feelings in both camps run at such a pitch that one risks getting torn to pieces by bringing up the question. But it is one thing to argue, to appeal to feelings, to faith, to reason, and to the conscience; it's quite another matter entirely to put the question to the vote. To do this is just as absurd as calling a referendum on the existence of God and then drawing up a law based on the result. Yet that is exactly what one of the oldest democracies in Europe, Switzerland, did by holding a referendum on abortion. The result (80 percent against and 20 percent for) might be of certain interest to some, but it is hardly a matter for legislation. If 80 percent of the population has no intention of practicing abortions, no one is trying to make them have one, nor could it be forced upon them, no matter what the referendum said. But by what right can they decide for those who favor the practice, or force others to bow before their beliefs or moral values? These are questions that each individual must decide only for himself, not for his neighbor.

I fear that the consciousness of law in the West is even more rudimentary than the one typical for the Soviet populace. For example, the Constitution of the United States guarantees the right to "the pursuit of happiness." It is hard to imagine what that really means. It is common knowledge that happiness is an elusive psychological state, and that there are some individuals who are organically incapable of being happy. On the other hand, there exist a considerable number of people whom this "pursuit" would inevitably bring into conflict with the law. Let's say that a man can achieve happiness only by killing his wife. Can it be his right to do so?

It is amusing to note that it was again in the same United States that none other than our chief specialist on law, Aleksandr Volpin, learned firsthand of the Western public's indifference toward the law. As one would expect of him, he began to study the local laws after settling in Boston. And he discovered to his great astonishment that according to the laws of the state of Massachusetts, "a married person is prohibited from having sexual relations with another person." Accustomed as he was to a close reading of the laws, Volpin was stunned by this wording. Not only can that other person be one's legitimate spouse ("another person" with respect to whom? with respect to oneself, obviously: interpretation is plausible enough), but in the case of Volpin, the important point was that before leaving Moscow he had not gotten divorced, so therefore he was legally still "a married person."

In vain did his friends reassure him that this law had long since ceased to be enforced and that, in spite of the fact that it was still officially on the books, no one in all of the state of Massachusetts had ever heard of it. But ignorance of the law, Volpin remembered, is never a mitigating circumstance. The problem was that Volpin planned to become a naturalized American after the required five-year wait, and as part of the solemn ceremony each future citizen is asked whether he has ever broken any American law while on United States territory. Afflicted by a "pathological truthfulness," Volpin could not even conceive of the possibility of concealing his illegal activities from the authorities. He checked the law of the other states and discovered similar statutes just about everywhere (with the exceptions of Louisiana and Arkansas, I believe, both of which are rather far from Boston).

I do not know how he would have managed over the five-year period, if the proximity of Canada had not saved the day.

Of course this story sounds like a joke, but why should a man have to lie in order to become a citizen of the United States? Have not most of the Soviet émigrés left the USSR because they could no longer stand having to lie day in and day out? And a further question relevant to our discussion of the awareness of the law: why had no one else paid attention to this silly law before Volpin?

Alas, Americans are not only ignorant of their laws, but consider this a normal state of affairs. The one legal right with which everyone is familiar is the right to say nothing until one's lawyer arrives, if one gets into a "spot." Pretty small stuff. In the USSR too, people know it's wisest not to talk too much in front of the authorities. In our case, of course, no lawyer will be allowed in until the "investigation" is complete, at which point nothing can be changed. We are certainly not spoiled by our rights, and we have a bit more respect for the law, since it exists only on paper. To appreciate the law, one has to have lived for a long time where it is absent.

◆ ◆ ◆

But perhaps our ideas about democracy were simply wrong, contrived, and overly abstract, and the people of the West have no need either of any particular tolerance or of a clearly defined sense of law. Perhaps democracy is nothing but a perpetual struggle between forces, groups, factions, differing points of view, in the course of which the legal norms and relationships are constantly re-examined and adjusted? What is the use of learning all about the laws if they represent merely a temporary compromise, while the only constant factor is the struggle itself?

I suppose there is much truth in such reasoning. The most essential aspect of democracy is the right to defend one's interests, one's principles. Injustice and oppression can occur in any society, but only in a democracy can no one prevent you from fighting against them. You can write appeals, put up posters, organize demonstrations, cast about for sympathizers (you will always find some), turn to the press (it will give you some coverage, if only because of a taste for novelty), appeal to celebrities (one out of ten will support you), or bring pressure to bear on the politicians (at least one will join your campaign, for he is looking for voters). All the mechanisms of democracy are at your disposal and, what is more, they encourage you to make noisy demands. It seems that no matter how foolish the cause you are championing or how absurd your demands, the result will be approximately the same in each case.

The mechanisms of democracy are neutral and cannot act in a selective manner. Only two conditions must be met: you have a *problem*, and you are making a *demand*. The more unreasonable or scandalous your actions are, the better your chances, and if in the course of the campaign you break the law, that is better still. Let the lawyers figure out who's right and who's wrong; that is their business. The current trend is to assure that society is guilty always and in every instance, a position to which society readily accedes. Your problem then becomes a national or even an international one. At this point you become unassailable, and nothing remains but to satisfy your demands, because all-powerful *publicity* is on your side. You have a mass of supporters and imitators, and your ideas gain general acceptance. A few "reactionaries" may still try to resist, but your sympathizers will move quickly to overwhelm them, to hound them into oblivion, and to keep them on the run. These adversaries, it is true, can reconquer their dominant position if they can demonstrate equal energy and initiative, that is, if they carry out a campaign in your style.

If you accept democracy as such, then you must also accept its excesses, since the system precludes any supreme wise man who could rule on what constitutes an abuse. The trouble is that one has to shout louder and louder to make oneself heard, and if one makes no energetic demands, then one gets no results whatever. These demands are, in effect, laid on the doorstep of each of us, for after all we make up society.

Demonstrations and petitions begin to lose their impact: there are too many of them. And that is why the "oppressed minority" finds it necessary to fall back on more effective methods like the taking of hostages or the bombing of beer halls.

I am aware that many "reactionaries" will frown at the very word *hostage*, yet the truth is that the taking of hostages has been a respectable method for some time now. It is not only the extremists who use it. Trade unions of unimpeachable reputation keep children hostage in British hospitals or make hostages of their fellow workers who have gone to take their holidays on the Continent. When you stop to think about it, virtually every major strike today creates a hostage situation. For the traveler it is of little consequence whether his plane has been captured by terrorists or held up by striking air controllers: in either case, money is being extorted by someone with whom he does not have the pleasure of being acquainted.

From whatever angle you look at it, democracy today seems to consist of the exercise of terror by "oppressed minorities," be they national, political, or social. Try writing the slightest criticism of feminists, especially in America. (I am only using this as an example, I swear I have nothing against them, it is simply that some group had to serve as an illustration.) So what is left to the "oppressed majority" except to give in? And anyway, the majority has to earn its living, it does not have the time.

It is astonishing how easy it is for the oppressed to become the oppressors, for the exploited to turn into exploiters. Art Buchwald wrote a very amusing column about the system of affirmative action current in industry, where the best way not to be hired is to be white, young, healthy, male, with an unblemished police record, and with no sign of narcotics abuse. Firms receive no governmental subsidies for hiring such an individual. This is not a joke: certain whites have gone to court protesting reverse discrimination. And the trade unions? Only yesterday they had to fight hard for the right to exist, but today they already insist on the dismissal of any worker who does not wish to become a union member. The right to strike had no sooner been won than thousands of British workers were complaining to their representatives in Parliament that without secret balloting, they dare not oppose strikes called by the union. And it is hardly necessary to add anything about the terrorist acts of political minorities, since their aims are undisguised and often include an explicit desire to destroy democracy.

But wait. All this seems suspiciously familiar: terror exercised by a minority on a majority, censorship, forced membership in a trade union, sometimes combined with membership in a political party (in England and Sweden, for example, the votes of trade unionists go automatically to the Socialist party). Why, this is our glorious Soviet Union in all its splendor! The difference is that in our country, the terrorist minority seized power in a time of crisis. This was followed by terror on a national scale, a frightened "silent majority," a feeble, disorganized resistance mounted by the army, and more terror. The country is huge, communications have been disrupted, one end of the country does not know what is happening at the other end; devastation, famine, mutinies, looting, turmoil on a scale that would make the most draconian measures to re-establish order seem acceptable even in the West. I am convinced that no European democracy would survive a crisis comparable to the one Russia faced after World War I.

"I beg to differ," counters the learned historian. "You're forgetting traditions, culture. Democracy has endured in Europe for centuries, whereas it never existed in Russia."

There is no intellectual pursuit more useless, not to say harmful, than history when it comes to the matters that concern us here. There are as many historical theories as there are historians, or rather as many as are needed to justify the various ideologies of the day. History is nothing but a huge assortment of facts that can be arranged to suit any conceptual framework. One can always play prophet after the event. If a totalitarian regime were to come to power in France tomorrow, historians would be quick to enlighten us about the baneful French traditions. The Convention period with its guillotine would certainly be brought up, also Napoleon and the Paris Commune. Moreover it is a fact that democracy does not have a long history in France and has never been very stable. Not so long ago, if General de Gaulle had not curbed democracy, it might no longer exist today.

Just as it is possible to write an obituary of someone who is still alive, so one could discern for each country possible causes of totalitarianism. Indeed, with the exception of Britain, Holland, Switzerland, and Scandinavia, no other country has had a democratic government without interruption over a period of several centuries. America cannot be counted in: slavery was abolished there two years after it was done away with in Russia. And it might be noted that the process was peaceful in Russia—the result of an imperial decree—whereas in America, abolition took a civil war lasting several years and was opposed by nearly half the nation.

On the other hand, we have witnessed the birth of new democracies, without benefit of any democratic tradition whatsoever (such as Japan and Germany), that seem to carry on without particular difficulties. The other half of Germany, a stone's throw away on the other side of the barbed wire, has remained a fascist state with but a change in color.

It seems to me that we assign too much importance to traditions. For example, how much is our political thinking influenced by the beliefs of the older generation? If anything, the influence is negative, since new generations tend to reject the convictions of their predecessors. After all I had heard about the youth movements of the 1960s, about "hippies," "beatniks," and so on, I was struck by the conservative appearance and mentality of today's students. Once I got into a conversation with a young man at my college, who seemed particularly straitlaced in his suit, tie, and vest, complete with a gold chain. It became clear that he had been traumatized by the life-style of his parents, and he described in comic terms how they had arrived at the graduation ceremony of his school, while he tried to stay out of sight of this odd-looking couple with their uncombed hair and torn blue jeans, pretending that they were strangers. Everything about their appearance raised the apprehension that they might slap him on the shoulder and offer him a "joint."

Something similar seems to have happened, though perhaps on a lesser scale, to this whole generation. For the most part, the students are as apolitical as they have ever been, working seriously at their studies, hard as that may be to believe about Western universities.

I think each generation makes a reappraisal of past traditions. The only limit to this dialectic is the national character, if this expression still means anything in our day. But even in that perspective, East Europeans are by no means suited for totalitarianism. We are unsubmissive, difficult to discipline, and have always had little respect for authority. For example, if all the prison regulations had been carried out to the letter, we would never have survived. The warden on duty is supposed to make a count of all prisoners every two hours. At night this would entail switching on the lights periodically and perhaps opening the doors to the cells. It goes without saying that inborn laziness scotched that, so the light is left on all night, which is unpleasant enough, but something that one can get accustomed to. In East German prisons, I am told, the rules are applied with Germanic thoroughness, and each night becomes a torture for the prisoners. Our legendary Russian muddle spared us some hardships!

As to traditional democracy, I strongly doubt that such is possible even in theory. The history of ancient Greece consists of continual swings between democracy and tyranny. Plato was of the opinion that one inevitably engendered the other. Besides, if the tradition were really so important, it would follow that people need to be taught freedom and democracy, much the way they are taught trigonometry. The argument becomes a vicious circle: it is impossible to pass from a tyranny to a democracy without being educated in the latter. Yet how can such an education take place in the absence of freedom?

All this quibbling over traditions would make more sense if the popular memory retained events from the past. But that is not the case. Judging by the national holidays celebrated by the democracies, their history is an unbroken series of victories and humanitarian acts. They reflect nothing except national vanity. In contrast, tragic events of no more than thirty or forty years ago have left little trace in people's memories. The American TV series on the Holocaust unleashed a veritable tempest. Even the older generation was stunned, as though the massive extermination of the Jews by the Nazis was some kind of news. One might have thought that the Nuremberg trials had never taken place, or that the long list of books and films on the subject had never appeared. Does not the hunt for Nazi war criminals still go on, from time to time, somewhere in Latin America? Are not the men who liberated the concentration camps still alive, as well as some of those who were locked up inside? Every schoolboy knows all about it.

> Where is the Life we have lost in living?
> Where is the wisdom we have lost in knowledge?
> Where is the knowledge we have lost in information?[2]

The only consequence of fascism and of World War II has been a reckless veering to the left, wherever that might lead. To be of the left has become a sort of fetish; any politician who is to the right of the socialists can be branded a fascist. As a result, the world is closer today to "red" fascism than it was to the "brown" variety before the war. So much for tradition.

Paradoxical as it may seem, the peoples of Eastern Europe have a far better memory for history. We live more in the past, for the present does not belong to us, and we have no future. Our peoples have experienced both the Nazi invasion and Soviet domination; that is why we are not drawn in either direction. Any antifascist book or film is interpreted by us an an anti-Soviet work (and sometimes gets stopped by the censor). Generally speaking, reading is far more widespread in our country. In the homes of even the poorest workers there will be a bookshelf; in the more educated circles, whole libraries are passed from one generation to the next. Books are printed in huge editions, and those that are rare or banned are sold on the black market. In the West, rare and classical books interest only the specialists, and the average period during which a book retains visibility is about one year. When in 1978 I was looking for a place to rent in Cambridge, I visited nearly a hundred homes, and the only book I saw regularly was the phone book. Note that this was Cambridge, not some working-class slum.

I am sure that my comments relate not only to Great Britain. I have visited other countries less frequently, and thus know less about their life-styles, but my brief glimpses reveal a very similar picture. In America, books are bought less to be read than to be put on view. Works by Solzhenitsyn can be found in most homes; it is in poor taste not to have them. I was curious to know what people thought of his writing, so I usually asked them whether they had read the book on their shelves. "Oh yes," was the answer in most cases, "but not personally."

I was at a loss to understand how one could read a book if it was

---

[2] T. S. Eliot, *The Rock.*

not personally, until a Russian acquaintance threw light on the matter: many people, so as not to appear ignorant in the conversation, simply rely on reviews they have read in the newspapers.

Finding myself in Marseilles, not so long ago, I naturally asked to be shown the Château d'If. All my friends burst out laughing, since that is what Russian visitors invariably ask to see. Some other foreigners are also curious, but not the French. French children don't read Dumas!

It is to the credit of smaller countries that they read a great deal more. Iceland is particularly renowned for it. But in the large nations the situation is atrocious. Television is alleged to have destroyed the reading habit. I am not at all sure that is true. But I would agree with the philosopher who said that the only knowledge that stays with you is that which you steal. For us, reading is like a drug, a means of escaping the drabness of daily life. Our leaders want us to ignore the past, to be cut off from universal culture. So we set about stealing the forbidden fruit. In the West, meanwhile, thousands of books appear yearly on every conceivable subject. There is no time to examine the past.

◆ ◆ ◆

But if it is not a question of tolerance, or of a consciousness of law or tradition, what is it that enables people here to be free when we are not? Is it even appropriate to formulate it that way? We are so accustomed to mouthing banalities about freedom here, and servitude there, that we begin to lose our grip on the concepts involved. The inevitable simplification typical of conversational speech has led to absolutization and externalization. Freedom is discussed like an object or a product that can be found in one store but not in another. All that remains is to determine the price per pound. Words become our enemy, for they can twist matters to shift all responsibility away from us, reversing cause and effect. In the twinkling of an eye, instead of the phrase "I am free," there appears "I live in a free country." It is such a handy idea, that one easily slips into the habit of treating freedom as a geographical concept, one whose meridian is the Berlin Wall. At best we distinguish "external freedom" as an institution from the inner freedom that is the freedom of choice. Completely disoriented, we start to ask ourselves if the Gulag is the product of a lack of freedom or if no freedom exists because of the Gulag. One day I was asked to what extent I felt freer in the West. A strange question. My life is obviously easier, and it is safer. But is it freer?

In the fairly harsh conditions in which I spent thirty-four years of my life, I was as free as I am now. What is more, everyone whom I met was equally free. We had censorship, but this led to a more subtle writing style and a sharpening of the reader's eye. Eventually, it brought about the *samizdat* movement. Of course, people were, and still are, put in prison for *samizdat* distribution, but has this destroyed freedom of expression? Words have simply acquired a greater value, and the sense of freedom has gained in profundity. Of course there were those who have opted for security, but they too had the freedom to decide this.

Yes, we were in prison there, but who can say that there is no freedom of choice in a prison? It is possible to buy one's way out with a betrayal. One can try to escape. One can grovel to gain a pittance. One can resist. In prison, finally, one can acquire inner freedom.

For those who lack inner freedom, who want to convince themselves that no choice exists, there is a wide range of alibis that always seem more sensible and humane than the arguments for freedom. One of these could salve even the conscience of an executioner: "If I don't do it, somebody else will. Let it be me, for the other man might be more cruel."

Many times have I heard that argument put forward by prison wardens, interrogators, and prison psychiatrists. And I have heard it again from the mouth of a businessman in West Germany: "If I don't sell pipeline sections to the Soviet Union, then my competitors will. In that case I would be condemning the 1,500 workers in my factory to unemployment." During this same period, we prisoners were refusing to work, having decided that it was shameful to contribute our labor to strengthen the system of universal oppression. For this we were placed in punishment cells and solitary confinement, but each one of us knew: "If I don't do it, who will? When will it be done, if not today?" Tell me, who is more free in this case?

In prison, there is always something to lose. Even when you are in solitary confinement, in a cell that has no light, no air, no bed, nothing to read, and a bowl of dishwater served to you every other day, they can always extend the period of punishment if you continue to resist. Of course the West is still a long way from the punishment cells of Vladimir Prison, yet it is already getting into the habit of staying in the good graces of the prison supervisor. Western politicians have allowed themselves to be trapped by the choice foisted upon them by the Soviet Union: either slavery or war. The policy of reckless concessions has already resulted in the increase of Soviet influence all over Europe. In the course of a visit to France by Brezhnev, for example, French television was prohibited from showing a film considered "anti-Soviet." The man might get angry! He barely has to knit his brow in the Kremlin to have the best and brightest of the West falling over each other in their rush to give assurances of friendship. May I ask, gentlemen, whether you wash your hands after all those handshakes?

And if it were only the politicians who did this! Millions of people both here and in the USSR are shackled by the same chains of fear and are busily digging their own graves. Are they free? Of course they are. But it is ever so hard to *choose* freedom and so terrifying to have to answer for its consequences. If only it could be done quietly and inconspicuously . . .

An accommodating imagination readies numerous self-justifications for you; they differ very little on either side of the Soviet frontier:

"What can I do by myself?"

"If it won't be me, it'll be somebody else."

"Best to do nothing, or things could get worse."

"All regimes are authoritarian. Let's stick with the one we've got."

"They can't possibly want war. They're human beings like us."

"It's best to do nothing. Time will work things out."

There are hundreds of these alibis, all of which have but one message: don't do anything. Submit. Just as the road to hell is paved with good intentions, so the road to slavery is lined with self-justifications.

Are we better people? Are we worse? Neither one nor the other. As I look at the faces of people walking by, I have no trouble picking out familiar types. This one would be a quiet and downtrodden bureaucrat. But the one over there would be the secretary of the local party organization. This one would become an informer, while that one would end up in prison. Characters from a familiar drama. The only difference is that they are dressed a little better and that their movements and faces do not yet express an understanding of their special talents and the roles that could be theirs.

Yes, the greatest discovery of all is that people everywhere are astonishingly similar. That is a hopeful discovery to the extent that it suggests that one day life in our country will resemble life in the West. But it is also a melancholy discovery that suggests that the West could grow to resemble our country. There is no way of explaining this, no matter how long one shouts. It is simply that we already know it, while the West does not know it yet.

CHAPTER THREE

On Capitalism, Socialism, and the Migrant Apparition

I continue to think that the idea of equality is metaphysically empty, and that social justice needs to be based on the dignity of each person *rather than on equality.*

Nicholas Berdyaev, *Dream and Reality*

Egalité *does not bother with* fraternité, *brother.*
That should be pondered one way or other.

Joseph Brodsky, *"Speech Concerning Spilt Milk"*

RESETTLING in a new and unfamiliar country is difficult for anybody. But emigrating from the USSR is the equivalent of jumping off into space without a parachute. Such a foolhardy person is not merely entering a different country inhabited by strangers with unfamiliar ways of doing things and speaking an incomprehensible language; he is irrevocably plunging into another world that is totally different from his own.

"What in the world has gotten into him?" grumble his friends disapprovingly. "It won't be like it is here, you know, where it's possible to loaf all day. Over there, you'll have to hustle, really put your back into it."

And the future émigré himself understands the foolhardiness of his impulse; after making his decision he can only marvel at his own desperate courage. In the sleepy kingdom of the Soviets, official government work generates nothing but endless jokes. Who can take it seriously? As they say, "We pretend to work; they pretend to pay us a salary." And thus we believe, as we cross the Soviet frontier, that we have come to a world where work and compensation have real meaning, where million-dollar deals are worked out right on the telephone, without any red tape, and where a man, after making his million, can become his own master, free to rub shoulders with kings and dignitaries.

"Ah, well," our man thinks, "I'll adjust somehow. Of course it'll be tough, but at least it's the beginning of a real life without that endless Soviet ambiguity, without the spectral existence in a world without a future. Everything will now be for real."

We are convinced that we are stepping into the world of capitalism. But the initial admiration and surprise begins to wane, and life settles into its normal routine. The quality of goods in the stores no longer evokes astonishment, the politeness of the sales personnel seems normal, and reading the local press becomes a habit. At this point one begins to notice what at first had escaped attention. It suddenly becomes clear that efficiency and competence are the exception rather than the norm in the economic life of the West and that people are not at all concerned about earning something extra. In the big stores, the sales clerks do not know what they have in stock and are not familiar with the prices. The employees of large enterprises (in Italy, for example) pass their time in exactly the same way as their Soviet counterparts: reading on the job, lots of conversation, and an eye on the clock for quitting time. From my window I watch workers putting up a house: they move slowly, pausing frequently for a smoke. The tempo is not a bit faster than what you'd get in the USSR. Yet their salaries are five or six times higher!

At first glance, life in the West is well-run and comfortable. Everything seems to be in its place, but you are in for a surprise if you need something in a hurry and a little out of the ordinary. I moved into my house in the dead of winter and due to my inexperience neglected to notice that I had run out of heating oil. As it happened, the weather was very cold. I immediately got on the phone to the fuel-oil dealers, but with absolutely no success. Wherever I called, the invariable answer was that the firm was overloaded with orders, and that nothing could be done for me until the start of the following week.

"But I'm ready to pay extra for a special delivery," I proposed in my innocence.

"Heavens, no sir!" was the polite answer. "That's impossible, that would be an illegal profit!"

An illegal profit? But where in the hell was I? Wasn't I in a capitalist country, whose economy is supposed to be based on supply and demand? It must be some kind of joke. Back in the socialist USSR, I would have flagged down an oil truck on a highway, and for ten or twenty rubles, I would have had all the fuel I needed.

Take the example of British Leyland, a company perennially in the red and on the edge of bankruptcy. The company is forever trying to sell cars no one wants, while at least two of its models are extremely popular—the Jaguar and the Range Rover. Yet it is precisely these last two models that British Leyland never succeeds in producing in sufficient quantity. Both in Britain and outside the country, one has to sign up long in advance to be able to buy one, sometimes as long as one year. There exists a whole network of speculators who sell their place in line illegally. It is exactly the same thing that happens with the Zhiguli cars in the Soviet Union. The chief executive officer at Leyland explains the short supply by saying there are insuperable technical problems. Yet there cannot be any *valid* excuses if we really live in a capitalist country where "demand creates supply."

Perhaps four years is too brief a time, but so far I have yet to discover any capitalism in the West. To be sure, no one will stop you from opening your own little shop, but that would also be permitted in Poland or Yugoslavia. Even in the USSR, one can legally set up a private shoe repair shop. But no one has ever gotten rich doing it, either here or there. I don't seem to have heard of any newly rich industrialists. The vast majority of the newly rich are connected to the world of entertainment: singers, musicians, writers, actors, and football players—along with their managers and lawyers. One can also include dealers in art objects and luxury items, and owners of sports establishments and gambling places. Industry, on the other hand, has long ago become the realm of failure, caught as it is between the state, with its regulations and taxes, and the trade unions. And there are virtually no more private owners of large enterprises. Industry is either nationalized or controlled by collective bodies. In both cases the results are in many ways the same as in the USSR: "collective irresponsibility," a total lack of motivation among the employees, unprofitability, and shoddy goods.

Granted that my knowledge of these questions is very limited; these are no more than impressions, based only on my experience in Britain. I am not trying to present a methodical economic analysis, complete with charts and graphs. Not that I have much faith in such an approach. It seems much more important to get a feeling for the psychological climate. I note that doctors can assemble a lot of graphs of temperature and blood pressure variations, combine this with the lab test results, and produce an overall picture that looks fairly normal. Perhaps just a few small deviations from the norm without any clearcut scientific explanation. Meanwhile a patient gets worse and worse, and it is obvious to any untutored observer that he is in a bad way. Before you know it, in fact, the patient is gone.

The period when editions of my book were being prepared in nine different countries was especially instructive. At first I wanted to avoid writing it altogether. What is enjoyable about stirring up a past as hopeless as mine? My one desire was to forget all that, start life anew without looking back, as if I had been born all over again. In any case, I loathe writing; every part of me revolts against such an enterprise. And I was dead-tired: after six years in prison and then six months of hectic travel, I wanted to catch my breath. But a friend convinced me to change my mind.

"Until you have told the whole story of what you have been through," he argued, "you won't be left in peace. People will constantly be harassing you with questions. No matter what you say to the press there will always remain things you have not talked about, things that stir up curiosity. But a book will be like a shield: when they attack you with questions, you can take cover behind your book."

The contracts were signed quickly. The editors urged me to hurry, pointing out with some justice that public interest in the West is short-lived. From their commercial point of view it was best to get into print as soon as possible. In short, the manuscript needed to be ready in three and a half months. I could never have accomplished it without my friends, the Churchills, who offered to put a cottage at my disposal and assured me of complete privacy.

"If you want to write this thing in a hurry," Winston said to me, "cut yourself off from the world. Whatever you do, don't give anyone your address, don't get on the phone, and keep your phone number secret. Disappear. We'll keep you in food and whatever else you need."

I accepted. My hosts let me take care of my own quarantine, and I followed these rules religiously, convinced of their soundness. My greatest fear was missing the deadline and disappointing the confidence the editors had in me. I didn't want to appear unbusinesslike or unreliable, or to have people say "Russians are all the same, you can't do business with them." This was my first encounter with the world of business, and the Soviet legends about capitalism gave me the most serious of expectations.

At times I thought I would lose my mind. After a few weeks I could neither sleep nor eat. Everything turned topsy-turvy: for some reason I wrote through the night until eight or nine in the morning, then slept during the daytime, and got up to return to my forced labor. Reality and imagination, past and present, night and day, were all mixed in a chaotic jumble. I hardly saw my hosts except at an occasional dinner, which for me was breakfast. My half-crazed appearance must have made a strange impression on them. Perhaps I am unusual in this respect, or perhaps it is a common experience, but I lived through the events I was describing with far greater intensity than when they had actually happened to me. Unconsciously in the process of life we try to take the edge off our feelings, to bury our emotions, to put distance between ourselves and events, to turn things into a joke and avoid looking at the future too closely. Time shrinks like mercury in a thermometer on a cold day, and in your mind the past and present somehow manage to occupy the same day, or even the same instant. Our organism protects itself by letting us reflect as little as possible, by not taking things too seriously, and never allowing us to count on a rosy future. That is why life always seems somewhat tolerable and we always find something that gives us pleasure. But when we begin to unravel our tangle of memories at a later point, this protective anesthesia no longer functions and we are like a postoperative patient whose nerves can now feel the pain. What is more, one must leave certain things unsaid when one is speaking about real events and real people. Many of the reasons that justified one's actions must be omitted or simplified, for there is no way to explain everything, there would not be paper enough, nor would it be understood without massive detail. This first book probably cost me ten years of my life; it really was forced labor. But I did meet the deadline.

But it was more than a year before the book reached the public. I have never understood why I was expected to put forth this superhuman effort and why my publishers thereupon frittered away a whole year, since they themselves had explained to me that public interest is short-lived. But it turns out that the commercial interests of publishers exist in theory only, that their level of professional competence is alarmingly low, and that they exhibit a total disregard for common sense. For the most part I have found them to be astonishingly obtuse, lacking in initiative, and devoid of any real interest in their trade.

Book publishing is not an easy matter in the West. Today's reader prefers his books to be 250 pages or less, and that has an obvious impact on the quality of the texts, for a great many things cannot be accommodated within such limits. And people here read remarkably little. One needs something to attract the reader, to capture his attention. Being an inveterate reader myself, I know very well that before buying some documentary book, one always glances at the photographs. A book without illustrations immediately loses half its interest: it lacks the feeling of authenticity that pictures provide. But I got nowhere trying to make this point to my publishers. Of those nine, only the French agreed to an edition with photos in it.

The title and the structure of the book took endless discussions, real battles. I don't know if it was a matter of differences in taste or (as it seemed to me) a lack of taste on the part of the publishers, for they insisted that everything should be told in chronological order and that the title should be either *My Life, Memoirs,* or even worse, *Memoirs of a Dissident.* The Americans, with whom I had the longest arguments, had concocted the title *Reflections of a Man in Handcuffs,* and expressed great surprise at my displeasure. I simply could not force myself to write in chronological order. It was physically impossible to begin by writing "I was born on December 30, 1942." That would exhaust the subject, and the only appropriate follow-up sentence would be "and died on . . ." And I was not ready to write my memoirs, not at thirty-five or thirty-six.

Strange to say, the American publishers gave me the most problems. The much-touted American reputation for efficiency, which we accept sight unseen, is in reality only a pose, a sort of camouflage. One has to *look* efficient in America so as not to stand out. The huge publishing firm with which I had a contract pressured me more than anyone else, but was the last to get the book on the market. It refused to include any photographs on the grounds that it would make the book too costly, and then put out a huge, dull-looking brick of a volume at a very steep price (over seventeen dollars). On top of everything, the publishers were forever trying to introduce emendations into my text. It was not a question of politics. I am now convinced that large corporations bear a striking resemblance to Soviet enterprises in terms of their lack of flexibility, the indifference of their employees, and the bureaucratic buck-passing. No one takes responsibility: John sends you to Peter, and Peter to John, and you can't get to the bottom of a question no matter how hard you try. For a long time I could not understand why the editors kept pestering me with proposals for changes, sometimes very silly ones that involved shifting the sequence of passages or phrases. It was an endless battle against the invisible forces of entropy, which were bent on destroying structural integrity, blurring meaning, untying all the knots, and ironing out all the wrinkles that are necessarily present in a literary narrative. I felt as if I were wrestling with a broken computer. Much later I discovered that this in fact was close to the truth. The giant machine had to justify its existence, and in the process of digesting my unfortunate book it inevitably transformed it into its own likeness—a tangle of absurdities. At the time this titanic struggle was going on, I had started my university studies, and it was particularly infuriating to have to go over each batch of proofs with minute care, checking them against the original, rather like an archeologist trying to reconstruct a broken vase. At last I received the final page proofs, corrected and mutually agreed upon, now ready for the press. The title page announced, in large letters: *To Build a Castle: My Life as a Deserter*, instead of *Dissenter*.

It is a strange way of conducting business. For some reason I was expected to perform several duties simultaneously: I was the author, the proofreader, the translator, the publicity agent, and the distributor. Why should this be? I am only the author; all I was supposed to do was write the text. Why should it be so difficult for this huge staff to publish my manuscript just as it reached them? In another country (which will remain unnamed), the translator had taken it upon himself to "improve" the text, judging it to be poorly written. Obviously this is a matter of taste, but even supposing he was right in his evaluation, why should it be his concern? Fortunately, the friends to whom I had entrusted the work of supervising the translation, and who had learned from bitter experience not to trust anyone, discovered the problem in time. (I might note here that translations fare much better in the USSR than in the West. The typical translator in the West is a failed writer, or a person devoid of literary flair, but who for some reason has the reputation of "knowing the language." In the USSR, in contrast, the best writers have had to earn their living by their work as translators since their own writing was not being published. As a result, the Soviets have extraordinarily high standards for translation and a strong tradition in this regard. Due to the high esteem in which foreign literature is held, having served for decades as a kind of safety valve for the intellectually starved people of a huge country, it is considered an honor to be a translator. In the West, however, it is poorly paid work and no self-respecting writer would take it on.) But it turned out to be almost impossible to change translators. They seem to be a sort of clan, almost a Mafia. Privately they would admit that a translation had been poorly done, but in public or in their evaluations submitted to the publishing houses, they would swear to high heaven that the work was first-class, that it would be impossible to expect anything better. One of them, a highly respected person and, in truth, a topnotch specialist, told me in all frankness that one simply did not criticize the work of a colleague; it was considered "unethical" and incompatible with the spirit of professional solidarity. "No matter how shoddy the work might be, there wouldn't be a single professional translator to say so. I would not do it myself, for the others would eat me alive."

I found myself in a desperate situation. The editor did not believe me, thinking that I was being difficult. How could I prove my point to him when I did not speak the language? I finally discovered a translator who was not part of the clan. But a great deal of time was irreparably lost, and that edition came out after a six-month delay. It was a nerve-racking and exhausting experience.

I learned later that a "Mafia" of this type is generally the rule among specialists. One rarely finds honest competition today. It is the law of least effort, for it is much easier to set up such a mutual support group than it is to strain and struggle for the client's business.

But what struck me the most was the overwhelming inertia that exists in publishing circles. My British publisher, a thoughtful, kindly person who was genuinely well disposed toward me, announced with pride that things were going well.

"You'll be glad to know that we are putting out a large printing of 7,500 copies."

I was thunderstruck. Only 7,500 copies for Great Britain and the Commonwealth! For whom had I written this book, at the cost of night after night without sleep?

It was explained to me that it is the booksellers who decide how large an edition will be in Britain; the size of their order determines the number of copies that are printed. They place ther orders without having read the book, and often without knowing anything about the author. Naturally enough, this strange system of buying "a pig in a poke" leads to highly conservative ordering; sometimes only a couple of copies will go to a large bookstore. It was again with pride that I was told that one of these large stores had actually ordered five of my books and that three of them were displayed in the window. The first printing was sold out fairly rapidly, but Western readers are not like their Soviet counterparts, they don't insist noisily on more. Books in the West are so costly that people buy them primarily at Christmas or in order to give them as a birthday present, and in this context they are not so carefully chosen. You have to be unusually interested in a book to place a special order for it (in Britain this will take from four to six weeks). As a result, some months later I was flooded by letters from readers asking where they could get copies of my book. I now acquired the additional job of bookseller, or so it seemed. Ridiculously enough, it was just like in Moscow, with people getting in line to read the book, passing it from person to person, and then telling about this with great pride in their letters to me. The British can sometimes be very touching. If something evokes their sympathy, they will spare neither time nor effort to express it. An elderly gentleman wrote me from London that when he could not find the book at the bookseller's, he borrowed a copy from the library and made a Xerox for himself and his friends and acquaintances. So much for the supply being created by the demand!

Second, and this is the least logical thing about book publishing in the West, books are divided into two categories: hardcover editions and paperbacks. I have never been able to fathom the point of this tradition, or to understand its business advantage. The fact remains that the hardback is published first, at an outrageous price (the British edition cost seven and a half pounds), and in a small printing. The vast majority of potential readers cannot afford such a luxury, and they await publication of the cheap and mass-produced paperback edition that should (but may not) appear a year and a half or two years later. After such a delay, everyone will have forgotten all about you and your book, for all the reviews, publicity, and so on accompany the publication of the hardback edition only. In the intervening years so much will have happened in the world, so many new books will have appeared with their own publicity campaigns, that it is a very long shot that your readers will have sufficiently strong memories to remember you. Even in the best of times, public interest is a highly perishable commodity, and due to the relatively low interest in reading in the West, the majority will be satisfied by the reviews alone. Whether or not your book will appear in paperback format is theoretically decided by the sales of the hardbound edition, a consideration that is unrelated to the intrinsic quality of the book, as I have tried to show above.

Getting ahead of my story a little, I will note here that no paperback edition of my book was published either in Great Britain or the United States. Nor is this likely in the future, but the reasons were entirely accidental. In Britain, the rights to the paperback edition were bought by Penguin, which shortly thereafter changed ownership. All projects underway were canceled. In the United States, the editor-in-chief, the editor, the legal adviser, and even the head of production had left the firm by the time the decision had to be made. Those who took their places resolved to start back at square one with all work under consideration. Once an author has signed over his rights of publication, it requires a long legal process to get them back, perhaps even litigation. I just did not have the patience.

But the absurdity of all this aroused my interest. I like to ferret out bureaucratic ineptitude, for this usually reveals a great deal about the system. And so I decided to look into the cause of the absurdities in the publishing world, to the extent this was possible with my limited time and my lack of specialized knowledge. For example, why could not the process be reversed, with a cheap paper edition coming out first and an advertising campaign to promote large sales? If the venture were successful, an expensive hardbound edition could then be brought out. The markets for different editions don't overlap, after all, and the collectors of fancy editions will buy them whenever they come out, while those who cannot afford such items would in any case have awaited the paperback.

But my editors were taken aback. "Heavens, no!" they cried. "That would be impossible! Who would ever review a paperback? That simply isn't done."

One must conclude, incredibly enough, that books are published not for readers, but for reviewers. As far as I am concerned, the critics can go to the devil. So what if they don't write their reviews? Certainly I had never intended my book for them. To tell the truth, most of the reviews of my book that appeared in England struck me with their low professional standards, their myopia, and at times with their political hostility. On the evidence of these reviews I can say with certainty that many of their authors had not even troubled to read the book, having at the most scanned its pages diagonally. The absurdities they concocted are hard to believe. It is against tradition to respond to reviews or to argue with reviewers. But to give a small inkling of what I mean, here are a few examples. A very worthy lady—who later admitted to not having read the book, saying that her editors had not given her enough time to do so—wrote that, according to Bukovsky, nothing in Russia had changed since Stalin, while we all know that this is not true. The remainder of the article was a homily on Khrushchev, and had absolutely nothing to do with my book. I do not fault her for not having had the time to read my book; that can happen to anyone. But even if she had only scanned it diagonally, she would have realized that I deal precisely with the changes that had come about. And it might have occurred to her that in the course of my thirty-five years in the Soviet Union, I had probably heard of Khrushchev. Why start from the assumption that the author is an imbecile who knows less than she does about his own country? She could at least have written something vague and noncommittal, as did so many other members of the press.

Another review, once again authored by an entirely respectable individual, stated that "the author would have done better to describe the day-to-day course of his life." I am curious to know whether the reviewer had ever tried to write his own biography in this fashion. How many volumes would he have needed? And of course the readers would have died from boredom. It is hardly possible to remember each and every day, especially if quite a lot of them were spent in prison.

Others simply used their reviews to settle political accounts, inventing all manner of accusations against me. A zealous young leftist thinker asserted that postwar Moscow was much better supplied than Bristol had been. I have no idea how he arrived at this conclusion, but I sincerely hope he never has to experience such abundance. He is the same one who accused me of having "naive views of sex," because in a passing remark I had sympathized with the young men raped by common criminals in the camps and then reduced to a bestial level by prison-camp mores. I might know something about prisons, he allowed, but that did not make me an expert on "the free life." I shall be glad to ask the author of the review, after he has been raped some-where in transit between prisons, whether he has become more naive as well as a greater expert on liberated life-styles. At least such re-viewers could have had the honesty to admit that they disagreed with me politically, as did the Italian communist paper, *L'Unità,* which car-ried a perfectly decent and sensible review.

For the most part, it was fairly easy for me to predict the kind of review that would appear in a particular paper, and I also knew that there was no point in expecting either courage or honesty from the British left. Its members consider it chic to live like "moles." Reviews are a most handy genre for them, for one is not supposed to either offer rebuttals or get angry at these texts. And yet your book depends on such critics.

With time I realized that there was more to it than traditions and reviews alone. It turns out that the first edition has to cover all the expenses incurred in its publication. These expenses are sizable, and there is considerable risk involved in launching any new book. Books thus suffer the same fate as the transportation system, with the man-agement carelessly reducing its own market. The fewer consumers there are, the smaller the printing and the higher the cost per volume; the higher the cost per volume, the fewer buyers there will be. It re-minds one of the British railway system or the airlines in Britain in the days before Freddy Laker came on the scene. Meanwhile the costs keep rising due to all sorts of economic factors (inflation, wage scales going up across the board, and so on). My ultimate conclusion, based on considerable observation, is that the main reason certain goods or services have disappeared is the obtuseness of a management that has grown decrepit, is afraid of taking risks, and clings to outdated con-cepts. A modern businessman needs to be a revolutionary if he is to succeed. But the revolutionaries in the West don't go into manage-ment. They prefer holding up a bank or setting off a bomb in a pub.

The prognosis is not very cheerful. If no Freddy Laker appears in the domain of book publishing, we will soon have to turn to a Western type of *samizdat.* The appreciation of books is in danger of disappear-ing altogether. If it still survives in Moscow, it is thanks to the enthusi-asm of book lovers, increased tenfold by the communist prohibitions. The general economic principle, though, is perfectly obvious to me, even though I have spent most of my life in a "socialist" country. Yet those who were born and bred in the "capitalist" world of the West don't want to admit it.

To be fair, I should note some exceptions to my comments. The Italians, for example, brought out an inexpensive little book, with an attractive cover, and they were rewarded for it. The best edition of my book was the one in France. Neither of these countries have the custom of starting with a hardback edition. They publish something much less expensive and more accessible. The French editors also made use of my photographs, took a great deal of care over the text, and did not have to contend with the bookstores determining the size of the printing. The book became a bestseller, appearing in further editions, both in a hardbound version and as a cheap paperback. Each edition succeeded very well.

It goes without saying that every domain, not just publishing, will benefit from initiative, ingenuity, and the readiness to accept risk. Some businessmen have divided huge enterprises into smaller components, with no more than four or five hundred workers in each, so as to make work a more creative experience; various diversions were used as a means of motivating the employees. One manager told me that he had a swimming pool installed to be used by his workers during working hours. The result was an increase in productivity. At a later point I will say more about my theory that the mentality of people has changed. For many reasons, money has lost its power as an incentive. People are ascribing a higher value to leisure, rest, and entertainment. It is time to rethink the system of incentives in industry. It is not my job to judge and give counsel; I am only an observer. I shall merely note that a rolling stone gathers no moss. The old ways of doing things are not going to stand up for too much longer. As long as the majority insist on sticking by the old ways, things will continue to decline. Really top-flight businessmen are the exception rather than the rule. It is very hard for them to beat their way through the network of government regulations and the atmosphere of inertia that surrounds them on all sides. It is a state of affairs where everyone loses: consumers, workers, the whole economic system.

Marx defined capitalism as an economic system ruled by the laws of the free market and the forces of competition. He then went on to say a lot of silly things about how the capitalists were necessarily so stupid and greedy, and the workers so rebellious and intelligent, that the whole system was doomed to collapse. Were he to take a look at modern capitalism, the old boy would shed many a tear in his shaggy beard. Whatever has become of competition? The spirit of the Mafia has long since taken over, and the markets have been divided up. It is unthinkable that a large and hopelessly inefficient corporation would be allowed to go bankrupt. That would seem almost the equivalent of a national disaster.

It makes little difference who is in power in the government, whether socialists or some other party. The process of socialization is advancing with an unbelievable speed, for socialism has become an integral part of the Western mentality. It has become part of the tissue of the modern world. One only has to read today's press, of whatever political tendency, to see that firms no longer exist to produce. Their principal reason for existence is to *provide employment*. And so the firm can permit itself to be less than productive or to produce shoddy goods.

None of this was a surprise to me. While I was in prison, I had read once in the newspaper about how workers somewhere in Europe had occupied their factory because their management was planning to close the plant. It was no longer making profits. The boss lodged a complaint with the authorities, but the police refused to intervene, saying there was no crime involved. I could not believe my eyes. What it meant was that if a thief rifles your pockets, that's a crime, but if your plant is swiped from you, it is quite all right. Later on, I was expressing my astonishment to a young diplomat whom one would hardly have suspected of socialist tendencies. "Don't you understand?" was his answer. "What is at stake for these workers is their jobs, their place of employment. That gives them every right."

This explanation did not satisfy me in the least, and to this day I am puzzled by this strange logic. If a woman comes once a week to clean my home, does that give her rights over her place of employment? Would she be able to occupy my apartment and refuse to leave if for some reason I had to dispense with her services? Would the police make the same observation that no crime was involved, and that this was simply a labor dispute?

There is no point in looking for the logic of all of this. Logic ceases where ideology begins, especially in the case of socialist ideology. "Whatever serves the workers is good" is the first principle of this doctrine (but of course it is not the workers who are being served but the trade-union bigshots, irresponsible demagogues, and shady politicians). I think all mass ideologies are bad, for they allow men to hide behind easy alibis, to follow their lowest instincts in the name of noble purposes. Killing is wrong, but it becomes permissible for worthy ends. It is despicable to steal, but if it contributes to the happiness of mankind, there is no reason not to. To use torture is the lowest of the low, but if the well-being of all depends on it, it would be criminal to abstain from the practice. In short, of all the self-justification we employ, whether deliberately or unconsciously, mass ideologies are the most despicable. They make men into a herd of sheep. And of all the ideological mass movements, socialism is the most dangerous, for it removes all responsibility from the individual. According to its lights, if a man should become an alcoholic, a drug addict, or a torturer, it would be despite himself. The blame is put on society, on the social environment in which a person lives.

I make trips to the United States fairly frequently. In 1977 I was on a speaking tour that included fourteen cities, mostly sizable industrial centers. Since I was the guest of the American trade union, I met mostly workers, teachers, and students. My hosts regularly showed me the most rundown slum areas of the cities as well as the wealthiest residential areas—in order that I could see the "contrasts existing in American life." While the residential areas were certainly impressive, the slums shocked me not at all. The housing looked quite normal and even average to Soviet eyes, although it would be less than honest to apply Soviet norms inside the United States; such things are relative. What struck me was the psychological atmosphere of these places. Having spent my own childhood in slums like these, I know perfectly well that genuine, "honest" poverty does not consist of picturesque rags that proclaim your need to the world. It entails, instead, clothes that are painstakingly mended, forced smiles, and a desperate effort to "look like everyone else." Twelve families could live together in one barracks, separated by plywood partitions, but there would be flowers planted and the door would have fresh paint. In the United States, on the contrary, every detail seemed to testify that the slum inhabitants had no desire to improve the quality of their life. It does not cost very much to spruce up an entrance, to put something in the place of a broken window pane; it costs nothing to clean up dirt. But instead I detected everywhere the spirit of ostentatious defiance. The worse it looks, the better, because *society is to blame* for everything and it is the *duty* of society to take care of everything. You can, if you wish, judge me to be cruel and inhuman, but I could not force myself to feel the slightest pity or compassion for these people or for this society. Even when we found ourselves spending years in our prison cells, we always made the effort to have a clean floor, to get hold of a rag to wash it with, to cut out a calendar from a newspaper in order to have something to put on the wall. Each one managed to dress halfway decently. Even when one was transferred into a dirty cell for a couple of days, an effort was made to make it livable. Nothing surprising in that: it was our living space, after all. These American slum dwellers, in contrast, seemed to be waiting for the guilt-ridden society to bring them everything on a silver platter.

A goodly half of Western economic problems are engendered by this parasitic attitude. In Italy, for example, I learned that the government, in an effort to remedy the economic backwardness and poverty of the south, launched a program of subsidizing industrial enterprises in that region. Huge sums of money were invested, and factories were built, but the local population would not work in them. There was no choice but to import some manpower from the north.

Northeast England, an area of many coal mines, has the greatest unemployment and the most severe poverty problems in the country. The reason for this is simple: the coal reserves are dwindling, the mines are closing, and the level of employment has fallen drastically. The government does all it can to provide retraining programs, even offering some kind of financial benefit to those who enroll in them. No effort is spared to lure workers into other sectors of the economy or to other parts of the country. But it is a hopeless task. The unemployed are willing to spend years of their life sitting in pubs and repeating with indignation: "Why the devil should I change my profession? My grandfather and my father were miners. I'll stay in the mine!"

We Russians are absolutely astonished at this immobility, this passivity, this sureness that aid will come from an outside source. From our earliest childhood in the Soviet Union it is drummed into us that society owes us nothing and that, quite to the contrary, we owe it everything. Take for example this famous matter of unemployment. If Western criteria were applied to the USSR, the unemployment figures would be as high as in the West, if not higher. To start with, the Soviet state flatly refuses to admit that unemployment exists. There is no agency where one can go for help or to report that one is out of a job. It would never cross anyone's mind to give financial aid to someone who is out of work. The famous "right to work" in the Soviet Union in no way signifies that one will be able to find work in the field for which he has been trained. It's a matter of a right to *work*, not a right to carry on with one's profession. If a fitter does not find an opening in his field, he had better become a lathe operator, a truck driver, a construction worker, a warehouseman, or a garbage collector. No one takes an interest in all this. But if you go too long a time without working, you get called in by the police and ordered to find work immediately, because "parasitism is a crime." If a month later you are still without work, you'll land a two-year prison sentence. In the camps, work will always be found for you, whether cutting down trees or in the great building projects of communism. For, as they say in the USSR, "those who don't work don't eat."

Let's take a look at some of the realities of unemployment in the West. Anyone can sign up as unemployed, even if one is actually working. Verification is hard to enforce. You are the one to state what your profession is, or you can refer to jobs previously held. It makes no difference that you may have been fired for incompetence. Next, you will get offers of a job in the field that you have chosen, and it will be up to you to accept or refuse them. This can go on for months and months. And all this time you go on drawing your unemployment benefits. If the conditions of new employment offered to you are not as good as those of your previous job, you are within your rights to turn down the offer. It goes without saying that new job offers will be for work in the area where you live, and not in some distant part of the country. Add to this picture the young people leaving school each year who swell the ranks of the unemployed, the students who sign up as unemployed during the school vacations, a certain number of do-nothings who have not the slightest desire to hold a job, and you get an idea of what is included in the Western unemployment figures.

After this I would defy anyone to tell me where socialism is operating, and how it can be distinguished from capitalism. It's worth emphasizing that the educational system in the West is different from ours. The number of students who enroll in a discipline is not determined by the demand in the marketplace for people with a certain type of training, but by the number of those who wish to enroll in one subject or another and by the number of faculty available to teach the subject. The state has no right to interfere in the internal affairs of the universities, even though later on it will have to foot the bill for the unemployment of thousands of specialists who upon graduation find that no one needs their skills. Whereas in the USSR there are dozens of applicants for each place in a university, in the West it is not hard to pursue undergraduate studies, for the majority of outstanding schools have no entrance exams. In France there is no selection process at all; in Britain the grades one received in secondary school have a certain influence. In Sweden, there are neither exams nor grades, since it is believed that grades and exams might traumatize the youngster and provoke feelings of inequality. In a word, education is considered a right in the West and not a privilege, as it is in the USSR.

This difference between the two systems is significant. In the West, one pursues a course of studies because one wants to, and one studies what one wishes to study. In the USSR it can be crucial for your future to enroll in undergraduate studies. If you have no diploma, it is impossible to find white-collar work; you will spend your life doing "dirty" work. Furthermore, such studies are the only way young men can avoid military service. Often they will sign up at any university, choosing the easiest one to get into, where the academic standards are not too difficult. The least important consideration is the profession in which one is going to be trained. After completing his studies, the young specialist is required to spend two years anywhere he may be sent, be it Siberia, Kamchatka, or Central Asia. If he refuses, he does not get his diploma, and all the work he's done is washed out. It is the state that decides where and how an individual will make himself useful to society. Half of the young workers are assigned to jobs for which they were not previously trained, leading to a bloated turnover rate in the country's work force. In spite of the requirement of internal passports, of residence permits to stay in a city, and of very strict rules against changing jobs more than twice in one year (an offender risks a prison sentence), our population is for the most part considerably more mobile and also more energetic than are people in the West. We simply know that no one will help us.

After a twenty-year interlude, I have once again become a student, and it is interesting to compare the social aspects of education in the West and the USSR. Although just about everyone who wants to can pursue university studies in the West (whereas competition for a place is much tougher in the USSR), the percentage of students with a working-class background is just about the same in both systems. (At Cambridge University the proportion may be a little lower than at Moscow University, but then Cambridge is something of a special case.) No doubt this reflects the view of education held by the working class everywhere, quite irrespective of country or social structure. Actually, university studies are free in both cases. I am probably the only one in my college who is paying out of his own pocket for his studies. All the other students are financed either by the government or by the municipal authorities. The size of the stipend is much larger than that received by Soviet students. During the 1960s, a first-year student at the University of Moscow received about thirty rubles a month, which was half of the minimum wage at that time. Moreover, the only students eligible to receive this much were those whose family incomes were not more than fifty rubles per month, per person. If the parents' income was higher than that, the student was totally dependent on his family. There is no way that anyone can live on thirty rubles a month, no matter how modestly. Just to give an example, one package of poor cigarettes costs fourteen kopeks. (It is true that the canteen meals at the university were very reasonable in cost.) At any time, a student could lose his scholarship as a punishment for cutting too many classes or for breaking rules (just as it was always possible to expel a student from the university). The majority of the students had to depend on their family's help or on part-time work. Often, we would do night work unloading trucks. In the West, students can treat themselves to a beer, buy books, have a party; I never saw anyone unloading trucks. Summer vacation is the time for Western students to earn money, but during the academic year there does not seem to be an insurmountable need to work.

◆ ◆ ◆

I don't understand why Marx came to the conclusion that workers are naturally inclined toward revolution and that "the proletariat has nothing to lose but its chains." As far as we can see, to the contrary, this part of society is the most inert, and readily hands over its freedoms in exchange for security.

The workers' movement, so stormy at its beginnings, finally led to the creation of the welfare state, to a distribution of wealth, and an implementation of a system of social guarantees. For all practical purposes, socialism has already been established in the West, to the extent that it can be embodied in a real human society. But this has brought about certain regrettable consequences. First of all, it has had a negative impact on productivity and on the level of competence of the workers; the quality of goods and services has declined, and the economic system has been destabilized. Work in general, and especially highly automated work typical of a modern industrialized society, is hardly satisfying. The introduction of social guarantees has removed any remaining incentives, since the quality of a man's work (or even his complete nonproductivity) has practically no effect on his standard of living.

Second, equality is an artificial condition that constantly requires artificial methods to support it. People are simply not naturally equal. Maintaining equality extracts an enormous price, in terms of a great burden placed on the shoulders of the competent and the hardworking, as well as in terms of the further corruption of the sluggards and the creation of a climate of parasitism. Moreover, one must have a constant organized force in order to maintain this equality, a force that tends toward domination in the society in a way that is hard to control. This applies to any rapidly growing bureaucracy, and to the bureaucracy-ridden trade unions in particular. We tend to forget that socialism, faithful to its principles, is not concerned with protecting the rights of individuals. It deals with groups, collectives, "classes." In fact, the ideology stresses that the interests of the individual must be sacrificed for the common good. And so it is not surprising that while Western trade unions are free of the state, they cannot be considered free in other respects. Individuals are no longer free to decide whether or not to belong to them and it is literally dangerous to vote against a strike supported by the executive committee. In short, the individual relinquishes more and more of his freedom in exchange for economic security.

Paradoxically, however, the individual gains no genuine security in this manner. Quite the contrary, for the system is far from stable. The economy begins to decline, the standard of living starts to slip. To keep its part of the bargain, the socialist system must constantly struggle with the rest of society, demanding that the status quo be preserved, for "the living standard of the workers must not deteriorate," no matter how poorly the economy is doing. Pressed from two sides, a business enterprise fails financially, and then, in order to prevent unemployment, there is nothing left but to nationalize the company, that is, to reduce it to a state of chronic inadequacy and unprofitability. And the state has no choice but to increase the tax burden, which in turn undermines those companies that have managed to remain profitable.

Who knows—perhaps my impressions are mistaken and the situation is not as desperate as it looks. Let us hope so. But I keep noticing all too many suspicious similarities between the state of affairs here and the Soviet economic system. It would seem that in the USSR the process was simply instituted with extraordinary speed under communist leadership, taking only twenty years to dismantle the economy and to reduce it to the state of absurdity that is evident to all. In the West, the process has been much slower, drawn out over a century or so. Forcibly introduced in the USSR, with the physical extermination of those who offered resistance, the process took very little time, while in the West the healthy elements of society continue to hold out. Might that not be the only difference between socialism in the West and Soviet socialism? One thing is clear: if in the West socialism is still in the embryonic stage and people are not yet accustomed to it, in the Soviet Union socialism is at what the journalists call an "advanced stage." This is a stage that inevitably leads to the black market, underground capitalism, and a fierce competitiveness among a substantial part of the populace. We are much better adapted to life, more enterprising, more active. I do not believe that the average Westerner could survive in my country, deprived as he would be of the welfare state. I now sometimes spend a whole hour waiting fruitlessly for a bus or a taxi. Innumerable private cars, trucks, service vehicles drive past, but it does not occur to anyone, as it would in our socialist country, to pull to the curb and offer me a lift for three rubles.

On innumerable occasions I got rides this way in the USSR: on fire engines, ambulances, fuel trucks, the limousines of bigshots! I even managed to get a lift from a chauffeur of the KGB. Business is business, and what family budget looks down on three rubles? What would stop a builder of communism from making a little money on the side during the lunch hour or after the workday is over? But here, in the so-called Kingdom of Capital, why should people make the effort? They'll get everything anyway.

Certain readers might get the idea that I take all these "isms" seriously, and that I have become an advocate of capitalism, considering it to be a cure for all ills. That is certainly not so. It is just that all around me I see socialism arousing the greatest sympathy; people see it as a genuine solution. And yet no one really knows what socialism is. There are as many different versions as there are socialists. I am irritated by the number of people all over the world who are persuaded that the way to solve human problems is by a simple redesigning of social structures.

And as for capitalism, I have never seen it and don't even know if it is possible. In any case, capitalism does not exist in the West today. This is not due to the dominance of socialist prejudices; there are deeper reasons for it. To begin with, technological advances have led to the so-called assembly-line method of production, where every operation has been broken up into simple component motions, endlessly repeated, thereby nullifying the creative aspect of work. It is difficult to expect enthusiasm from a person who spends eight hours a day tightening the same nut over and over again. This method of manufacturing, furthermore, inevitably seems to bring about a substantial growth of the industries concerned, while competition generates the huge and unresponsive corporations where employees no longer care about anything.

Perhaps it is too early for me to judge after four years in the West, but I think there is another reason for the degradation I notice around me. It seems that a great change in the mentality of people took place in the 1960s. It was then that the mass protests against consumerism took shape, along with the rejection of savings, the cult of material possession, and the economic rat race in general. My guess is that this was a revolt against materialism, against a life-style that consisted of a constant scramble to make money. Earn money so that you can spend it, then earn more to spend more. The cycle was endless. This is when people began to ask themselves whether it wasn't preferable to live on less, and to live more simply, while there was still time. Man does not need that much, after all. Tens of thousands of young people abandoned everything and started to rove from country to country, strumming their guitars and enjoying life, to their parents' envious consternation, proving by their example that man really can get by on very little. My suspicion is that the movement of the 1960s has influenced the whole world. The system of values changed. Relaxation and entertainment were now the principal ideals. From all this came an unprecedented expansion of the leisure industries and a renewed interest in religion.

I suppose that much of this is defensible. Certainly human beings deserve a better fate than a constant race for material rewards. But while the values may have changed, the problems have remained. Leisure and entertainment also cost money, and this money has to be earned. Unfortunately, time is money, but you have either one or the other, not both.

Simply to abandon the rat race is the great temptation that beckons us as the easiest way out. To hell with all your pointless hurry-scurry, your ceaseless quest for gain. What fools you are to get caught up in the struggle; I've got more sense, I am going to sit on the sidelines, soaking in the sun. But the trouble is that human beings are made up of contradictions: left alone, we feel bored; together with others, we feel cramped. A victory that no one else is aware of is of no use to us, but when we get together again, we begin to struggle for the number one spot. For we are not even capable of understanding ourselves by merely observing our neighbors. How else can we find self-expression and fulfill our potential except through struggle and competition?

It is possible to abolish money, to destroy articles of luxury, to institute stringent rationing of food and basic necessities, to require everyone to live in identical barracks, and to have husbands and wives dealt out by lottery; in short, it is possible to reduce human life to any kind of bestial level in the attempt to establish equality at any cost. But it would be a venture doomed from the start. The individual will always find a way of standing out, and people will unfailingly assign value to something of which there is not enough to go around equally—and which will then define their inequality. The only result of such an extreme experiment would be to generate unprecedented inequality and corruption, for under these conditions the slightest privilege would be perceived as a huge advantage. Brotherhood would go out the window. Just imagine how many secret policemen would be necessary to enforce such leveling.

For some reason Westerners prefer not to reflect seriously on the Soviet example. It is considered a corrupt instance of socialism, impure and debased. Not in the slightest. The Soviet leadership always acted in accord with the theory, in the interests of the workers. Our leaders simply were more consistent than those who preceded them or those who tried to copy them. Failures never discouraged them, but inspired them to apply the theory with even greater consistency.

I think the only ones to outdo them in the matter of consistency were the Khmer Rouge, but their reign was a brief one. The results produced in the USSR are far more interesting. For example, in the sixty-two years of its existence, the Soviet regime has failed to extinguish the instinct for private property, even though those who expressed this instinct were physically exterminated and continue to be persecuted. This goal has proved to be as difficult to achieve as destroying everyone with a pug nose and blue eyes. To the contrary, the instinct of possessiveness has erupted with tremendous force in all sorts of unexpected places. The Soviet experiment has resulted in the astonishing discovery that the desire for things and possessions is not a mere material need, but a deep spiritual one. For the great majority of people, ownership is a means of self-expression. One cannot expect most people to find their fulfillment in art or science; there are plenty of individuals who are simply not interested in these fields. And even among artists and scholars it is rare to find someone who needs no material goods whatever, whose only satisfaction is the practice of his profession.

Neither has the Soviet regime succeeded in eliminating social classes. The actual gap between rich and poor, between the bosses and their subordinates, is usually much greater than in the West. There are also certain privileges that cannot be given a dollar figure. How can we determine the "wealth" that allows one person to travel abroad at will, when another is not allowed to leave the country? Yet we began with complete equality.

No, the problem cannot be laid to the "accursed property" that has enslaved men, or to some meaningless "isms," or to an "unjust" social structure. The problem stems from our inability, as well as our unwillingness, to discriminate between the real world and our own desires and aberrations. It is rooted in our astonishing incapacity for thinking.

◆　◆　◆

We who are forced to fish out fragments of truth from the swamp of official lies can be forgiven when, in our ignorance, we confuse myth and reality. But in the West people also believe that they live under the capitalist system, and at least half of them ascribe all their misfortunes to this fact. We can be forgiven for thinking that our socialism is somehow different from the Western variety. But in the West, too, even well-informed, inquisitive, and intelligent people will automatically assume that everything good and noble is to be found in socialism. As a rule this is not even discussed, but is accepted as self-evident. Of course it is highly significant that socialism in the USSR is imposed on us by force, while this is not the case in the West. It is equally significant that Western socialists don't intend to institute "social justice" by violent means. But that hardly affects the question of whether one should consider socialism a synonym for everything that is admirable.

I have already enumerated several of the undoubtedly negative aspects of socialism. But the list is far from complete. One of its most harmful consequences is without question the surrender of personal responsibility to the state, an act that is the equivalent of renouncing this responsibility and the freedom that goes with it. These two concepts are inseparately connected. A normal person will understand, for example, that he should help those who are in need. But in the attempt to achieve institutionalized equality, we entrust this function to the state and make the state responsible for the welfare of the needy. It is no longer my affair, I've paid my taxes! The moral duty to help is thus transformed into a legal requirement, and I have lost the freedom to decide whom to help. Human misfortunes become a matter of indifference to me: I have paid off my duty. And the needy now no longer ask for help, but demand the share that supposedly belongs to everyone, that is, to no one in particular. As a result, the number of people who wish to be poor increases. In addition, my participation in the life of society becomes an empty formality, since I have no control over the distribution of tax monies. And the worst feature of all is the monstrous growth of the bureaucracy, which leads to an ever more powerful state (and which also consumes an increasing portion of the budget, bringing about spiraling taxes).

A swollen bureaucracy is an inevitable consequence of socialism. It is as if people have lost trust in their own sense of duty and justice, in their ability to solve their own problems. The state, represented by its bureaucracy, becomes the arbiter, the supervisor, and eventually the oppressor. But is there any other way to assure greater fairness and equality than through "neutral" people like bureaucrats? Bureaucracy, meanwhile, grows exponentially. It is the contemporary Frankenstein, which soon begins to lead an independent existence, governed by mysterious laws and pursuing equally mysterious goals. Bureaucrats are the same everywhere. They are not concerned with the duties that they have been hired to perform. Their principal interest is their own existence, and corruption and inefficiency are the direct result. In order to make them work and to keep them "neutral," one must set up regulatory agencies, that is, a new level of bureaucrats. Mommsen, in his history of ancient Rome, had already pointed out that the typical feature of all regulatory agencies is their tendency to protect those whom they are supposed to evaluate. This is not surprising, for an inspector not only inspects, but is held responsible for the state of affairs. If serious irregularities come to light, the inspecting agency bears some of the blame. For that reason ever new levels of internal control must be created, none of which adds anything to equality and justice. Ideally (and this is the case in the USSR), the entire population is bureaucratized, creating a country of universal bureaucracy, a process that under socialism is greatly facilitated by nationalization.

All of this naturally costs a great deal of money, so that taxes have to be raised, which deals a blow to the healthiest sector of society. But then that is what fairness is all about, is it not? Once the bureaucratic machine reaches a certain size, it attempts to control everything; certain principles of cybernetics seem to insure that it cannot function otherwise. It is at this point that one develops a vested interest in corruption, because otherwise life would be simply unbearable. It is a real misfortune if a bureaucrat in a socialist system does not accept bribes. Even minor difficulties become virtually insurmountable.

For the sake of greater justice, and in order to inject some regularity into the workings of the bureaucratic machine, the state has to keep issuing reams of laws, instructions, and regulations, which are impossible for a mere mortal to disentangle. It is already true today that a citizen paying his taxes needs to hire a special kind of lawyer unless he has specialized training. Otherwise he is at risk, as in Sweden, of having to pay 101 percent of his salary in taxes. A bureaucratic state tries to turn everyone into bureaucrats. You need to keep collecting endless scraps of paper, receipts, proof of expenses and earnings; you must keep filling out innumerable forms, constantly behaving like a person under suspicion who must justify his actions. What is the point of all this? Why must a man hire a bureaucrat or become one himself merely to fulfill a simply civic duty? Ah, but it is all done for the sake of fairness and equality.

It is the kind of social equality that for some reason is always achieved through the destruction of what is good rather than through the improvement of what is bad. I cannot explain it, but it probably comes down to the fact that it is much harder to build than to tear down. If you have a good house and your neighbor has a poor one, equality will be more easily attained by wrecking your house than by improving his. In the same way, if you have more money than the man next to you, it is easier to ruin you than to enrich him. I am not exaggerating a bit. In England there exists a private system of education, which is considered excellent, and a state-administered system, which is considered inadequate. So what do you think the specialists are proposing? Naturally, it is to shut down the good system. Better that no one should have it than just some; such are the demands of equality. And this coincides exactly with the ultimate achievement in all the socialist countries: an equality of universal and uniform poverty.

At the turn of the century, those who were termed "progressive" championed the development of technology, industry, and the sciences; all this was considered inseparable from the concepts of progress, humanism, and socialism. Those who warned of the danger of upsetting the equilibrium of nature were of course considered reactionaries and enemies of humanity. Today, more than half a century later, to be progressive is to oppose technological and industrial development and to champion closeness to nature and environmental protection. But oddly enough, this is once again perceived as part and parcel of humanism and socialism. I doubt that anyone among the crowds of young people storming nuclear power stations in the name of socialism is even aware that faith in the balance of nature is radically at odds with socialism—a teaching that is in all respects opposed to nature, based as it is on the premise that man is capable of rebuilding the world and correcting the imperfections of nature.

In the USSR, where theory is taken literally and is fully put into practice, the transformation of nature has become one of the fundamental aspects of the building of socialism. Not a single major river has not had its course changed or been dammed up at some point to create an artificial lake. The concepts of the class struggle and the defense of the oppressed have even been applied to the animal kingdom. The wolf, being a beast of prey, was likened to a capitalist who subjugated hares, deer, and so on. So do away with wolves! But after the wolves had been exterminated, it soon came to light that the hares and the deer had begun dying off in alarming numbers. A study revealed that the wolves were the "medical orderlies" of the forests, who winnowed out sick, feeble, and helpless animals, thereby preventing epidemics and degeneration. Wolves had to be artificially raised in order to stop the decline of their victims. Everything in nature serves a purpose, and this is even true of large-scale disasters. There is a certain kind of bird in North America that can only breed in areas of a recent forest fire. As the efficiency of forest-fire prevention increased, the bird declined in number. Fires had to be set deliberately in order to save the bird from extinction.

Why should different standards be applied to nature and to human society, with "socialism" as the justification for both? Why do we think it appropriate to preserve the balance of nature while we seek to destroy a similar balance in society, and why do we persist in seeing both acts as humane? It would surely be useful to reflect a little on these matters before railing against material goods, storming power stations, and shouting ourselves hoarse about injustice. As mathematicians will confirm, inequalities can be perfectly valid.

◆　◆　◆

Perhaps those of us who have lived under socialism exhibit the once bitten, twice shy syndrome. Perhaps Western socialism is in fact different and will produce different results. But we observe with growing apprehension the ominously familiar personality types, misconceptions, and attempts to institute this system of thought. The truth of the matter is that the various ideas that seem fresh and innovative to Western specialists have already been tested in the USSR. And if some of those experiments were eventually repudiated, it was not because socialism has been perverted in the USSR, as Western commentators claim, but because these innovations proved to be utterly unfit for real life. A cruel experiment half a century long has failed to alter human nature. Even the scientists admit today that "being determines consciousness" only a small part of the time.

I have no intention of denying the problem. It is certainly true that unchecked competition will result in abuses that cannot be tolerated by a civilized society. The struggle for existence leads to the selection of the strongest and most adroit, but what about the others? On the other hand, an artificial leveling of society promotes degeneration and the growth of parasitism. This is very much the tendency in the modern West, where it is much easier to live on the government dole and to depend entirely on the state. Moreover, if an individual attempts to stand on his own two feet and regain his autonomy, he will have to overcome great difficulties. The state, that monster with a thousand heads, instantly sets off in pursuit of him as if he were a criminal, robbing him at each opportunity and not letting go until he is once again a dependent. In the West, the role of the Soviet KGB is in part taken over by the gigantic agency in charge of taxation, with which anyone who earns his own living is in almost constant warfare. The issue is not money so much as keeping one's independence, an idea profoundly offensive to socialism.

I am sure, for example, that if I lived in Sweden I would have been in prison long ago. By the law of the land, every social organization is subsidized by the state, which means by the taxpayers. There are a dozen or so communist organizations in Sweden, all supported by people who thus may not have the remotest link to communism. As a staunch democrat I haven't any desire to see these organizations banned. But it is one thing to tolerate their existence, as an inevitable price of living under democracy, and quite another to have to finance them from one's pocket. This I would absolutely refuse to do, even at the risk of being hanged. It is a question of principle for me not to take part in a wrong when that wrong is perfectly evident. This principle cost me twelve years in Soviet prisons, and I suspect that it would keep me permanently inside Swedish ones.

In order to allow citizens to live by their consciences, the state in theory ought to make available lists showing where tax money is allocated. The citizen should be able to decide what he wishes to support. Shielded by the anonymity conveniently provided by the chic label, "the common good," socialism attempts to turn us into irresponsible parasites or else to place us outside the law. The process is slower and less visible in the West than in the USSR, but this makes it all the more dangerous.

Socialism is a fashionable idea with very little meaning. People have simply wanted to attach this appellation to everything that seems desirable and yet unattainable. It is even claimed that the early Christians were quasi-socialist because they championed equality. I doubt it. And in any case the reference to Christianity is not convincing, since no ground is gained by trying to invoke one utopia to justify another. Furthermore, as one of my friends has pointed out, the analogy does not hold: the Christians *voluntarily* shared *their own* belonging with others, while the socialist would use force to *compel others* to share *their* goods. One does not need socialism in order to share voluntarily. Nor would there be any need for bureaucracy, and the world would be a better place.

I've never been able to understand the socialists. To believe that human beings are equal (or that they even desire to be) is to live in a fantasy world, totally isolated from real human behavior. Even identical twins who have been raised and educated together are not absolutely equal. And what makes equality so desirable? What would be interesting about living in a world where everyone was alike? Why does material inequality provoke such a pained reaction in them? Why are socialists so envious, so mercenary? The majority of them are intellectuals who pursue the life of the mind. Their theories lack logic: they are forever criticizing consumerism, greed, and materialism, and yet these are precisely the aspects of life that preoccupy them most. They wish to establish equality on the level of consumption. Do they really believe that if everyone received the same ration of bread, we would all become brothers? Men become brothers as a result of shared hopes and common suffering, mutual help and mutual respect, and the acceptance of each other as persons. Can two men become brothers if one enviously eyes the other's income, and carefully counts every mouthful the other swallows? I would not want a socialist as a brother.

It is high time we realize that no rearrangement of society is going to deliver us from the problems brought about by our inborn characteristics, whether they are failings or virtues. It is time to grow up and get rid of the childish illusions begotten by the nineteenth century. An embodiment of these illusions stares us in the face, and their consequences are easy to predict.

Sooner or later, two phenomena will invariably appear in a socialist country: the black market and the disappearance of good workmanship. Part of the population simply loses the habit of working because it is no longer worthwhile: the principle of equality prevents one from earning more than the amount decreed for everyone, and the administration is powerless to fire incompetents or to demand better work. A more enterprising part of the population, meanwhile, seeks to make a little extra on the side. In the countries of Eastern Europe, the black market has become a perfectly respectable institution, one that has an almost acknowledged status. Western socialist countries like Sweden have an extensive black market in jobs. After putting in his official hours at his official job, the person who wishes to earn some extra cash works as a waiter, say—and, of course, without reporting these earnings to the tax authorities. It's just a matter of scale. The firmer the grip socialism has on a country, the more widespread the black market will be.

Naturally the state tries to combat such "antisocial" behavior. Detective and punitive forces grow apace, and with them the stifling atmosphere. So much for fraternity! The more energetic part of the populace begins to seek emigration to some country with a little less socialism. Naturally enough the first to leave are the most able specialists. This has an immediate impact on the quality of goods and services. And that in turn brings about a growth of internal and external debt and increasing economic difficulties.

Today the building of Western-style socialism has essentially been completed. The next phase depends entirely on the socialists themselves. In order to make the system work, it will be necessary (1) to close the borders; (2) to make work mandatory; (3) to intensify the struggle against "antisocialist elements," including the use of concentration camps to extract labor from them; and (4) to prohibit political activity, opposition parties, and newspapers that show themselves to be too independent.

Don't worry: this will not provoke a revolution. The people will understand how urgent it is to rescue the country from its desperate economic crisis. As you will agree, it is all being done in the interests of the workers.

Naturally, the Western socialists are far too decent to stoop to such methods. Naturally, too, the opposition parties will propose other ways to save the country. However—and this is of crucial importance in understanding the socialist experiment—the process is irreversible. It is impossible to rekindle good work habits in people. You have to wait for another generation for that to happen. It is impossible to remove advantages that are now seen by people as theirs by right. That is the way we are made: it's not hard to start distributing free milk; it is impossible to stop doing it. It would be too unpopular. It is impossible to discharge unnecessary or inept workers. You can hire them, but cannot fire them, for there is a certain level of employment that must be maintained. (At this point one wonders whether the science of economics has any purpose.) There is no way to get back the specialists who have the fled the country. There is nowhere to turn for funds to pay back debts. There is no way to cut down the level of taxation, to make work meaningful again, or to cut down the bureaucracy. Before our eyes is the example of Britain, and the desperate efforts of the Conservatives to save the economy. The bureaucracy resists fiercely. The government cannot order the local authorities to reduce its ranks rather than reducing service. All it can do is to cut the budget. It is up to the bureaucrats to do the rest, but we can be sure that reducing their number is the last thing they will do. Everyone else will be cashiered before one bureaucrat loses his post. The opposite is more likely, in fact, since a whole new bureaucratic apparatus is necessary to handle any cutbacks. Even Khrushchev in his time was powerless before the bureaucrats. No matter what he did, their ranks continued to swell. He divided district committees into industrial and agricultural sections and the staff doubled. He reunited them again, and the personnel doubled once more. He gave up at this point since he concluded that further tampering would make things worse still.

Have the British begun to produce better work? Have they agreed to stop demanding ever higher wages? I don't know, but I don't seem to get that impression. The dim future seems to display images of Tony Benn, a sort of Suslov à l'anglaise, and of general nationalization. In any case you can count on both like you can count on vultures.

That brings us to the last "flaw" of socialism: economically, ideologically, and psychologically, it paves the way for a power takeover by the Communists. One could say that it opens the gates.

◆   ◆   ◆

Ah, *mon cher,* for anyone who is alone, without God and without a master, the weight of days is dreadful. Hence one must choose a master, God being out of style.

Albert Camus, *The Fall*

It is striking how the majority of present-day Communists, and socialists too, seem to have nothing in common with the workers. They are intellectuals, representatives of the so-called middle class, often quite wealthy or the children of wealthy parents. In fact, the richer they are, the more leftist they tend to be, and vice versa. This has become the rule in Western countries. It used to give me a sort of aesthetic pleasure at first to hear them carry on about "the sufferings of the workers." Was it a sense of guilt, I wondered, or just a pose; was it stupidity, or the itch to play with fire?

In my opinion, the most insufferable people of this kind can be found in England. Although they are far more numerous in France or Italy, yet in those countries the proportion of naive and honestly mistaken persons is much higher. You can at least talk with them: they argue, but they listen. British politics, in contrast, is subject to the mentality of a social club.

There was a story about a British sailor who was shipwrecked and spent twenty years on a desert island before being rescued by a passing ship. But before he left his island, the Englishman showed his rescuers how he had passed his time: his work, his relaxation.

"This hut was the house in which I spent 20 years, and the hut over there was my club, where I used to go in the evenings."

"What was the function of that other hut, over there on the hill?" asked his guests.

"Oh, that one. That is the club which I try to ignore."

That is one of the few jokes about the English that gets close to the truth. This club mentality is tremendously developed, especially in politics. The followers of different political parties may live side by side and yet never in their whole lifetime meet each other, to say nothing of having an open conversation. Each one has his "club," his newspaper, his group. The compartmentalization is almost hermetical. If you belong to one chapel, it's best not to set foot in your neighbor's.

When I arrived in Great Britain, I happened to be well received by the Conservatives, who were then the opposition. I became friends with several of them. Faithful to the club mentality, the members of the opposing group decided to ignore me. For the longest time I did not succeed in meeting a single member of the Labour party; it was as if they did not exist in Britain. But time passed, the Conservatives were returned to power, and the Labourites became the opposition;

no doubt curiosity also played a role. The upshot was that I was no longer subjected to total ostracism, and little by little I was able to make contact with the other half of the British population. And of course I was always free to pick up the Labour papers that were on sale everywhere.

In the most general terms, the Labourites can be divided into two categories. First there are the refined intellectuals, the professors, the journalists—these are brilliant and witty conversationalists, highly knowledgeable in art and literature. They are terribly cultured and sophisticated, to the point that they would have been called some choice names in the Gulag. But consider this small example of the club mentality: for them there is no difference between a Churchill and a Hitler. And it is useless to argue the point: the moment you try, a faraway look comes into their eyes. As for the Soviet Union, they consider themselves well informed, thank you, and they can even quote some second-rate Soviet authors to you. Their conclusion is: don't bother talking to us about all this, it is just as bad everywhere else.

The other category is a larger group, made up mainly of young or young-looking people, who go around studiously trying to resemble workers, even though in their entire life they probably never lifted anything heavier than a tea cake. Needless to say, their overalls and deliberately plebian talk cannot conceal that fact. These pseudoproletarians can be distinguished from the other group by their abysmal ignorance. They probably read nothing but their own propaganda, for despite today's accessibility of good books, they stubbornly cling to the most ridiculous legends and prejudices. They will in all seriousness recite the propaganda line about no unemployment in the USSR, or about the all-but-universal illiteracy in Russia before the revolution. It is tedious and pointless to argue with them, for they are physically incapable of taking in any information contrary to their faith. Nor is there any point in trying to discuss the built-in contradictions of Marxism with them, for most of them have never opened a book written by Marx, Engels, or Lenin.

Like all religions, communism has no need of logical proofs and is inaccessible to logical argument. To the contrary, the more incredible an assertion is, the more it is believed. A description of failures does not seem to discredit the idea: if a priest sins, that in no way proves that God does not exist. If socialism has not been established in the USSR, then it exists in Cuba; if not, we must look to China, or to the far side of the moon. No matter what the reactionary astronauts or the cosmonauts may say, their tall tales can in no way shake our intense faith in a new society of a lunar type, free of inflation and unemployment, where misery and strife are unknown. In any case, anything that might be said will not unsettle the lunatic party in the least. Actual information can bypass this psychological barrier only with great difficulty and will make little practical difference.

Man can be viewed as a concept-generating machine. The more smoothly this machine functions, the more easily it can find a place for inconvenient facts within a conceptual scheme. Give a worker a couple of months in the Soviet Union and as a rule he will understand more than an intellectual will in a whole lifetime. The latter will always find a way to justify what he sees. During the 1930s, essentially all the information contained in the three volumes of *The Gulag Archipelago* was available in the West.

"Well," the defenders used to say at the time, "the birth of a baby also occurs amid blood and pain. But a strong and healthy child will come from it."

During the 1930s and early 1940s, everything was justified by the struggle against fascism; in the 1950s, postwar difficulties were the excuse. And the plethora of information about the dissidents and their persecution that has become available in more recent years has given rise to a new legend.

"Perhaps the intellectuals are treated badly, but at least the workers have many advantages. After all is said and done, how many dissidents are there? A few thousand at the most. But on the other hand there is no unemployment, no inflation, no exploitation."

And so we have the usual ready-made theory about the primacy of socioeconomic factors over civil rights. "Of what use is freedom of the press for the worker if he is hungry?"

But as fate would have it, the events in Poland in 1980 confronted the concept-builders with another dilemma. For here were millions of workers who not only destroyed the myth about socioeconomic well-being on the far side of the planet but who insisted on freedom of the press and of religion, and who demanded the release from prison of those very "dissidents" who were not supposed to count for very much. One would think that these events would have had an impact on a few minds. Not in the least; rather to the contrary.

"You see, it is after all the *working class* that is taking the lead, and not some obscure dissidents. Our theory is right!"

To be sure, the number of true believers dwindles periodically. Only the cleverest stick by their doctrine, being so subtle and sophisticated that they find an explanation for everything.

And yet a different tendency is also growing within the ranks of the traditional left: a yearning for realism, a desire to be rid of illusions, an interest in true information and sober reflection. This is especially true in France and Italy, where the Communist parties have enough strength to transform a utopian dream into a political reality. The consequences of such a potential change, as well as its irreversibility, is starting to get people back on earth again. But will it last? A Parisian friend of mine told me that in 1956, after Budapest, countless discarded party cards floated down the Seine; the same thing happened in 1968 after Prague. But only a few years later, the ranks of the builders of a radiant tomorrow were full once again. I think it would be hard to find someone in France who had not belonged to the Communist party during his youth, and who had not felt deceived by it as he became older, and yet this has not affected the behavior of the young. It seems to be a childhood disease, something like adolescent onanism that has persisted a little too long.

To a degree, this turn of mind is also based on a feeling of national superiority: "In our country, things can't go wrong like that, we are not some sort of Asians." I fear that this arrogant attitude has little justification: slowly but relentlessly, socialism is changing developed countries into underdeveloped ones. That really is the historic mission of socialism. One cannot take too much heart from the dwindling ranks of the European Communist parties. In 1917, there were only 40,000 Bolsheviks in Russia, compared to a population of 170 million. To put great stakes in some special level of civilization among Europeans would be naive: history suggests that they slit each other's throats just as readily as the Asians, once they are given a good enough pretext.

In the same way that our fear of responsibility and our desire for a life of security can lead us to illusions that, in turn, bring us to socialism, and just as socialism unlocks the door to communism, so does communism inevitably open the gate to Soviet tanks. So far, no one has succeeded in closing this gate once it is ajar. Indeed, it has not yet stopped swinging wider and wider.

CHAPTER FOUR

The Sparrow, the Cow, and the Cat

I hear today—finally—what happened when Nixon met Khrushchev that morning in the Kremlin. Khrushchev opens up strong. He tells Nixon he knows about him, knows he is an enemy of communism, of the Soviet Union, that he is a white knight of capitalism.

Nixon replies: He is a defender of capitalism, yes, but he began life as a poor boy, growing up on a small orchard in California, doing all the chores. Khrushchev rejoins that he himself started life as the poorest of the poor. Nixon can't even imagine what it was like to be so poor. He, Khrushchev, was a barefoot boy. He shoveled shit to earn a few kopeks.

Well, says Nixon, he too was a poor boy; he too went barefoot; he too shoveled shit.

Khrushchev snorts. So what kind of shit did Nixon shovel? Horseshit, Nixon replies. That's nothing, says Khrushchev. Shoveling horseshit is nothing. He shoveled cowshit. Much worse. Stinks. Sloppy. Gets on your feet and between your toes.

The vice-president: I too had to shovel cowshit.

Khrushchev seems skeptical. Perhaps Nixon shoveled cowshit once or twice. But animal shit is one thing. He had to shovel human shit. That is the worst.

Nixon does not try to top Khrushchev on this. He leaves the Kremlin in a state of shock.

Harrison Salisbury, "My Nixon File," *Esquire,* September 1980.

K HRUSHCHEV was surely right: poverty in America cannot really be compared to poverty in our country. When it comes to handling manure, however, it would be hard to find anyone more competent than the Soviet head of state, since the essence of his job is precisely the sorting of human excrement, all the nuances of which we involuntarily learn to recognize after living under socialism. There is just no way Nixon could beat that.

This dialogue between the leaders of two opposing worlds seems to be filled with symbolism, especially the outcome: Nixon's quick retreat and his departure "in a state of shock." Up to the present, all the conflicts between these two worlds have had the same result, and competition in "dirty tricks" or blows below the belt has never once brought the West any success.

It is of course very hard for a democracy to compete with a totalitarian state, whose limitless power permits it to throw all its resources into the competition and in effect to subordinate the life of the country to the goal of winning the struggle. The population can go hungry and be poorly dressed, the most elementary goods and services can simply cease to be available, but the army will have the most sophisticated weapons, and a good half of the budget will be spent on subversive activities against enemies and the financing of allies. No democratic government can force a whole society—the press, the church, the diplomatic sector, the arts, sports, and so on—to serve the goals of propaganda, falsehood, espionage, and ultimate victory at any price. The total secrecy and level of censorship that we have known for decades is unthinkable in a democracy. During the Vietnam War, for example, the press discussed the departure of every battalion for the war zone on the same day that it happened. In our country, when a huge military factory blew up in the Urals, the West only learned about it several years later.

As a result, those of us who grew up under socialism have learned to react, to conceptualize, and to evaluate in a radically different way. In a totalitarian state, an individual exists to serve a purpose, even if he himself does not believe in it. In a democracy, in contrast, an individual lives for his own pleasure, and it is no small task to get him to sacrifice anything for an abstract goal. Some fifty thousand Americans were killed during the Vietnam War; that is, roughly the same as the number of fatalities from road accidents in the course of one year. This called forth a powerful emotional outburst against the war, almost a revolution. In one year of the campaign in Afghanistan, the Soviets lost thousands of men, and no one dares even to talk about it. We have other scales of evaluation, other standards and criteria, and until the casualty figures climb to the millions, the population will remain passive.

Life in the West is too pleasant and too comfortable for people to accept having to die in some distant jungle, or even to go through the inconveniences of military service in peacetime. Carter had only to make a passing reference to reinstituting the draft for thousands of young people to demonstrate in the streets carrying placards that said: "There are no causes worth dying for." At the same time, the Soviet eighteen-year-old goes docilely to do his military service in an army where discipline and living conditions are incomparably more harsh than in the American army. No one will ask him if he is willing to kill or be killed, no one will ask him if he believes in the policies of the government. He has no way to refuse, unless he wants to end up in a prison camp, or, in time of war, to be shot for treason. For many years this has been accepted as the norm, and no one is surprised or scandalized.

The Western world is kinder and more humane; it does not easily accept the need for sacrifice. I was struck by a seemingly insignificant detail found in the press communiqué about the unsuccessful attempt to free the hostages in Iran. When the colonel in charge realized that the operation had failed and that eight of his men had been killed, he sat down and broke into sobs. I cannot imagine any Soviet colonel shedding tears in a military operation, no matter how many men he had lost in the process. During World War II, these colonels used machine guns to drive hundreds of thousands of unarmed, poorly trained adolescents against German tanks in the attempt to close breaches in the front, and none of them wept as the soldiers were massacred. That is how the war was won, at the cost of ten Russians for every German casualty.

How would the American high command react if an atomic bomb exploded over New York? Would the Pentagon drown in tears, would the Potomac's water level rise so that the population of Washington would have to be saved from the flood? I beg my readers to forgive me this cruel example, but it is crucial for understanding the psychology of the Soviet leaders, their perception of the West, their mindset. In Soviet eyes, the Western man is soft, unable and unwilling to fight, and will in fact not fight. Only the Americans are naive enough to believe that their marvelous technology will do their fighting for them: some kind of planes that cannot be detected, tanks with impenetrable armor, and ships that are unsinkable. Having fought two world wars and a civil war on their home soil, the Soviets know that no matter how important military hardware is, in the last analysis it is men who wage war and decide its final outcome.

I am not suggesting that the USSR wishes to start a world war. It certainly does not. Obviously neither of the two opponents desires mutual destruction. But the quality of the "non-desire" is radically different on the two sides. For when it comes to mutual blackmail or bluff, the winner is he who has less fear of losing (or who gives that appearance). In recent times specialists have been debating whether the USSR intends to launch a first strike. Of course it is the job of the military command to work out plans for every contingency. At the risk of contradicting the specialists, however, I submit that the Soviets have no intention of making such a move, at least not as long as they think that it would provoke a retaliatory strike of similar magnitude. Why should they take such an unjustifiable risk? It's much better to keep confronting the enemy with the choice of whether or not to push the button, while they themselves continue to spread "wars of liberation" in Asia, Africa, and Latin America. If the enemy does make the first strike, he will draw a counterstrike on himself and will be damned by world opinion. If he decides not to, so much the better. And so the Soviets continue to build giant submarines and aircraft carriers; they swell the numbers of their airborne troops as they prepare for distant campaigns. Most of the world lies defenseless before them. Would the Americans ever risk destroying the world for the sake of a Thailand, a Namibia, or even a Sweden? They did not do it for Angola, Ethiopia, or Vietnam. They are too humane.

In the eyes of the West all wars are bad, and every effort is made to avoid conflicts, to lessen the tensions, and to try to maintain some sort of equilibrium. The Soviets, on the other hand, divide wars into "just" and "unjust" ones: those serving the interests of socialism and those running counter. To them a climate of conflict, dissension, and instability is as important as the darkness of night is to a mugger. One of the parties is a natural predator, and the other is a victim; one is permanently on the offensive, and the other constantly on the defensive. For this reason, and for other reasons of which I will speak later, the initiative remains in Soviet hands. It is the Soviets who choose where and how to start a conflict, how and when to resolve it. The initiative is an immensely valuable element in any game. A chess player will tell you that the initiative is worth one or even two chess pieces. In a war, it is the equivalent of an army, and in politics it's worth even more than a faithful ally. And he who is at the receiving end will find that every move he makes in response can be disadvantageous.

It often puzzles us how it can be that the Soviets seem to have penetrated into all the "strategically important" regions of the world; we fail to realize that this is a misleading impression. It is simply a case of an area becoming "strategic" as soon as the Soviets establish themselves there. In this sense, their strategy is amazingly simple: they pick up everything left unattended and fill every vacuum carelessly left behind by their opponents. There are more than enough such vacuums. Using the same technique as a pack of wolves going after a herd of cows, they attack the weakest, the youngest, those with the poorest defense, while we scratch our heads and attempt to grasp their strategic design and to predict their next target. One must admit that the West, under these circumstances, acts much less sensibly than a herd of cows. The animals at least know that wolves are wolves, that they are after fresh meat, and that there is no way to persuade them to give up their habits or to come to an understanding with them. The herd knows that it must stay together rather than wandering off separately, that it must look after the weak and the inexperienced—those who out of curiosity would like to play with the wolves—and that, finally, all sides must be defended, not only the direction where the wolves can be seen, for the predators can set an ambush or lurk on the flank. The essential thing, however, is that once the wolves have set foot on your good pastureland, you have to give up a lot of things in the interest of survival.

But the trouble is that what suits one does not suit another, and human beings can't seem to grasp truths that are obvious to cattle. A cow is not a complicated creature, and at the sight of a wolf it is quite simply overcome with terror. A human being, on the other hand, immediately invents a thousand theories to prove to himself that wolves do not in fact exist, or that they are not at all dangerous (if a calf was brought down, it was simply because the wolves were famished), or, if we must be eaten, let it be done slowly rather than in one gulp, which would make the wolves sick. One could say that, in contrast to cows, we have to contend with the following afflictions: (1) diplomats; (2) political scientists (whatever this incongruous phrase might mean) and other Sovietologists; (3) politically oriented traders or trade-minded politicians, or some subtle combination thereof—in short, the forces of peace; and (4) numerous clever people who consider being eaten by wolves a fine and progressive thing.

And that is of course not all. The net result of the common efforts of all the above is that the average citizen has still not realized the extreme gravity of the situation. He does not understand that in the circumstances he must subordinate his various and sundry problems and difficulties to the only true problem: how to survive.

◆ ◆ ◆

It is such a sad tale that it is hard to know where to begin telling it, perhaps because it has no beginning. On the one hand, its roots go back to the beginnings of history; on the other, they plunge into the depths of the subconscious.

To describe it briefly is to oversimplify and thus to invite easy criticism. Yet to describe it in detail would require impossible length, and in our time who reads lengthy histories? The long and short of it is that the twentieth century has given rise to a novel phenomenon, one that is new in principle and for which we have no tested method of behavior. Attempts to find historical analogies result only in still greater complications. The problem is that the conceptual framework of Western diplomacy belongs to the nineteenth century. These principles have proved incapable of saving us from the catastrophes of the twentieth century—catastrophes that grew directly out of the psychological and moral climate of the previous century.

Stability and compromise are the fundamental principles of classical diplomacy. Accordingly, any and every neighboring state deserves recognition, provided it exhibits sufficient stability. Diplomacy exists to reinforce peace and cooperation, and any conflicts that arise

must be resolved through mutual compromise. This cheerful pragmatism of our grandfathers was based on "acknowledging reality"
rather than shaping it: if a "stable" power in a neighboring state had
legitimized cannibalism, this would of course be considered regrettable, but it would in no way affect the goals of diplomacy. The sovereignty of every other country must be respected and interference in
their internal affairs is inadmissible. Even with the most turbulent of
neighbors, a poor peace is better than a good quarrel.

But with the appearance of totalitarian regimes based on ideology,
these seemingly irreproachable principles—the product of long experience and common sense—have led to disastrous consequences.
Natural processes under extreme conditions can produce unforeseen
anomalies that seem illogical and paradoxical; it appears that the same
thing occurs in human relationships. Logic itself seems to buckle in
these circumstances. If one adds, divides, and multiplies two numbers, for example, inevitably one gets a new number. This obtains
with all numbers from greater than zero to approaching infinity. But
the rules disintegrate when one is dealing with zero or infinity, where
all mathematical operations produce the same result. While zero can
be visualized in some fashion, infinity defies our intuition entirely.

It has proved even harder to grasp the nature of a totalitarian
state. And the more "normal" and rational one's approach, the more
difficult the task becomes, because the kind of state that seeks to realize an ideological absolute is fundamentally irrational. The fact that in
this state no one, high or low, continues to believe in the ideology
makes no difference at all. Ideology in the Soviet Union exists not in
the minds of people; after half a century of heated debates it has crys-
tallized in governmental structures and institutions, in the way of life,
in the manner of psychological reactions, and even in the atmosphere
itself. It's like the science fiction story where an idea separates from
its creators, acquiring a concrete, physical, and entirely independent
existence.

No one is permitted to question this ideology, not even the chief
ideologist himself, for by definition it alone is right. You can think
what you like; but if you openly question the ideology, you will quickly
disappear. The men who will come to take you away will express sympathy and will even tell anti-Soviet jokes in consolation. The judge
will be even more eager to express his sympathy, and the party supervisor will secretly shake your hand and whisper a word of encouragement. But you will nevertheless disappear for many years. And if this
upstart should prove to be the general secretary of the party, well,
then, the country would simply wake up the next morning with a new
general secretary. The higher placed a member of the apparatus is, the

more he loathes the ideology. But what can he do? It does not matter if a priest does not believe in God: the church will persevere. And it is immaterial that parishioners have no real faith if *custom* nevertheless dictates regular church attendance, the christening of children, and Christian marriages and funerals.

The founding fathers of this surrealist state have defined its purpose for once and always, for there exists no mechanism for changing it. This goal consists of establishing "absolute justice" in the world, that is, of propagating the system to the entire globe. It would be correct to say that it is not a state in the usual sense, but rather a military base, a center of universal subversion. All the structures are organized to carry out this function, and the system can only exist in a permanent state of war. The "iron curtain" is a popular phrase in the West, but if one could in fact cut off the USSR completely from the rest of the world, the system would fold in the twinkling of an eye. Its very survival depends on the superhuman intensity generated by the superhuman goal. The system is fantastically unstable and unviable if it is deprived of enemies. Every ideology needs its devil, and for Soviet ideology this function is fulfilled by the noncommunist world. It is of no consequence that no one any longer believes in either God or devil, since an individual cannot be sure that all the others have also lost their faith. Nothing would change even if everyone learned the truth.

The Soviet leaders have exacted stupendous sacrifices from their people, they have killed off a substantial segment of the populace, and they continue to ask for ever new sacrifices—all for the sake of a mythical goal. What can the leaders do now? It is impossible to dismount from the tiger you are riding. The least hesitation, the slightest sign of weakness in the power structure could be fatal in this undeclared civil war. So the only possible course is to keep expanding, going on to ever new conquests.

The problem is that the West is so unshakably normal that it cannot understand the mechanism of this schizophrenia.

◆ ◆ ◆

"I have met with many Russians, and I must disagree with you," objects an old diplomat. "They are people like you and me—polite, well educated, well brought up. Like us, they yearn for peace and wish to avoid a nuclear catastrophe."

"It is not our business to make changes in the Soviet political system," I am told by a respected elder statesman, a former prime minister of a European nation. "Our duty is to find a way to get on with them, and to maintain the balance of power in the world."

And a distinguished university professor specializing in Russia assures me: "Russia under the Soviets is a country like any other. The political adventuring they engage in is the remnant of their old colonial ambitions."

How does one explain to these people that they are cruelly and inexcusably wrong? How does one get across to these very normal individuals that they are dealing with an abnormal state, one in which a single person, even if he should be the head of the state, counts for nothing? How does one prove that it is impossible to establish and to maintain the balance of power of which they speak unless the Soviet system changes? And what does the past have to do with it? What possible national interests are at stake for Russia in Angola or Vietnam? Would the classic sort of colonialist ever consider spending several million rubles daily to maintain a Cuba, say, twelve thousand kilometers away from the national capital and virtually on the opposite side of the globe? How does one visualize the fact that infinity subtracted from infinity yields infinity all over again?

When the methods and concepts of classical diplomacy are applied to a totalitarian state, it is not difficult to predict the outcome. Just as in the case of an individual living within such a state, for whom "accepting reality" means direct or indirect complicity in the crimes of the regime, so for a foreign state this is the road to dependence and complicity. Totalitarian regimes need satellites, not partners, just as they need slaves rather than citizens.

It is already a serious effort for a democratic state to give recognition to a totalitarian one: it is rather like entering into negotiations with terrorists. Recognition strengthens totalitarianism and disarms the other side morally, it confers legitimacy on the regime in the eyes of the enslaved population, and it lulls the vigilance of democracy. It encourages other states to follow this example. Most important, it opens the way to "cooperation," a process that inevitably reinforces totalitarianism and weakens the democracies, for the totalitarian state continues to wage a hidden (or sometimes not-so-hidden) war, while the democrats remain faithful to the precepts of classical diplomacy, showing loyalty and nonbelligerence. The totalitarian state intrudes into the others' internal affairs, aims to destabilize them by every means possible, while the other side cannot reciprocate. And it is hard to correct the error, for it is far easier to establish relations than it is to break them off.

Every democratic state is highly vulnerable to destabilization attempts. It always has its share of unsolvable problems; it has minorities with all sorts of grievances along with opposition parties of every description. And democratic principles make it impossible for the government to simply forbid its totalitarian neighbor from setting up organizations that openly disseminate propaganda within its borders. At the same time democracies cannot respond in the same coin. It is hardly possible to do so secretly in a totalitarian country and impermissible to do it openly. That would be an "unfriendly act." In a word, double standards and an unequal relationship are set up from the beginning.

Conflicts arise almost as soon as this "cooperation" has begun. Classical diplomacy is committed to resolving them by means of compromise. But it suddenly turns out that in the vocabulary of your totalitarian neighbor, compromise is a dirty word. It could not be otherwise, since in the eyes of an ideologue, to compromise with the devil is a crime. It is of course true that in practical terms totalitarianism will agree to compromise, but only in those cases when to do so is to its advantage. For this reason, the readiness to compromise is perceived as a weakness, a sign of spinelessness, and a signal to seek even greater concessions. The difference in starting position is very substantial: one side actively seeks compromise, while the other side is occasionally so kind as to accept them. Westerners are taught from childhood that compromise is a desirable thing and that it virtually guarantees success. But in dealings with totalitarianism, the opposite is true. One could say that democracies are not as a rule wedded to principle. When confronted with the choice between life and principles, the majority of Westerners would opt for life. This leads to what is to us an astonishing readiness to submit to oil blackmail or to enter into negotiations with terrorists. Such an attitude can be carried to ridiculous extremes. For example, New York City police have advised citizens to carry ten dollars on their person when they go out onto the street: if they are held up, they will have something to give the mugger, lest he become violent from the disappointment of finding no money on his victims. It goes without saying that a guaranteed booty can only increase the number of muggings. I cannot imagine such docility or such recommendations in the Soviet Union. We have a "backward" mentality that would brand such behavior as shameful. I guess that, for the most part, notions of honor and shame are no longer much in style in the West; they are considered obsolete. A European politician whose wife is found to have taken a Soviet spy into her bed no longer blows his brains out (as would have been the case a hundred years ago); he does not even resign, and all that is required of him is that he change posts.

All this can only reinforce Soviet beliefs about the weakness of the West and reaffirm the "infallibility of uncompromising Leninist policies." But what can the West do? Once you have accepted one "reality," how can you refuse to accept another? This is all the more true because over the years the Soviets have acquired the reputation of being "impervious to external pressure" ("those Russians, you know"). And besides, time is always on the Soviets' side, and they have no need to hurry. They have eternity before them, whereas a politician in the West has only a miserable four or five years at his disposal. The rule in the West is that if a certain policy yields no visible results in the short run, it must be changed. That plays wonderfully into the hands of totalitarianism—if a policy or a particular statesman is not to their liking, they have only to sit it out until more favorable circumstances come along. The initiative remains with them all along and this, it will be recalled, is worth two chess pieces.

But even that is not all, assuming the period of "fruitful cooperation" has just begun. Commercial links must now be set up. As the reader is undoubtedly aware, commerce is an authentic instrument for peace and for strengthening neighborly relations. That is surely the one domain where there cannot be subterfuge or unilateral advantages. We send them technology, they send us timber. We send them machines, and they send us vodka. We put up an automobile plant in exchange for caviar. Yes, but—these are new times; it is now standard practice to extend credit, to trust one's trading partner. And so we send them technology, machines, and factories in exchange for a receipt. And the question of who depends on whom—the debtor on the creditor or vice versa—is determined by the side that has the strongest nerves and the biggest supply of brazenness.

The establishment of trade opens up limitless possibilities for interfering in the internal affairs of a democratic country. The giving or withholding of a lucrative contract to our country (or to a particular company) can affect the level of unemployment, either in the whole country or in a certain region. To stop placing any orders after a long period of "fruitful interchange" can mean that the level of unemployment suddenly shoots up. There have been some rather curious occurrences, as when a leading firm received a huge contract from the Soviet Union *through the good offices* of the local Communist party, no doubt due to the goodness of its heart. Or take the case of the factory built for the Soviet Union and then dumping its products in the country that built it.

Socialism may have won a lot of ground in the democracies, but commercial transactions still enjoy a considerable degree of freedom in the West. A few years of trade are enough to blur many distinctions concerning ownership and jurisdiction. You think you are dealing with a respectable, long-established firm, but it may in fact be controlled by the Soviets.

Finally, it is difficult to enforce restrictions or controls on trade. If certain products cannot be legally exported to a particular country, it is possible to route them through a dummy firm in another country. That is how the USSR acquires items of strategic importance and sometimes even weapons. Antony C. Sutton, a scholar at Stanford University, has shown that during the 1920s and the early 1930s Germany alone built for the USSR seventeen artillery factories, all of its submarines, and plants to produce warplanes and tanks.[1] Sutton's research findings are of the greatest interest, especially to the Russian reader. It becomes evident that literally all the industrial complexes and major factories were built by foreign firms, sometimes using foreign credit and even foreign manpower. These were the very projects touted as the great accomplishments of socialism both at home and abroad.

By 1927 (shortly before the period of collectivization that brought death to several million peasants and famine to the entire country), 85 percent of all tractors had been supplied by Ford. The coal industry (especially in the Kuznetsk and Don basins), steel mills, rolling mills, the Gorky automobile factory, the ZIL car works in Moscow, the Dnieper dam, the industrial complex of Magnitogorsk, even the electrification plan laid down by Lenin—all of these were planned, constructed, and equipped by Western firms. Even the famous "Lenin light bulbs" were manufactured by a German-Swedish company (originally in Yaroslavl, then in Moscow, Leningrad, and Nizhni Novgorod). The Russian reader, unlike his Western counterpart, will note two significant points: (1) forced labor provided most of the manpower used in the construction work proper; (2) most of these giant projects, involving as they did energy, the production of metals, and machine-building, laid the foundation of the military might of the USSR. Once again we see the two aspects of totalitarianism, internal oppression and external aggression, going hand in hand, handsomely equipped by the Western democracies.

So perhaps it would be better not to hasten one's acceptance of such "realities." Perhaps there are some types of "stability" that don't deserve acceptance? Can we really afford to turn a blind eye to a neighbor who practices cannibalism? And maybe a bad peace is no better than a good quarrel in some circumstances?

[1] See Antony C. Sutton, *Western Technology and Soviet Economic Development*, 3 vols., Stanford: Hoover Institution Press, 1968–73.

Pragmatism is merely a polite way to describe a lack of principles, which is why it seems so convenient at first glance. Pragmatists prosper under every regime, and they are useful to every type of system, for they support power, regardless of what that power stands for. That is why they are invariably the objects of hatred, even more so than the executioners. The day will come when the latter are hanged; the pragmatists, however, will again manage to get off scot-free.

The perniciousness of pragmatic policies toward totalitarian regimes is but one side of the coin. In normal circumstances, the hatred directed at the pragmatists has little practical consequence. But in the context of global ideological confrontation, such feelings of hostility can provide fertile soil for the propaganda of the West's enemies. For it is nothing less than amazing that the United States, a democratic and essentially nonaggressive country, one that gives Third World nations incomparably more aid than does the USSR, receives nothing for its pains but an ever-mounting dose of hate. The USSR, meanwhile, despite all its aggressiveness, manages to be seen as the good guy. What is the source of this unanimous anti-Americanism?

Of course there is no simple answer to this question. One factor is that the people of the nonindustrial countries have not yet developed an immunity against "the childhood disease of leftist thinking," which is a consequence of their economic difficulties. Another factor is the great skill with which Soviet propaganda has portrayed the timid steps undertaken by America in its own defense as the desire for world hegemony. One must also consider the socialistic mindset of the Europeans, who are always ready to assume that the rich man must be responsible for the poor man's poverty. But the main enemy is pragmatism and the incredible blunders committed by American politicians. This ineptitude is rooted in the basic paradox of US policy. Traditionally, and by every natural inclination, the US would like to be isolationist, and yet circumstances (above all the Soviet menace all over the world) have propelled it into a position of leadership of the democratic world. It is a role for which the United States is quite unprepared. As a result, American intervention in world affairs has not been energetic enough or global enough to protect the world effectively, but it has been sufficiently great to draw negative reactions. The ambivalence of this stance leads to half-measures that in turn pave the way for failure.

The scenario of these failures is depressingly predictable. Following the precepts of pragmatism, the United States hastens to accord recognition to "stable" authoritarian regimes and to cooperate with them. Naturally, better relations with China must be sought. And all the problems are of course due to the fact that the pragmatists were not sufficiently heeded. Indeed, their view is that Cuba should be recognized as quickly as possible, since Castro heads a stable system—to say nothing of the Cuban troops that are stabilizing Angola. If one took the advice of the pragmatists, the world would have become incredibly stable long ago.

None of this is appreciated by people who have grown up under a "stable" dictatorship, nor is it even comprehensible to those who are filled with revolutionary fervor. One's own experience is always more persuasive, and for such people experience suggests a very clear, black-and-white picture in which the Americans are the "bad guys" and the Soviet Communists are the "good guys." Sooner or later such clarity, helped by a push from the "good guys," will bring our "stable" dictator to the verge of collapse. At this point the pragmatists are faced with an unsolvable dilemma. On the one hand, one must not abandon an ally in difficulty, since this would have negative repercussions on other allies and alliances. Moreover, the "stable" new regime that promises to replace the old exhibits inordinate hostility. On the other hand, helping the present regime means intervening in a conflict that is unpopular, unnatural for America, and obviously doomed. Who knows, it might even involve calling in American troops, and then "American boys will start dying," something that will never be tolerated on the home front.

One should add to this a further American misfortune: inept leadership. Some time ago my friends and I happened to meet a Vietnamese officer, now in exile. We asked him:

"How did you manage to lose the war? After all, you had American troops on your side, as well as the best military equipment in the world. Or were you blind to the consequences of losing the war?"

"We knew, all right," he answered bitterly. "But how could we win when the American equipment came with endless conditions? Shoot this way, but not that way; bomb this, but not that. One cannot fight a war this way, especially since the Americans were totally ignorant about our country."

Later on, when I was more familiar with the American style of leadership, I understood better what that Vietnamese was saying. For lack of space, I will only cite one minor example, but it illustrates the problem very well. It concerns Radio Liberty, which broadcasts in Russian and the other languages of the USSR.

At some point after the end of World War II, right in the middle of the Cold War, the Americans finally understood that they had to make at least some kind of response to Soviet propaganda. At a minimum, they could provide the people of the USSR and of Eastern Europe with a source of information that would be free of Soviet censorship.

But instead of openly proceeding with this very commendable goal, it was decided to regard the enterprise as an intelligence operation, "just in case." The venture was secretly financed by the CIA, which naturally denied this vociferously. I will never understand why it was deemed necessary to conceal the operation. It has been argued that Congress would never have voted the money, for in its eyes the program represented a "hostile act." (At the same time, the Soviets were spending billions for anti-American propaganda, which they spread without the least embarrassment.) And what possible harm can there be in giving information to people misinformed by the Communists? Radio Liberty was financed secretly, but a secret in America is sure to be followed by an exposé. And that always suggests illegitimacy, if not criminality. Predictably enough, clever peace-lovers like Senator J. William Fulbright used this association to demand the closing of this radio station, calling it an impediment to friendlier relations with the Soviet partner. The existence of the station hung in the balance until someone had the idea of financing it openly. Why not, indeed? And that is what finally happened, but not without drawing the criticism of all the Fulbrights in America.

Nonetheless a certain air of impropriety remained, reflected as it was in a system of censorship. The Washington office with jurisdiction over the station regularly published political directives that were filled with incredible nonsense. For example, the announcers were not to have a hostile tone of voice, Soviet propaganda must not be answered head-on, nothing should be done to encourage people to flee from Soviet Russia (in other words, don't paint too rosy a picture of the West or people might want to escape from their own country), and of course no uprising against the authorities was to be incited. If by some misfortune such an uprising were to take place of its own accord, efforts should be made to calm the Soviet population, and under no circumstance should any advice be given to the rebels. In short, just as in Vietnam, there were instructions on where to shoot and where to bomb. If the journalists of Radio Liberty were to follow these directives strictly, the result would be indistinguishable from the programs put out by Radio Moscow. And that is in fact what happened during the "détente" period, for Radio Liberty followed the winding trail of American politics. It is a curious fact that a radio station named "Liberty," one whose task is to spread democracy among those benighted Russians, should institute political censorship. It seems that in fighting for democracy, the Americans don't trust democratic principles. But that is only half the problem.

What happened next seems to be the usual fate of American governmental institutions: the number of bureaucrats started to mushroom while the number of more or less gifted journalists shrank alarmingly. Perhaps in keeping with the formerly "illicit" nature of the enterprise, the bureaucratic additions consisted mainly of failed diplomats and CIA operatives who had not proved their worth elsewhere. The station instantly became the refuge for incompetent functionaries whom it was inconvenient to fire outright and much easier to "kick upstairs." All the while, the budget rose as the quality of the programs went down. The station's own calculations showed that the number of listeners in the USSR was declining. A discriminatory pay-scale seemed to arise of its own accord: Soviet émigré specialists began receiving much less than the Americans who performed the same functions (a reminder of the good old colonial days). The yearly budget reached the astronomical sum of 94 million dollars, which equals the cost of four bombers. Yet even this amount was deemed insufficient for the station to function effectively. I submit that if the U.S. Congress were to dispense only one-fifth of this sum to émigrés from the Soviet Union, the USSR would soon be cracking at the seams. But that seems to be exactly what the Americans fear, since the equilibrium must not be upset! And besides, how can one let these people work without supervision?

I don't know how fair it is to extrapolate from this example to other initiatives that the Americans have undertaken on a larger scale. And yet there is surely something typical here, at least in the ambivalence of purpose: on the one hand, an attempt seems to be made to resist an outlaw state, yet on the other, there is a desire to retain "equilibrium" and a stable relationship with the same regime. In a word, the Americans still don't know what they want.

In contrast, the Soviets have not the slightest doubt about their goals, and they work furiously to enlarge their sphere of influence in the Third World, exploiting every blunder made by the United States. No nation has yet been able to escape from their grip to be able to tell their neighbors that "American imperialism" is child's play compared to Soviet "liberation."

A Russian parable relates that during a fierce cold spell a sparrow was flying from one hay rick to another. Overestimating its strength, it flew too far, froze, and fell rigid to the ground. A cow was passing by, took pity on the unfortunate bird and covered it with a large warm cow pat. As the sparrow regained its warmth and its strength, it poked its head out and discovered that it was stuck in a foul mess. Full of indignation, it started to shriek: "Help! Save me! This is an outrage! I've been buried in shit!" About this time a cat was passing by. "Who ever did that to you, poor thing?" the cat purred. "Don't get upset, I'll get you out of it," whereupon the cat ate the sparrow. This fable has three morals: (1) whoever covers you with shit is not necessarily your enemy; (2) the person who pulls you out of shit is not necessarily your friend; and (3) when you find yourself deep in shit, sit quietly and don't cheep.

But the problem is, as Khrushchev has wisely observed, that cow dung is not the limit of human knowledge.

◆　◆　◆

When you reflect on the foregoing, it is amazing how durable democracy is despite all. But if anything is capable of bringing about its collapse, it will be the Sovietologists and the specialists in political science. Educated people, especially those with degrees, are held in extraordinarily high regard in America. But using one's brain is considered inferior to book learning. The more diplomas you have, the less you are expected to use your powers of reasoning and your intuition. The sad outcome is that these professors, in keeping with some unwritten rule, are always named to key positions in the government. It is typically American to place great store in specialists; and they have a specialist for every occasion. Thus if an American falls in love, he does not sigh at the moon and does not write poems, but instead consults with a specialist on love. The moment you have a problem, you go to the appropriate specialist, who is supposed to solve it for you. The USSR is a "problem"; this is something all Americans understand. It follows that the "Sovietologist community" exercises enormous influence in the handling of this vital issue.

Very often these professors do not even read Russian; in the best of cases, they may have had a few years soaking in the artificial climate of the American embassy in Moscow. And yet these are people who are called upon to elaborate theories and concepts that will guide the president and the State Department in their policies. Some of them are even given key posts and the chance to put their theories into practice.

In the long run it is often difficult to tell who influenced whom, for the dominant theories generally correspond in a striking manner to the interests of a particular segment of the "establishment." I do not know why this should be so. Are the theories created with this goal in mind, or are they prized because they happen to coincide with certain interests? Whatever the answer, the essence of the problem is unaffected, and the results have been brilliantly described by Lev Navrozov in an article entitled "What the CIA Knows About Russia" (*Commentary*, vol. 66, no. 3, September 1978).

In any case, this combination of selfish considerations, ignorance, and dogmatism, all formulated scientifically and presented with conviction, is translated into policies so dangerous that they may cost the West its last chance to survive. Even in the rare instances when there is an opportunity to put pressure on the adversary, this possibility is carefully avoided on the advice of our experts.

Here is a small but characteristic example. In February 1972, President Nixon traveled to China, where he was received by Chairman Mao. Photos of the event showed the two leaders in confidential conversation, and it aroused in the Soviet leaders a panic that they could barely conceal. Even we who were in prison and were able to read only the Soviet press could feel the alarm and consternation of the men in the Kremlin; we knew that the Soviet leaders would go to great lengths to be able to publish a similar photo of Brezhnev talking to Nixon. It was a golden opportunity to strike for significant concessions from the allegedly "unyielding" Soviet regime, and to do so without risk, by exclusively diplomatic means. The initiative fairly cried out to be taken, and the more intractable Nixon would have been in his negotiations, the more he could have gained. A skillful player might even have attempted to effect a real turnaround in the relationships of the two blocs, for the USSR is immensely afraid of China. In fact China is perhaps the one menace that the Soviets seriously fear. But nothing of the sort happened. A mere three months later, Nixon was in Moscow, without having made conditions of any kind, and was warmly kissed on both cheeks by Brezhnev. The much-desired photo of the two leaders in conference was obtained by the Soviets at no cost.

We spent hours puzzling about this. As usual, the optimists maintained that some secret concessions must have been gained from the Soviets: the Americans could not have been so stupid as to throw away the trump cards they were holding. Now we know, however, that this is precisely what happened (see the *Memoirs* of Richard Nixon). In fact it had been the wise Dr. Kissinger himself who had talked Nixon into going to Moscow as quickly as possible, because "one must not exert excessive pressure on the Russians." A point to Nixon's credit is that he hesitated, since his intuition suggested a different course of action. But the arguments of the renowned professor won him over. It is significant that the Moscow authorities prepared for the visit by ridding the city of dissidents; many of them paid for Nixon's visit with their liberty. The distinguished visitors must have been aware of this campaign, which was widely reported in the Western press. But they made no attempt to stop even this, being preoccupied with more lofty plans. The only thing they gained was lodging in the Kremlin, an honor that had fallen on no foreigner since Napoleon.

And just as in the case of Napoleon, the road to Moscow led to disaster: a "détente" that had been launched on an unsound basis could not have yielded anything else. The very doctrine of détente is a striking illustration of how leading political analysts help the West to go down in defeat in the most effective and speedy manner. The four basic principles of this doctrine are all false; what is more, they contradict each other. They are not even genuine principles, but rather glossy clichés:

1. *The USSR is a state just like a Western one. It desires peace just like we do.* I've already tried to explain that this assumption is far from the truth. It is obviously false even at first view by an untutored observer. But of course the professors are always there to enlighten poor untutored oafs like us. There are whole libraries of books written to help us swallow this wisdom.

2. *The two adversaries have no option other than détente. The choice is cut-and-dried: either war (and hence world destruction) or détente.* This seems ominous and categorical. But the man in the street cannot help being puzzled: the West has survived in the same world with the USSR for more than sixty years, so why this dire urgency? What has occurred to make all other options disappear all of a sudden? And besides, if they want peace as much as we do, why would war be inevitable in the absence of détente? Perhaps the inevitability appears only if we accept it, that is, only if we allow ourselves to embark on all that détente implies?

3. *Détente works for the liberalization of Soviet society.* But just a minute! Why does it need liberalizing if it is a society just like our own?

4. *It is wrong to put too much pressure on the Russians, to ask too much of them.* Absolutely incomprehensible! If the USSR longs for peace as much as we do, if it too has no other option than détente, why should we be limited as to what we can talk about together? And besides, who is to say how much is too much? (In practice, as we know, this principle amounts to *applying no pressure at all and asking for nothing whatever.* There is no other alternative, don't you see.) How is one to interpret this strange principle? Let's say we sign an agreement with the USSR, knowing in advance that the USSR may not adhere to it (we must not ask too much of the Russians), while we are completely bound to observe the agreement (we must not exert pressure). In any case, all this is not too serious since they are just like us. We are gentlemen and so are they.

In reality there is nothing new about "détente," which is simply a mistake that the West has repeated periodically. Each time the moribund Soviet economy brings the entire system to an impasse, the Soviet leaders suddenly become conciliatory and propose "normalizing relations," instituting détente, and, naturally, the setting up of commercial links. Each time the West takes this at face value and rushes into the arms of "the Russians," exclaiming: "You see, we were right! They are just like everyone else . . . they too desire peace!" Emotional speeches are made about peace and about one's responsibility toward future generations. "This time the Russians are sincere"; "The Russian bear may be a little coarse, but he is a likable beast all the same." The euphoric dreams include visions of general disarmament, mutual confidence, a sky full of doves. (For the men in the Kremlin, meanwhile, this means no more than a change of tactics: if you want to break a wire, you need to bend it back and forth.)

The important thing is that the economy is once again in a sorry state. Nevertheless, "the ideological struggle is not affected by this fact in the least." The paradox here is that this above statement was made quite openly by Brezhnev. (Lenin, Stalin, and Khrushchev were just as open in analogous periods of détente with the West.) Yet no one wanted to take these words seriously. The Sovietologists among the professors are quick to explain to us that this was simply a sop given to the hawks by the doves within the Soviet power elite. They're just like us, don't you see, with hawks and doves just like we have here. It follows that the nice man Brezhnev (or Lenin, or Stalin, or Khrushchev) is an undisputed dove who is deceiving his comrades in the party in the name of friendship with the West and peace in the world.

All this Western eloquence is aimed only at the general public, the uninitiated. In reality, détente is a period in which, once again, the West attempts to buy peace by paying off the robber. Perhaps it will work this time. They need our help? Let's give it without stinting. A well-fed Communist is better than a hungry one. Perhaps they will settle down at last? This is the typical logic of a victim, a pattern of behavior that I often had the chance to observe in the transfer prisons when the hardened criminals robbed some inexperienced newcomer. "But of course, fellows," he would mumble, "I have nothing against it, I'll be happy to help."

The result is that he will be stripped of everything, will get a clout to boot, and will end up sleeping under the bed, the whipping boy and laughingstock of the whole cell. An underground millionaire caught by the KGB exhibits the same mentality. The stool pigeon who has been placed in his cell whispers to him:

"You think they are after you, old fool? They want your money, your gold. Hand it over to them and they will let you go."

The interrogator makes similar insinuations. And how could one fail to believe that a friendly understanding can be reached with one's own Soviet authorities? After all, they too are human beings. Result: the millionaire is shot, the stool pigeon gets an administrative pardon, and the interrogator receives a commendation and a bonus.

And of course there are hawks and doves, how could it be otherwise? It's a method as old as the hills, used both by the KGB and by professional criminals. For example, one interrogator takes on the role of hawk while the other plays the dove.

"Will you come clean, you bastard," snarls one, "or will I have to give you the works, you dirty son of a bitch?"

"Now, now, Ivan Ivanovich, easy does it," purrs the second. "You're going at it too hard. 'Give you the works' and so on. What might a man think of us? We're not beasts, are we? Why don't you go and take it easy while we talk things over here. He's not such a bad man, you know. I'm sure we'll end up agreeing with one another. Why would we want to harm a good man like you?"

Such planned duplicity is the cornerstone of all Soviet politics. There will be the "peace-making" side—the Foreign Affairs Ministry—and the "militant" side—the Comintern (or its successors). It's a perennial method, and don't tell me the West is not wise to it. The merry-go-round of "détente" and "Cold War" is no more than a KGB comedy featuring hawks and doves. But the way the world is built, there will always be the hardened crooks and the naive prisoner, and each side will continue to play its role.

How can one seriously believe that importing foreign goods can help liberalize the Soviet economy? Even a child counting on his fingers would figure out that the opposite is true. *Only the absence of outside aid will force reforms to be undertaken.* And how can anyone accept the proposition that Comrade Brezhnev would deceive his colleagues? He would not last one day if he tried a trick like that. No, Virginia, the Kremlin is not a bird farm. Some years ago the Norwegian psychiatrists at the Honolulu Congress who had voted against condemning psychiatric abuse in the USSR explained their reasons to me. It turns out they had been persuaded by the Czech delegation.

"If the resolution passes," argued the Czechs, "the Soviet delegation will withdraw from the World Association of Psychiatrists, and we will have to follow suit. We don't want to leave, we want to cooperate with you."

It goes without saying that when the resolution did pass, the Soviets had not the slightest intention of leaving the association, any more than the Czechs did. "Clever guys! They tricked us this time," said the Norwegians, amused. "The next time we won't be fooled."

It was an entirely traditional stratagem, complete with hawks and doves. So if anyone has doubts, I recommend turning to the psychiatrists for advice. They are specialists, after all.

But let us come back to détente. In the attendant climate of immoderate dreaming, every action of the USSR is interpreted in a positive light. You say the Soviets are continuing to build up their arsenals? It's because they are afraid, don't you see. We've given the poor fellows such a scare in previous years (?) that they have developed a persecution mania. *Let them acquire an advantage and then they don't need to fear us any more.* But no one takes the trouble to think this through. Of whom, in fact, should the Soviets be afraid? Of their best friend Giscard d'Estaing? Of their equally dear friend Willy Brandt? Perhaps of Great Britain, which is toying with the idea of unilateral disarmament? Of America, which has put off indefinitely most of its military projects? Of Japan, which has no army? An ordinary man without diplomas would be surprised at the thought that generals who won a world war should spend the last thirty-five years feeling so much fear and insecurity. And anyway, this unenlightened creature will wonder, what is the difference to us if we are occupied out of fear or as a result of calculation? But of course professors aren't supposed to think in these terms. Their duty is to apply their erudition.

As times goes on, the situation deteriorates. The treaties are not observed. Soviet expansionism increases, new countries become its victims. But even that does not matter. The experts assure us that the essential thing is to keep open a golden bridge, an escape route in disguise, so that the Soviets can retreat without losing face. The war is still going full blast and the people of Afghanistan continue to resist, but Western statesmen race each other to Moscow in the effort to help the Soviets save face. What worries them is not that another country has disappeared from the world map, but that détente could be undermined. So they've invaded Afghanistan? This is nothing more than "a Russian tradition," the eternal Russian quest for warm-water ports. And they certainly must be freezing, poor things, they need sun! The only regret of the specialists is that their Russian friends had not sent in Cuban troops. There would have been so much less fuss.

You say Soviet influence is growing stronger in Europe? What's bad about that? Finland is a model of cooperation that should be emulated. Its security is guaranteed: "It's better to live under a foreign flag than under the moral pressure of America" (*Stern*); "Finlandization is better than being atomized" (Channel 1 on German TV); "Finland—a policy of common sense" (*Le Monde*); "If we are occupied, the USSR will continue to supply us with natural gas" (Austrian parliamentarian); "It's better to live on one's knees than to die standing up" (French writer Cavanna speaking on French TV).

All this reminds one of the Soviet saying, "Let's hope war comes soon so we can be taken prisoner." But how in the world did we get ourselves into such a situation? We started off with the premise that both parties were *equally* interested in peace, that neither side had any alternative. So why is it they do have another option, and we don't? And yet it was they who first came looking for help, who were the asking party. Should we have allowed ourselves to get drawn into a game from which it becomes impossible to escape? It means giving up one's independence from the start and accepting the inevitability of having to live on one's knees.

In response you will hear many worthy arguments and even entire theories. What I am struck by is not that there should be such theoreticians, but that they should find such a wide audience. There is something pathological about the readiness to believe any soothing and reassuring nonsense that comes along. There is no need to be a psychoanalyst to realize that all these torrents of words have their source in *fear*. The same fear shackles us all, both in Russia and in the West, in a single chain that knows no frontiers. It is petrifying, animal-like, irrational fear that one is ashamed to admit to. But until we have overcome it, neither we nor you will be able to escape anywhere.

It brings to mind a sad joke that is current in my country, where people like to tell stories at their own expense. A prisoner on death row is talking with a pal:

"Let's make a break for it . . ."

"But what if the outside is worse?"

◆ ◆ ◆

It will be objected that détente had been designed with the primary purpose of bettering conditions in communist countries. Did it not envisage a guaranteed respect for human rights? Does not the free exchange of ideas and of people serve the interests of the dissidents themselves? Could it be that there was nothing useful in these efforts?

This is a typical objection that proves one more time that people are poorly informed about what happens in practical terms when one attempts to embody a superficially attractive idea. Particularly if we ignore the true intentions of the parties involved, where one side has the will and the desire to give life to the idea, while the other side aims only to make sure that their opposite numbers go through with it.

It goes without saying that we would all welcome a more open exchange of people and ideas, so long as this exchange is genuine and not merely a phrase on paper. In the Soviet Union this would mean open, or in any case, more open, access to uncensored information, in particular to foreign books, periodicals, and newspapers. At a minimum, it signifies the *right* (see Article 19 of the Universal Declaration of Human Rights) to seek, receive, and disseminate information or ideas for any purpose, by any means, and irrespective of national boundaries, and hence without risk of prosecution for such actions.

The signing of the Helsinki Accords in 1975 did nothing to change the situation in the USSR. Arrests, heavy prison sentences, and other forms of persecution for perfectly legitimate activities continued unabated. It never crossed the mind of the authorities to bring their practices and their laws into line with the new international agreement. The Western press and Western books did not acquire legal status on Soviet territory. At the border it remains standard procedure to confiscate copies of the Bible. Thus from the very moment of signing the Helsinki Accords, the Soviet authorities have demonstrated a complete unwillingness to abide by the obligations they had agreed to.

On the other hand, the Western governments who signed the final pact showed no desire to insist that the USSR live up to the declarations concerning the free exchange of information. Reserving their protests for only the most flagrant violations, the majority of these countries followed the principle that "one must not ask too much." They stubbornly repeated their belief that "protests end up hurting the dissidents," something the dissidents themselves, even those in prison, had explicitly and often rejected as false reasoning. Even President Carter, whose administration started so auspiciously with a strong defense of the dissidents (this campaign had saved a good twenty of them from prison), soon came to side with the "experts," despite all the information we were able to get into his hands. In any case he discontinued his open campaign and did not resume it during the rest of his term in office. Even when he undertook the boycott of the Moscow Olympic Games, he never mentioned human rights violations as one of the reasons for this action. When we had started the campaign for this boycott in 1978, world opinion was far more open to it than after Carter's initiative in 1980. Part of that reflects anti-Americanism, and part of it was the unwillingness of people to support the professional politicians in *their* games. But I am convinced that the lack of world support for that campaign was the result of Carter's inexplicable and excessive prudence in matters dealing with human rights in the USSR. The debate on the question of a boycott took on a completely different tone, which allowed those who were in favor of the Moscow Games to ignore the human-rights-based arguments we had elaborated, arguments that were well-crafted, often irrefutable, and meaningful to the common man.

But governments and their special advisers stressed the advantages of "quiet diplomacy," something that of course cannot be easily monitored by an outside observer, and which in the case of the Soviets is much less effective than open public protest. This method furthermore places the West in the weak position of having to make a secret request for something that is guaranteed by an international agreement. The very legitimacy of the Helsinki Accords thus seemed to be put into question.

In fairness I must note the USSR's one concession: it agreed to stop jamming most of the Western radio broadcasts beamed at the Soviet bloc. However, this improvement was to a considerable extent nullified by the precipitous change in the tone and content of the broadcasts: the sudden "softening" made it possible to suspect that an agreement with the USSR had been reached on this score. In 1980, at the height of the events in Poland, jamming was resumed at the former level.

Thus détente had very meager practical success in this sphere. In fact one could argue that the net result was regression, to the degree that détente led to a change of tone in the radio programs and to governmental insistence upon "quiet diplomacy." Many Western countries accepted de facto the Soviets' view on the international defense of human rights: this was an "interference in the internal affairs" of the Soviet bloc. At the same time, Soviet propaganda efforts and their subversive activities actually grew under the guise of "increasing the exchange of ideas and information." What is more, the Soviet Union largely succeeded in foisting its own interpretation of this concept upon the West. Although no formal recognition of this fact was ever made, it was nonetheless quietly agreed that in fact the only acceptable kind of exchange was one that had received official Soviet approval, and the only ideas and information to be exchanged were those that had passed the official Soviet censorship.

I cannot remember a single instance in which a Western government made vigorous and public attempts to expand the narrow interpretation imposed by the Soviets in this matter. What I do remember is the example of Malcolm Toon, the U.S. ambassador in Moscow, who gave strict orders to his embassy personnel not to receive any *samizdat* material from Soviet citizens nor to distribute books banned by the Soviet censor. By so doing, he was tacitly agreeing with the Soviet contention that the section of the accords that dealt with increased exchange of ideas and information should be limited by another section that stipulated "respect for the internal legislation" of the countries taking part. In point of fact the accords do not foresee such a limitation. On the contrary, there is explicit language to the effect that all signatories undertake to make their laws conform to the provisions of the accords. The USSR did not fulfill this promise, and the Western nations did not make a protest. And since the U.S. government did not see fit to react to our complaints about Ambassador Toon's actions, one must conclude that the United States accepts his interpretation.

If any positive gains were made, they came about not because of the policy of détente but in spite of it. They were achieved by individuals and organizations who took strong exception to the amoral policy of détente and made a point of opposing it.

Much the same could be said about the other humanitarian clauses of the Helsinki Accords, for example, the important question of scientific and cultural exchange. Although exchanges of this type did experience some temporary growth, here is another area where the Soviets succeeded in imposing on the West criteria and rules that were advantageous to their side. Trips abroad remained under stringent and high-handed control, with travel documents denied or granted in accordance with the regime's evaluation of the particular individual. It seems that a large number of outstanding scientists and artists are deemed unreliable and cannot hope to receive permission to travel, a point that is surely at variance with the whole purpose of the Helsinki agreement. At the same time other individuals are regularly allowed to travel abroad. This has become a device whereby the regime seeks to gain the conformity or collaboration of its intellectual community, since foreign travel is one of the highest goals for a Soviet citizen, and especially so for an artist or scientist.

Using this artificial means of discrimination, Soviet authorities can promote a specialist and create the aura of an international reputation for him, thereby increasing the influence of their hand-picked people on specific professional fields. Although Western colleagues have often protested against this discrimination, I cannot recall a single instance of a Western government intervening openly and forcefully. In fact, the official exchange agreements signed between the USSR and the various Western countries (except Sweden) all lack the provision that one side has the right to invite *specific* individuals and that the other side must honor this invitation. It is a defect that can, and frequently does, render the whole exercise pointless, since meaningful scientific and cultural cooperation must as a rule be based on interaction with particular specialists whose work is familiar and interesting to those abroad.

Scientific and cultural exchanges thus ended up a hollow formality, for they did nothing to bring about greater freedom of creativity in the USSR or to strengthen the links between Soviet professionals and their colleagues in other countries. These exchanges simply gave the authorities one more lever to use in controlling the intelligentsia and buttressing the official party line. What is more, by carefully cultivating ideologically congenial Western intellectuals, those "friends of the Soviet Union," the USSR is to a certain degree able to influence the Western intellectual elite as well: for a Western writer, for example, the typically huge editions of his book in the Soviet Union are by no means immaterial. When the Soviet authorities issue invitations to particular individuals, this does not and cannot meet with objections from the Western government involved. It goes without saying that what the visitors from the West will see is only what the Soviets wish to show them, and that things will be so arranged as to establish contact with predominantly "reliable" people. All this behind-the-scenes planning is not nearly as obvious as one might think, for the Soviets are past masters at staging these events.

I have a friend who lives near a tiny railroad station in Moldavia, who told me that each time there were foreign delegations passing through on the way to Moscow a troupe of actors and dancers in national costume would appear on the platform, singing and dancing. Goods that normally were not to be found here (chocolate, etc.) would be displayed on the station platform, at prices that were laughably low, during the fifteen to twenty minutes the train would be in the station. The inhabitants of the little town of course knew all about these extravaganzas, but they were not allowed into the station lest they immediately buy up all the goods that were meant for display. The canniest of the local kids occasionally found their way in and took advantage of their good fortune. What Western visitor would even suspect that such a large-scale operation had been orchestrated especially for him, and in some tiny town where the train stops only briefly? Upon his return home, our "eyewitness" can become an unwitting instrument of Soviet propaganda.

Thus even tourism, the most elementary form of exchange between countries, is exploited by the Soviets for its political advantage. The Soviet tourist who goes abroad is by definition a privileged and "reliable" individual; the foreign tourist entering the USSR is a potential agent of disinformation. And of course he is also a source of much-needed foreign currency. In general it is laughable to regard tourism in the Soviet Union as a means of improving mutual understanding between peoples, given the rigid itineraries and compulsory tours of endless buildings and monuments. Indeed, tourism serves the Soviet authorities as a means to conceal the truth. The authorities will explain that 99.99 percent of Soviet territory is off limits to foreigners because of military secrets, whereas the true reason for the restriction is to hide the horrendous living conditions of the population. A foreigner cannot legally go more than forty kilometers beyond Moscow without getting his itinerary approved by the authorities, a process that may take many months.

Moscow, Leningrad, and Kiev—the cities most frequently seen by tourists—are in fact just store windows, something like the railroad station mentioned above. Supplies of food and quality of life in general are here far better than in the rest of the country. If meat becomes scarce in Moscow, that means that in the provinces none has been available for months. There is no way a stranger can come to understand the nation in the space of a couple of days. The visitors who came for the Moscow Olympics, although they had been repeatedly warned by journalists that the authorities would stage a major effort to impress them, did not for the most part notice any deceit. According to some of their impressions that appeared in the Western press, the Russians are "polite, helpful, friendly, and have no wish for war." It had been wonderful at last to find oneself "in a place where no one talked about nuclear weapons or wars." One visitor wrote that during the nine days he spent in Moscow he noticed "not the slightest amount of propaganda." Another said he found the stores full of merchandise, almost too much so. A third told how in all his stay he had seen only one police officer. A fourth spoke of being struck by the "freedom and normalcy of the common people." It will of course be impossible to convince these people that they were duped. After all, they saw all this with their own eyes.

Of what possible use is "increased contact between people" when each and every Soviet citizen has the duty to be a soldier in the ideological war, while a man from the West may not necessarily be a defender of democracy? Where is the sense in lofty phrases about peaceful cooperation, when one of the parties carries on an unceasing war?

It might seem strange that since the beginning of the "era of détente" conditions in the USSR have steadily deteriorated. In reality it is not surprising. First of all, the population needs to be shown in the most convincing way possible that all the words about peace, decreased tension, and the various rights so frequently mentioned in the press are meant not for their ears, but for the benefit of foreigners.

Second, once the West has given what was expected of it, what reason is there to pretend that the society is about to be liberalized?

I come now to what is perhaps the most symbolic and vivid example of the practical consequences of détente. Some two years ago, seven people succeeded in getting inside the American embassy in Moscow. They were members of two Christian families who for many years had tried to obtain permission to leave the USSR; they wished to settle in a country where they would not be persecuted for their faith. In the Soviet Union they had already experienced prison, insane asylums, and the revocation of parental rights for giving their children a religious upbringing. For sixteen years they had suffered for their faith, and their one hope during all this time was to leave the country. About ten years earlier, the father of one family had managed to enter the American embassy; he had been promised aid and protection. When he walked out of the building, he was arrested and thrown in prison. Now, several years later, the family decided to follow up on the earlier contact. It is not possible to simply walk into a foreign embassy in Moscow, since it is guarded by uniformed police and KGB men in plainclothes. The only way to get inside is to break through physically. If you don't make it, you get a prison term, but if you do get past the guards, they will nab you on the way out. In this instance everyone got through except one son, who was savagely beaten and eventually released. After witnessing the brutal beating, the rest of the family refused to leave the building and has been living in the embassy ever since. They were extremely fortunate to be able to do so, even though the ambassador (the same Malcolm Toon) did all he could to try to persuade them to leave. They were made to live in one room in the basement, were not allowed to meet with journalists, and had to listen to a long succession of embassy officials who tried to convince them to depart voluntarily, hinting that otherwise they might be evicted by force. The ambassador and his aides knew perfectly well that once these people set foot outside the embassy, they would be dragged off to prison and insane asylums. The American bureaucracy and the KGB could understand each other admirably in this matter. "If you allow one person to do it, then there will be thousands tomorrow"—all this is what both sides are thinking.

It was forbidden for this family to send or receive mail by the diplomatic pouch. And of course the KGB blocks any mail from going through the Soviet postal system. But they were able to communicate with me regularly by illicit channels. According to their calculations, from ten to fifteen people are arrested daily in front of the embassy, frequently whole families. Here is a portion of one of their letters:

It is painful to watch people being dragged away in front of our window while an American official simply stands by, smiling. We throw ourselves like animals against the window bars shouting and screaming, for it is impossible to watch such a sight without reacting. For several hours afterward we tremble as in a fever. Recently we saw an entire family being arrested, a husband, his wife, and three little girls of about nine, seven, and five years of age. The wife was led off first, and four policemen carried away the husband by his arms and legs. All five, including the children, were crying out: "Help us, Americans! Help!" The children first ran after their mother, then returned to embrace their father who was yelling for help.

Every effort is now being made to keep us from seeing these arrests, to the point of diverting the vehicle carrying the arrested people so that it no longer drives by our window. They passed word through the consul that they don't want us to shout when we see people dragged off. We squarely laid the shame on "them" in our conversation with the consul, and explained to him that they have no more respect for Americans if they dare to transmit a message like that. They don't even attempt to hide the fact that those arrested were simply trying to enter the embassy, since the embassy personnel also do not wish to have people coming to them for help. Peace and quiet is what they want. The poor, unfortunate Russian people whose lot has been to suffer almost as much as have the Jews!

There exists a Soviet-American consular agreement that stipulates that citizens will have *free access* to these facilities in order to receive information on the procedures for emigration. How is it that the government of the United States allows its embassy in Moscow to be made into a place of ambush? Why does the embassy not protest each infraction of that consular agreement? Obviously if there were free access to the embassy and people were not punished for trying to enter, there would be no need to fight one's way in or to refuse to leave. Why sign such an agreement if there is no intention of keeping it? Is it to create a "climate of cooperation" at the embassy?

There is no sense in signing treaties with the USSR unless one has the intention and the means for forcing it to respect its commitments. The signing of a treaty with the USSR is not the conclusion of an effort but the beginning of a struggle. A "dialogue" with the Soviet Union—that eternal dream of Western liberals—is only possible by cornering the Soviets in such a way that they cannot wiggle out. They do not understand dialogue in any other form and one can count on them to do their level best to pin you to the wall. The more courteous and conciliatory you are, the worse things will be for you.

Once in the camps I met an old man from the Ukraine, a teacher of literature who was extraordinarily courteous and who would not have been able to hurt a fly. When the other prisoners would start to swear, he would blush like a young girl and attempt to move out of earshot. Yet for some reason the KGB officer in the camp kept picking on him, putting him into solitary confinement, canceling his right to get packages and to receive visits from his wife. It began to interest me and I questioned him about his relations with the KGB man. He answered sadly:

"He calls me in to try to persuade me to collaborate."

"So what do you tell him?"

"What can I tell him? I ask to be excused on account of my character. I tell him that I simply don't know how to do those things. How would I ever be able to look those I had denounced in the eye?"

I took pity on the old man, and for a whole week I tutored him in the juiciest of swear words. It was hard going for him at first, and at times it brought him to the point of tears. Yet at the end he learned to spit out some oaths firmly and without blushing. The question was whether he could muster up a sufficiently convincing tone of voice when faced by the guard. By good luck, he managed to act entirely contrary to his real character. The next time he was called in, he got fifteen days solitary for "using obscene language," to the great astonishment of his fellow prisoners. But he was never again summoned by the KGB.

This is not only a joke. The mentality of the Kremlin leaders is exactly the same. In fact, quite a few of them rose through the ranks due to their work in the KGB. The problem is that I cannot open a school for teaching obscenities to Western diplomats and politicians.

♦ ♦ ♦

I have no idea why the reflections of "Russian travelers" invariably turn into discussions about shit. You'd think we had nothing better to talk about. Why not dream of something beautiful, even though it might be rather improbable? But it seems that in our country things resemble the story of the man troubled by vivid dreams. Sometimes he would see fabulous grottoes full of priceless gems, or sometimes piles of gold. Gold everywhere, lying within easy reach of his hand. Gold, gold, gold. His wife wakes him up:

"What's the matter with you, groping around the bed? What are you looking for?"

"I dreamed there was gold all over the place."

"For heavens sake go back to sleep, stupid. Gold! What an idea!" He goes back to sleep, only this time he dreams that there are mounds of shit everywhere. He is surrounded on every side.

"Looking for gold again?" grumbles his wife.

"No, this time, it was shit . . . loads and loads of it. Oh, but wait a minute, I think it's true . . ."

Epilogue

IT is four years since I found myself in peaceful Zurich, stunned and blinded as if by a blazing light. Four years is not a long time, but these years have passed very quickly. How many changes, how many events? I no longer wake at dawn thinking I am hearing the guard rapping on the door with his key, yelling at me. The past becomes more and more blurred, I become more accustomed to my new life, as if I had lived here always. It is no longer clear what "in our country" and "in their country" means, what is "ours" and what is "yours." It is just that when I get news of another arrest or a new trial in Moscow, I get a lump in my throat.

Good things, just as bad ones, fade from memory with extraordinary rapidity. Recently, a reporter from one of America's leading newspapers startled me:

"Tell me, how did you manage to emigrate? Did you get an Israeli visa?"

Another surprised me even more when he tried to persuade me to make a visit to the United States:

"You know, it's worth the trip. You should see the country, Washington, the White House."

One question is asked repeatedly and with great insistence:

"What do you think of the West?"

Each time, I try to avoid an answer. It is impossible to answer briefly, and no one would listen to an answer in depth.

Basically that is the reason for this book. Writing it was the last thing in the world I wanted to do. As God is my witness, I never would have undertaken it without the extraordinary urgings of my publisher. The immediate past is too recent and too fresh in my memory. All I can offer are impressions, the nature of which is to reflect the experience and general mentality of the observer to a greater degree than they reflect the subject being observed. Impressions are always categorical and lack nuance. Presented in brief form, they will inevitably contain broad generalizations, some of which may be quite unjustified. Finally, impressions are always contradictory and inconsistent, haphazard and unreliable. What is more, some of the most interesting impressions must be omitted because they are related to specific individuals. It will not do to make fun of good people simply because they had the bad luck to stumble across your path.

The publisher remained unmoved.

"All right," I said angrily. "You'll have a book. But don't complain about it afterward. You and I are going to be stoned, reviled, burned at the stake like the heretics during the Inquisition."

And it is indeed a strange undertaking. It reminds me of a foreign traveler crossing the breadth of Russia on the Trans-Siberian railway, on a train that never stops for more than twenty minutes anywhere along the route. What can he see from the window of his compartment? The natives will be indignant when they read his reflections on the trip.

But then again, it all depends on how you look. I too have traveled many thousands of miles in the trains of Russia. Bored, I used to count the number of cars in the freight trains we met; at dawn I would listen to the long, yawn-like whistles of the locomotives, and then I would drink tea in a glass held in the inevitable metal holder. All those monotonously similar platforms, sidings, and tiny godforsaken villages leave almost no trace in one's memory.

All that is left are *impressions*. Whenever the tracks passed close to a village, some children would unfailingly come out to watch the train go by. Whatever the weather, two or three small silhouettes, motionless, would stand as the convoy passed, with a kind of poignant sadness, as if their lives were speeding away.

Never in the West have I seen children watching trains that way.

1980

Appendix One

IRONICALLY, no sooner had the ill-famed 1984 passed by, ringing in celebrations of George Orwell, than the Free World displayed once again a remarkable ignorance of the communist system's very essence, thus leaving us to wonder: was it ever properly understood, along with Orwell's writings?*

We can hardly pretend, however, that it was totally unexpected: we have already witnessed similar outbursts of Western euphoria each time Big Brother suddenly disappears from public view after a bout of mysterious Russian cold, and instead of the usual propaganda sombre music is heard from Moscow. But each time one hopes that the previous lessons have not been entirely forgotten. And each time we are forced to admit that all our efforts to explain the difference between the totalitarian and democratic worlds, all our books, articles, speeches, piles of evidence, and miles of testimonies are just swept away by the inexhaustible desire of the people to be deceived.

And so it was this time again. While a solemn procession of goose-stepping soldiers and stumbling gerontocrats was slowly moving towards Red Square, numerous commentators of Western television, radio, and newspapers, breathless with excitement, were warming up to proclaim a "new era." And the closer the procession moved towards Lenin's Tomb, the more optimistic were their forecasts, a growing crescendo with every goose-step, as if the communist ideology it-

*This address was delivered at "Beyond 1984," the Conference on Communism and Liberal Democracy organized by the Committee for the Free World, which took place in London on 18–20 March 1985.

self, and not just one of its humble servants, was about to be buried in the Kremlin wall.

Of course, the new Big Brother was immediately described as "charismatic," brilliant, young, energetic, expert in the economy, a great reformer and a peace-lover. And who was not, from Comrade Stalin onward? Particularly charismatic was Comrade Khrushchev, who charmed everybody by demonstrating his shoe to the United Nations.

Surely, the new Big Brother must be a liberal, perhaps from the same closet as Comrade Andropov. Why? Oh, because his wife is slim and handsome, not one of the usual Kremlin milkmaids. It takes a liberal, you know, to break with such respectable tradition. And she is not just a wife, she is a philosopher, one of those people like Spinoza and Einstein. What does she do? Oh, she teaches Marxism-Leninism to kids.

And he is very well educated too. He studied law in the '50s. Soviet law, of course. Although he does not speak English, not yet, he might understand it, as a British MP has assured us. Just a bit more training, a few more trips to Britain, and he will be speaking alright. Have patience, he is still young and growing.

Suddenly, this kind of drivel has filled the newspapers, jammed the radio broadcasts and occupied all the television channels to such an extent that one cannot switch on without running the risk of being overwhelmed. I am afraid even to use my vacuum cleaner, for fear that it will start babbling about a new Soviet leader as soon as I switch it on.

Thus, we are told that Comrade Gorbachev is a great expert on the economy. To be sure, he was in charge of Soviet agriculture for a few years, but if there were any great improvements in this long-suffering branch of the Soviet economy, we have failed to notice them. The Soviet import of grain continued to grow steadily, while production of meat, eggs, and milk declined even further.

We are also told that, due to his exceptional talents, Comrade Gorbachev has made the fastest career ever known in the Soviet hierarchy. Indeed, he has. What was not widely publicized, however, was that his talents had very little to do with this achievement. Or, should we say, certain talents other than those implied are responsible for his success. He simply used to be the party boss of a district frequented by Andropov for purely medical reasons—because a famous mineral water resort is located there.

This type of career is anything but exceptional in Soviet history. Khrushchev used to be a local party organizer in the place where Stalin's wife worked. Being young, bright, and charismatic, Khrushchev did not miss this golden opportunity and always praised Stalin's policy of collectivization to Allilueva, a policy Allilueva disagreed with. Sooner or later, it became known to Stalin and Khrushchev's career was made.

In a similar way, Chernenko made it to the top, first by being a petty functionary under Brezhnev, and then, later, by being his nurse, valet, and errand boy.

♦ ♦ ♦

But the greatest significance is given to Comrade Gorbachev's young age. He is not, we are informed, one of the old guard. He was only eight when the Second World War started, he was only 14 when it was over. Neither the crucible of the Revolution, nor the bloody battles of the last war could temper his will. Thus, it was solemnly proclaimed by the Western media, the new generation has come to power, pushing aside the old Bolsheviks.

One can hardly imagine a more ridiculous statement. Whatever his age at the end of the war, Comrade Gorbachev was brought up and educated in one of the worst periods of the Stalin era. He was only 21 and a second-year student at Moscow University when he joined the Communist Party. This alone indicates a more than average zeal and a desire to serve the authorities. Particularly so, if we bear in mind that this was in 1952—a year of great purges and the last political campaign of the Stalin era: the campaign against "cosmopolitans," Jews, and intellectuals. Once again, as in the late '30s, mass persecutions were dramatically increased while the Jews were being prepared for a mass deportation in the wake of the "doctors' plot." According to those who were at Moscow University at that time and knew Gorbachev personally, he was quite active in this campaign, earning himself the reputation of a faithful communist.

Subsequently, for the next 33 years he was nothing but a party *apparatchik*. From being a district secretary of the Komsomol in 1955, right after graduating from the University, till the present day, when he became General Secretary of the Communist party, he was steadily promoted by the very "old guardsmen" whom he has allegedly "pushed aside." They have selected him and made him what he is now.

So, why should we suddenly become enthusiastic? Indeed, he is younger than the others and might be more energetic—so much the worse for us. Why should we prefer a younger and more energetic enemy, who might have a good 20 years to deal with us? For that matter, why are we so eager to endow him with better qualities, better education, bigger talents and experience than he actually has? After all, it is not in our interest to have a gifted enemy.

This seemingly irrational behaviour has a very simple explanation: neither the Soviet system, nor the communist ideology have ever been quite understood in the West. With the exception of those who have either lived under communist rule, or have otherwise had some first-hand experience of its ideology, people in the West are probably incapable of understanding them. Irrespective of their political orientation and of the number of books they might have read on the subject, they still believe in the depth of their hearts that the difference between the two worlds is not so great, after all. Those on the Left tend to perceive the other side as a mirror image of this one. They talk about "superpowers," as if the term meant anything. No matter how many crimes of communism we disclose to them, they would always come up with an equal number on this side, whether they be real or imaginary.

Unfortunately, those on the Right are not much better. At best, they perceive the Soviet system as a peculiar Russian form of dictatorship, as something inherited from Ivan the Terrible, and therefore they do not rule out the possibility of better relations, of a constructive dialogue, or of a new "pragmatic" leader coming to power in Moscow.

The current fit of Western euphoria is particularly depressing precisely because it has affected conservatives. Official Washington is reported to be "high on hope" and has hastily proclaimed an "era of new relations" with the Soviet Union. Leaders of West European countries rushed to Moscow and lined up to shake hands with the new "pragmatic" leader, vying with each other in inviting him to visit their respective countries.

Even Margaret Thatcher has been widely quoted as saying that she can do business with the new party boss and that neither she nor Comrade Gorbachev are going to change each other. What a nice basis for "constructive relations"! Business as usual—you will give them credits and technology, and they will pay you back, in hard currency . . . through economic subversion. You will build them a truck factory, and they will send the trucks to Afghanistan filled with soldiers. Don't bother to change them—they will change you anyway. This is exactly the type of economic reform Comrade Gorbachev is looking for: the West will build the Soviet economy, while they build communism in the rest of the world.

Unfortunately, this is not a joke, but a sad reality. The current mellowing of mood in Moscow is well calculated and dictated by the grim conditions of the Soviet economy. It is true that the growth of their GNP is about to cease, that over 60 percent of their industrial equipment is obsolete, that due to barbaric exploitation of the natural resources they cannot continue to satisfy their needs in oil or energy and that due to the legendary inflexibility of their centrally planned economy some 30 percent of consumer goods and services are provided by the flourishing black market. But it is also true that no real reform is possible without loosening the party control over the country, and therefore, without a total collapse of the system. The only reform they can afford is a return to *détente* as it used to be in the '70s, that is, a one-way street which will allow them to enjoy Western technology and cheap credits while preserving their system intact.

I can only hope that the West will not repeat the same mistake twice within 10 years. There is absolutely no need for the West to hurry and once again save the most vicious system ever known in history, a system which openly proclaims the destruction of liberal democracies as its ultimate goal. Its need for your help will grow dramatically with each year. So, let them pay in advance, let them return what they grabbed in the past, let them fulfil their past promises and long-forgotten obligations. Let them do it first, before you even consider any improvement in relations.

The time has come to mount the pressure, not to relax it. They know they cannot afford the multi-billion Strategic Defense Initiative program. So, for God's sake, don't cancel it! Not for any promises in the world.

They know they cannot at present support the most remote parts of their empire, such as Angola and Mozambique. But they also calculate quite well that the West will do their job for them. Indeed, current American policy in that region is a disgrace. At the moment these two communist regimes continue to exist only thanks to American money and diplomatic support. Rather, Americans should support popular resistance movements in these countries, thus totting up an extra pressure on the Soviets and making irreversible changes in their empire. With each year this pressure will inevitably result in more and more changes in our world.

It would be a tragic mistake if the West once again bailed out the Soviet economy without imposing irreversible internal changes. Scared by the spectre of nuclear holocaust, frightened by hysterical crowds demanding immediate peace at any price, restrained by numerous self-imposed limitations, the West is too impatient to utilize the advantages of its situation properly. Paradoxically, our eagerness to live in peace prevents its achievement.

The current wave of conservative euphoria shows us once again how little the West has understood the nature of the Soviet regime.

Contrary to popular belief the Marxist-Leninist ideology is far from dead or forgotten. It is not just an absurd relic of the '20s and '30s, but is still the ruling ideology of the whole system. Sixty years after Lenin's death, the Soviet Union remains the same ideological state serving the purposes of world revolution as he conceived it. It does not matter that no one believes in communist dogma nowadays. In their everyday life the Soviet people may perceive it as a nuisance, or as a source of numerous jokes shared equally by the people and their rulers. But at the end of the day, the Communist Party is still in firm control of every aspect of Soviet life, and communist ideology is never challenged within the party.

The contradictions between the communist and non-communist worlds are still defined as "antagonistic" (i.e., irreconcilable), as are those between the opposing "classes of capitalist society"—the proletariat and the bourgeoisie.

What was once a utopia, a dream, has become a structure, an institution, and a day-to-day job for millions of people. The Soviet Union is not a state in the traditional sense of the word, but a huge and well-organized army of ideological warriors, a fortress.

What do you expect a "pragmatic," "young and energetic" Gorbachev to do? Even if we accept that he wants to change the system, he has even less chance to do so than the average worker. Any deviation from the glorious path of the victorious ideology will immediately be used against him by his rivals. Besides, nobody wants to introduce any changes which might upset the established equilibrium. The party is proclaimed to be infallible, and as long as it remains so in the eyes of the population, the hypnotism of absolute power remains with it. Surely, we cannot expect Comrade Gorbachev to approach people who have been forced to make the utmost sacrifices for half a century, and announce: "Sorry, folks. It is all our fault. We'll start all over again."

Indeed, Comrade Gorbachev has already confirmed in his acceptance speech his commitment to the main principles of the ideology, including a pledge of support to liberation movements, the forces of "progress and socialism" around the world. The old declaration of war against the non-communist world, which is solemnly repeated every five years at each Party Congress, is thus confirmed again by the new charismatic and energetic leader.

In fact, it does not matter how young, energetic, educated, and experienced the General Secretary may be because he is not a human being—he is a function. Even if he does not exist at all, the system will continue to live and function. Big Brother Andropov, Chernenko, or Brezhnev could be practically dead at the end of their reign, yet their letters, decrees, and interviews continued to appear. Their function continued to exist as if nothing had happened, like communist ideology continues to exist and control Soviet life, although nobody believes in it. The reality of a totalitarian society, brilliantly defined by Orwell in three old party slogans: "War is Peace," "Freedom is Slavery," "Ignorance is Strength"—is still unchanged.

What kind of "constructive relations" can the West hope to have with this machine? Or, should I better ask: is it possible to have the peaceful coexistence of a tiger and a rabbit in the same cage? Quite possible, if you maintain a steady supply of fresh rabbits.

It is time to understand that there are no quick solutions to our problems. It is time to understand that Soviet aggressiveness is inseparable from its internal oppressiveness.

As Andrei Sakharov wrote in a letter to the President of the Soviet Academy of Sciences:

> A most important concept, which in time became a cornerstone of my position, is the indissoluble bond between international security and trust on the one hand, and respect for human rights and an open society on the other.
>
> As long as a country has no civil liberty, no freedom of information, and no independent press, then there exists no independent body of public opinion to control the conduct of the government. Meanwhile, the [Soviet] military-industrial complex and the KGB are gaining in strength, threatening the stability of the entire world, and super-militarization is eating up all our resources.

Thus, Western policy should be always calculated to help the people in the communist world, not their rulers. It should promote the democratization of these societies. We have a common cause to serve, in the East and in the West: the cause of freedom and democracy.

Indeed, we are connected in this common struggle, more strongly than a chain can bind prisoners, by invisible ties. Only together can we score a victory, and if one of us fails the rest are dragged down even further.

When the crowds of hysterical people in the streets of your cities demand unilateral disarmament of the West, when they demand peace at any price and surrender to Soviet blackmail, not only is your future betrayed but the future of Poles and Czechs, Vietnamese and Russians. For what hopes are left for them, where can they find the strength to resist against all odds if the people of free countries choose to be red rather than dead?

Yes, this universal struggle for freedom does not know national borders or linguistic barriers, but stretches from the Polish shipyards to the mountains of Afghanistan, from the jungles of Angola and Nicaragua to the deserts of Ethiopia, from the streets of Western capitals to the Siberian labour camps and Cuban prisons.

I wish this simple truth were always remembered by the people and the governments of that small and constantly threatened patch of land called the Free World. For it is ultimately for your survival that the Afghan peasants are fighting with almost bare hands. The West is not even grateful enough to supply them with medicine, food, or weapons. Instead, several European governments have decided to buy Soviet natural gas, perhaps the very same gas that is being pumped out of Afghanistan by the Soviet occupation authorities as compensation for "liberating" Afghanistan.

We may shake with indignation whenever we hear about the Soviet invasion of yet another country. We hate these obedient soldiers, ever ready to do whatever they are told. But what do we propose that they should do? Do we honestly expect them to rebel and face a firing squad, while the entire world continues to provide their executioners with goods, credits, and modern technology? If we really are allies in this universal struggle for freedom, is it fair to expect the people in the East to sacrifice their lives, while the West is not prepared to sacrifice its profits?

Equally, when the American Congress cowardly refuses to support the popular resistance to the communist regime in Nicaragua, or when we hear about the intention to recognize the communist government in Angola we must consider it a defeat for us all. Surely, the cause of democracy and freedom will suffer if communist slavery is spread further in Africa or Central America. Neither will it encourage the people behind the Iron Curtain to risk their lives in our common struggle, but it will show them that they are alone against the most oppressive system in the world's history.

And what else should they think when they hear all these conciliatory speeches of the world's leaders about "normalization of relations" and "negotiated settlements," about "trust-building" between the East and West, in which their rights are not included? Is it considered "normal" by the Western Allies when 17 million Germans are kept by force from joining their nation? Is it "normal" to see Polish "Solidarity" crushed, or the Baltic states still occupied under the Molotov-Ribbentrop pact?

What sort of "normal relations" or "coexistence" will it be if just in order to send their Olympic team to Los Angeles the Soviets wanted a kind of martial law to be proclaimed in California, censorship imposed on the press, demonstrations prohibited, a special *gulag* to be built for their athletes and anyone of them who might defect to be dragged back in chains? Yes, that is exactly how the Soviets understand "peaceful coexistence": it is when the West builds communism for them and helps them to keep their population in obedience. But in that case, would it still be a "Free World"?

We, in the Soviet Union, understand our common cause differently. It is also for your freedom that members of the Ukrainian Helsinki Monitoring Group Oleksa Tikhy and Valeri Marchenko have recently died in prison, while dozens of their colleagues from the Helsinki Groups were jailed or sent into exile. Right from the moment the Helsinki Accords were signed in 1975, these people knew that the Soviet regime was not going to respect its obligations and would try to deceive the West by false promises. They also knew what it would cost them to expose the Soviet cheating, but they never hesitated to stand up and be counted.

And what did the West do with the information obtained at such a high price? At the first review conference in Belgrade it was decided "not to demand too much" from the Soviets, which in practical terms meant not to demand anything at all. The Western countries happily signed a Final Document with the Soviets as if nothing had happened. The human rights violations were not even mentioned. The results of the second review conference in Madrid were hardly more encouraging, although it went on for three years. At the end, the West conceded the most important part of the agreement—the link between security, cooperation, and respect for human rights—and agreed to have a separate conference on security and "trust-building," while the human rights problems were again shelved.

Thus, the Helsinki Accords have lost all meaning by now. I wonder what they discuss behind the closed doors of the Stockholm conference: Clearly, one is ill-advised to trust a governing clique which does not allow its people to know the truth and to discuss it, which deliberately pumps hostility and hatred towards other nations into the heads of its population. Surely, there can be no trust between East and West unless an independent public opinion is allowed to exist and to serve as a control on the government. Surely, trust should first be built between nations before it becomes possible between governments. So, what kind of security can we have without respect for human rights?

Although it would be only logical to declare the Helsinki Accords null and void because they were never implemented by the Soviets, the West still clings to this remnant of *détente*. After its human rights provisions were so blatantly violated, after "Solidarity" was crushed in Poland and Afghanistan was invaded, after an attempt on the Pope's life had been masterminded by the KGB, after Andrei Sakharov nearly died in exile and practically *all* members of the Helsinki Monitoring Groups were persecuted—what sense does it make to cling to this piece of paper? Just to encourage the Soviets to violate other international agreements?

Instead, the West is eager once again to rush to the negotiating table with the Soviets, only to procure another piece of paper which the Soviets will not respect. Aren't you tired of this endless paper game?

Scared as they are by the constant Soviet blackmail, and in the absence of a clear political concept, the Western people have become obsessed with a desire for "Talks." "Keep talking"—is a political prayer of our time, as if "talking" ever helped in dealing with the Soviets. Just as a frightened child, lost deep in the woods, starts talking loudly to calm itself down and to dispel the dark shadows, so the West believes that by talking to the Soviets it might dispel the threat of war.

It is time for us to become politically mature people and to forget our childish fears. The time has come to understand that only together with the hundreds of millions of enslaved people in the communist world can we successfully serve the cause of freedom, peace, and democracy. It is they whom we should trust and their needs that we should keep in mind. They are our greatest and most reliable ally.

1985

Appendix Two

No matter how much evidence is amassed of Soviet deception during the last 40 years—violation of international agreements, manipulation of public opinion, subversion and terrorism, covert coups and overt aggressions—a large part of the Western public still finds it too difficult to accept. If nothing else, the sheer scope of this Soviet activity and the utterly inhuman methods the Soviets employ should make a "balanced" Western observer suspicious.

Even the most undeniable facts—like the shooting down of the Korean airliner a few years ago, or the invasion of Afghanistan—failed to change public opinion in the West. Instead, the very absurdity of Soviet behavior in both cases has prompted many to look for a more "rational" explanation of Soviet motives, or even for a justification. And more often than not, these explanations tend to blame the Western governments rather than the Soviets.

Unfortunately, such an attitude is only natural. Any textbook of medical psychology describes a similar pattern of behavior displayed by a patient with terminal cancer. In general, whenever a person is confronted with something mind-boggling, something utterly horrible and beyond his control, he goes through a succession of mental states ranging from denial to guilt, from fantastic rationalizations to acute depression.

Indeed, what can be more traumatic than to face a mortal enemy who stops at nothing and who can destroy the Earth five times over?

*This article, originally titled "Mesmerized by the Bear," was published in the *Washington Times* on May 27, 1986.

An enemy who subjugates country after country, slowly but steadily, for half a century, who penetrates every sphere of our life and ruthlessly exploits our every weakness—all for no apparent reason. In the course of history, the West has tried practically every possible approach, from containment to détente, and nothing has worked. As Alexander Solzhenitsyn suggests, communism is like a cancer and, therefore, not surprisingly, our reaction to it is similar to that of a cancer patient.

So, the most important reason for Soviet success is the reluctance of the Western public to face the danger, to recognize the source of threat. Soviet behavior ceases to appear so frighteningly irrational as soon as we understand that the Soviets regard themselves as being at war with the rest of the world.

Yet, we refuse to believe that the Soviets routinely employ the methods of warfare by supporting and manipulating all kinds of extremist groups around the world. The facts are undeniable, but it seems just too mean to be true.

Strictly speaking, we cannot blame the Soviets even for waging an undeclared war against humanity: this war was actually proclaimed at the turn of the century by the founders of Marxist-Leninist ideology under the banner of "class struggle," and it has continued unabated ever since. Every five years, at each party congress, the Soviet ruling clique solemnly reaffirms the declaration of war by pledging its full support to "liberation movements" and to the "forces of progress and socialism." The West simply does not want to hear this.

Another reason the West is so receptive to Soviet influence is ignorance. Indeed, we know more about a remote galaxy, or about a minuscule part of a living cell, than about a political system existing just a few thousand miles away. Just a small but illustrative example: each time a Soviet leader dies in Moscow it is automatically perceived in the West as a signal for change of the Soviet regime. Media, the public, and even so-called experts become extremely excited.

Apart from the usual wishful thinking we discussed earlier, this example shows a remarkable ignorance in the West of the Soviet system. Even after 69 years of its existence, the Western public and decisionmakers still don't know that it is not an autocracy but a totalitarian regime where the death of a leader does not mean anything at all. And that is exactly why the Soviet system is so dangerous: autocracies disappear with the death of autocrats; a communist system continues.

But most depressing is the level of knowledge among so-called experts, Sovietologists, Kremlinologists, etc. Few notable exceptions aside, they are the least qualified to tackle the problems of East-West relations.

Who are these people? What are their credentials? Usually, somebody who worked a few years in the U.S. Embassy in Mongolia, or took a guided tour in the Soviet Union and then wrote a popular trash book, or better still, who used to be a government official with "experience of dealing with Russians."

These modern astrologists have done incalculable damage to popular understanding of the Soviet problem. They have made impossible any meaningful public debate on the subject of East-West relations: once the truth is not an objective to be reached, your guess is as good as theirs. Disinformation is as good as information.

Another reason for the Soviet success is the ideological affinity of a certain part of Western society. I don't mean by that the extreme left or the Communists, but rather a certain tendency of those on the left of center to perceive danger only from the right. There is no way to persuade these people that any dictatorship is far better than the communist system, simply because their reflexes are opposite. Besides, the Soviet Union, in their perception, is still a "revolution which went astray." That is to say, something made with good intentions that went wrong through somebody's mistake. Therefore, they feel obliged to justify intentions, if not the results.

These people actually constitute a large and very influential part of Western society, while being an excellent conductor for Soviet disinformation. They introduced certain moral and intellectual dishonesty into our public debate, social attitudes, and reactions. Can anybody explain why it is all right to be a Communist and absolutely socially unacceptable to be a fascist? Nobody can. But if you try to treat a Communist with the same disgust as his less fortunate brownshirted colleague, Western society will brand you "intolerant," "unpluralistic," and "undemocratic."

It is quite all right to "remove" dictators like Ferdinand Marcos or Jean-Claude Duvalier (even though it requires interference in the internal affairs of a neighboring country), but it is absolutely unacceptable to support "contras" because they want to "overthrow" the "legally elected" government of Nicaragua. In short, when we deal with a dictator, then he has a problem; when we deal with a communist system, then we have a problem.

The Soviets, however, have a few problems of their own. Created according to a nineteenth-century doctrine, a doctrine which became obsolete even before it was implemented, the Soviet system still has to spread its ideology, even though nobody believes in it any longer. It has to "liberate" mankind without alerting it and, above all, to make the world cover the expenses of its own "liberation."

What used to be a belief, a revolutionary passion of the founders, in due time became a structure, social order, and a job for millions of people. Sixty-nine years after its creation, the Soviet system cannot survive without the ever-present threat of war, which has gradually become a substitute for the attractiveness of communist ideology, both at home and abroad.

At home, a threat of war is the only excuse for a totalitarian regime, lack of rights, misery, and privileges of the ruling elite. Abroad, it is the only device to keep the empire together, to spread further Soviet influence, and to blackmail the West into providing credits, goods, and technology. Therefore, peace has become the main subject of Soviet disinformation, while "struggle for peace" has become a substitute for "class struggle."

How does it work in practical terms?

First, the Soviet Union generates constant conflict, a threat of war, either by shifting the balance of forces with the West, or by its adventures in the Third World. Then, the Western response is used to generate military hysteria at home, and to utilize "peace hysteria" abroad. These two hysterias feed each other: when Soviet people see on the screens of their television sets millions of Westerners marching against "American missiles," clashing with police, chanting slogans against their "war-mongering" governments, they begin to believe Soviet propaganda about the aggressive plans of "American imperialism."

On the other hand, when thousands of peace activists, "bridge-builders," and "citizen diplomats" visit the Soviet Union, they are confronted by genuinely concerned and scared people, asking them: "Why do Americans want to burn us in the nuclear holocaust?" These visitors see only people craving peace and traumatized by the losses of World War II, endless monuments and museums dedicated to the last war, and Soviet officials with their inevitable toasts for *mir i druzhba*. Being what they are, these peace activists never understand the difference between the people and the system, and they go home firmly convinced that "Russians" do not want war.

Of course, in the process of their trips, these visitors are interviewed by Soviet media at every location. Surely, as respectful guests, they do not mention SS-20s or Afghanistan. They condemn Reagan's "militarism" and Star Wars program, thus strengthening even further the military hysteria of the Soviet population.

Exactly the opposite happens when Soviet people are allowed to visit the West. With their families left at home as hostages, these carefully selected envoys simply repeat slogans of Soviet propaganda. Of course, Western people, as polite hosts this time, do not ask them about Afghanistan, either. Once again, we hear only about bad Reagan and the purely peaceful intentions of the Soviet Union.

One might ask: what do the Soviets gain by scaring these millions of Westerners into a peace hysteria? After all, missiles were placed in Europe, peace hysteria notwithstanding, and peace movements have never reached a sizable proportion of Western society. Shouldn't we consider their "struggle for peace" just as their participation in the public debate, quite legitimate in the democratic societies?

Even if we leave aside the unilateral nature of this "debate," which is never allowed to spread into Soviet territory, the Soviets are still left with enormous advantages:

1. Peace hysteria makes any decision to strengthen defenses (particularly nuclear defenses) so unpopular that the Western governments become more and more reluctant to consider such measures, while the Soviets are totally free to build up their arsenal with impunity. Sooner or later, this will lead to Soviet strategic superiority.

2. It constantly threatens to split the Western alliance.

3. It shifts the focus of public attention from the aggressive nature of the Soviet system as a threat to peace in our world to the number of warheads, missiles, planes, and other quite innocent hardware. As a result, Western governments are forced to engage in a senseless and self-defeating process of arms control negotiations, while the public perceives both sides as equally responsible for the ever-present danger of a holocaust.

4. It gives priority to questions of security over the issues of human rights in the Soviet Union, issues too dangerous for the Soviet regime to tolerate as a subject of public discussion. Thus, launching a new round of the "struggle for peace" in 1980, the Soviets came up with a slogan: "The people have the power to preserve peace—their basic right" (*Pravda*, Sept. 24, 1980). The message was unmistakable and very effective: if you want to survive, forget about human rights problems in the Soviet Union. And they did. "Better red than dead" became a rule of the time. And skillfully cultivated attitudes of the Western public were a great help for the Soviets in their effort to destroy the human rights movement in the Soviet Union.

5. Finally, after years of artificially created tension and peace hysteria, no government can reject a Soviet offer of détente, although a recent spell of détente has left little illusion about its real nature. It became clear that the Soviet system cannot relax for a prolonged period without eroding. Détente is necessary to catch a breath, to lull the Western vigilance, to gain access to Western technology and credits, to gain as many concessions from the "imperialists" as possible, to improve the military balance, and to grab as many new countries in the Third World as time may permit, before the West becomes alerted once again. Then, a period of "cold war" will follow, with all "progres-

sive mankind" blaming American "imperialism" for "overreacting" and for "not recognizing political reality."

In short, détente is simply another version of the "struggle for peace," another weapon of psychological warfare. Aimed at softening Western resistance, it does not affect internal life in the Soviet Union, where the climate of "cold war" never relaxes.

Thus, in the 1970s we witnessed several examples of successful disinformation campaigns. One was a theory, created in the Kremlin and popular among "Sovietologists" and politicians, a theory according to which the Soviet regime was proclaimed "paranoiac," not aggressive.

In a typical and quite deliberate confusion of the Soviet system with the Soviet population, the theory claimed that repeated foreign invasions and persistent Western hostility have made the Russians paranoiac. Therefore, if we relaxed and allowed them to gain strategic superiority, then the Soviets would also relax internally and externally. This ridiculous theory became a central doctrine of East-West relations for nearly a decade, giving the Soviets the legitimate right to improve their strategic position, and to swallow Angola, Ethiopia, Mozambique, and, finally, Afghanistan.

An equally ridiculous theory popular in the same Western circles was the theory of "hawks" and "doves" in the Politburo. I have little doubt it was invented by the Soviets, who even tried to play an old-fashioned police trick of "good guy" and "bad guy" in their dealing with the West.

Yet another favorite subject of Soviet disinformation during the 1970s was the need for quiet diplomacy in East-West relations. Thus, contrary to numerous protests of Soviet human rights activists, and even political prisoners, the West accepted the Soviet idea that open pressure is counterproductive, that "dissidents need détente"—a popular argument of that time.

And, of course, an idea that East-West "economic cooperation" is the best instrument of peace was quite popular among experts. How did they know it? Oh, Georgi Arbatov himself secretly told it. Fortunately for us, this nonsense was stopped by Sen. Henry "Scoop" Jackson.

But the most successful Soviet trick of the détente era was, of course, the Helsinki agreement signed in 1975. To be sure, the whole affair was presented to the Western public as a great victory for the cause of human rights. In reality, the Western politicians knew perfectly well that the Soviets were not going to respect their obligations, and the Soviets knew equally well that the West was not going to demand seriously that the obligations be respected. Meanwhile, the Soviets have presented this agreement to their public as a postwar peace treaty and recognition of their territorial acquisitions, a clear message to Estonians, Latvians, Lithuanians, Poles, Czechs, and Hungarians that their national aspirations are not supported by the Free World.

Why do we need to recall today all these mistakes, particularly the mistakes of détente?

First, because they are still very much alive and continue to affect popular perceptions of East-West relations. We can see it every day. Our mass media still describe these relations as "normalizing" whenever the West makes concessions to the Soviets, and as "cold" when the West takes a firm position. We still cannot discuss the need for strong defenses without being called warmongers.

But most important, we must remember these past mistakes because the Soviets are about to offer a new spell of détente to the West, and the West is about to repeat the same mistakes I have just mentioned.

Due to a catastrophic decline in productivity, due to general backwardness of the Soviet economy, the Soviets cannot successfully continue their military competition with the West, and they cannot support their ever-growing empire. These are the real reasons behind Mikhail Gorbachev's well-advertised economic reforms, not a concern for the well-being of his people.

Should we give them a break now, should we relax in military competition or reduce pressure on their empire, should we give them credits, goods, and technology, there will be no reforms endangering power of the Communist party at home. After recovering from the present crisis with our help, they will continue their expansion in the Third World, their threat of war, and "struggle for peace." Next in line will be Pakistan, Mexico, and perhaps, South Africa.

Should we, however, deny them the credits and technology, should we go ahead with the Strategic Defense Initiative, and continue support for the anticommunist resistance, the need for reforms will increase dramatically. Nobody can predict how far such reforms might lead the Soviets in dismantling a totalitarian society, but it is in our interest to force them to go as far as possible.

The combination of Soviet psychological warfare and Western willingness to be deceived has paralyzed the will of even the most resolute and wise leaders. Even the current American administration has not learned how to resist it, and is reluctantly sliding into détente. Meaningless arms control negotiations are still on the top of the American agenda, while issues of human rights are at the bottom. In the joint statement issued after the recent summit meeting in Geneva, human rights problems are barely mentioned and described only as "humanitarian cases." But, as long as we do not understand that human rights in the Soviet Union is the central political issue, not a humanitarian one, we will continue to play into the Soviets' hands, helping their propaganda.

At the end of the Geneva summit a "new" agreement on cultural and scientific exchange was solemnly signed. This agreement, however, is new only in name. In fact, it is a precise copy of an agreement signed in 1972, which gives all the advantages of exchanges to the Soviet Union. Once again, all the contacts between East and West will be channeled through official Soviet institutions, giving them the right to control information and people.

We are told, once again, that "understanding" is the best way to peace with the Soviet Union. But the choice is limited: one can have "understanding" either with the Soviet people or with the Soviet rulers.

Détente is upon us once again, this time by default. Conservatives don't want to criticize "their president," liberals don't want to criticize "their" politics. I am afraid we are going to witness a repetition of the same mistakes a second time within a single decade, something without precedent in human history.

1883

7833